CELEBRATE!

A Toast
to Fine Food
and Good
Friends from
the Junior
League of
Sacramento

CELEBRATE!

A Toast to Fine Food and Good Friends from the Junior League of Sacramento.

DESIGN
Gwen Amos Design

FOOD STYLING
Mitchell B. Miller

PHOTOGRAPHY
Keith Jensen

WRITER/EDITOR
Cheryll Cochrane

SET DESIGN
Paulette Trainor

CONCEPT & DEVELOPMENT
Cathy Levering

Opposite: White Chocolate Cheesecake

Published by:
The Junior League of Sacramento, Inc.

First Edition
First Printing, June, 1991
Second Printing, September, 2007

Copyright © 1991
The Junior League of Sacramento, Inc.
Sacramento, California

**JUNIOR LEAGUE OF
SACRAMENTO**
Women building better communities®

ISBN: 978-0-9630857-0-2
Library of Congress Control Number: 2007935938

Manufactured by:
Favorite Recipes® Press
An imprint of

FRP.

P.O. Box 305142
Nashville, Tennessee 37230
1-800-358-0560

The Junior League of Sacramento, Inc., is an
organization of women committed to promoting
voluntarism, developing the potential of women,
and improving communities through the effective
action and leadership of trained volunteers. Its
purpose is exclusively educational and charitable.

The proceeds realized from the sale of CELEBRATE!
will be returned to the community through the
projects of The Junior League of Sacramento, Inc.

Additional copies of CELEBRATE! may be obtained
by writing:

CELEBRATE!
The Junior League of Sacramento, Inc.
778 University Avenue
Sacramento, CA 95825
(916) 921-1096
Web site: www.jlsac.org

Printed in China

JUNIOR LEAGUE COMMITTEE

CHAIR
*Cathy Levering

WRITER/EDITOR
Cheryll Cochrane

SET DESIGN
Paulette Trainor

RECIPE COORDINATOR
*Marget Kingston

RECIPE DATABASE
Martha Carle

DESKTOP PUBLISHING
Mindy Bazlen

PROOFING EDITOR
Dornie Burr

CATEGORY CHAIRS

APPETIZERS
Karin Harris

BREADS, VEGETABLES
Jeannie Frisch

SOUPS & SANDWICHES
Suzie Smits

SALADS
Jennifer Smith

SEAFOOD
Kathie Frasier

POULTRY
*Mardy Fellenz

MEATS
Jody Schauer

PASTA & PIZZA
Allison Lintner

DESSERTS, BEVERAGES
*Marget Kingston

COOKIES & BARS
Cindy Fores

COMMITTEE MEMBERS

Carol Bowman
* Diana Davis
Toni Farrell
Kathie Frasier
Bev Geremia
Sally Gibson
Marlene Gidaro
Caroline Gwerder
Helen Home
Hely Jones
Gloria Knopke
Allison Lintner
Gail Lohmann
Laura Lyon-Diepenbrock
Tricia Meister
Nancy Miller
Mary Beth Morris
* Cindy Mullins
Margaret Noisworthy
Susie Orlady
Lauren Poage
Rebecca Regan
Amy Scherschligt
Julie Steacy
Rene Stwora-Hail
Catherine Taylor
Marlene Ward
Linda Wodarski

* Indicates three-year contribution

INTRODUCTION

Welcome to Sacramento, the Capital City of California. Sitting proudly in a fertile valley where two rivers meet, it is truly one of California's premier cities. It is a community which combines reverence for the past with promise for the future. Sacramento is a beautiful city often called "the city of trees" because of the thousands of trees which offer a blanket of dappled shade to the entire community. Beautiful old mansions share midtown with well designed modern office buildings. Capitol Park with the magnificently restored State Capitol dominates the city center with splendor and grace.

Visitors to Sacramento are delighted to find remnants of the city's exciting past. Old Sacramento, a carefully restored version of the 1849 Goldrush scene, offers stately examples of nineteenth century architecture, cobblestone streets, and fascinating museums. The California State Railroad Museum is renowned as one of the nation's best. The Crocker Art Museum, the oldest art museum in the west, is considered one of the finest anywhere. Sacramento offers many cultural attractions such as opera, symphony, ballet and theatre. Opportunities for outdoor recreation abound. The Sacramento and the American Rivers offer not only boating, rafting and fishing, but also miles of bicycle trails.

Sacramento is the heart of a vast agricultural domain. The fields, orchards, and vineyards of central California supply much of the world's food. And the volume and variety grown in this area are unsurpassed anywhere. The Sacramento Valley and surrounding areas produce much of the world's rice, tomatoes, walnuts, almonds, asparagus, and wine and table grapes Some of the finest wine in the world is produced only a few miles to the southwest in the Napa Valley.

Sacramento's most valuable assets by far, however, are its citizens. For over one hundred and fifty years people from all over the world have been drawn to Sacramento making it a community of many diverse cultures. The Native American, Spanish, Mexican and Chinese all figure most prominently in Sacramento's history. More recently other Northern and Southern European, African, and Far Eastern and other Asian cultures have played important roles in the nurturing and development of this community...They have each brought with them art, music, cuisine, customs, hopes and dreams. The State Capitol brings government and agriculture brings business, but the citizens bring the pride and vitality that make the community strong.

The Sacramento Community is proud of its people, its history, its commerce, its cultural achievements, its ethnic diversity and its beauty. To live in a community such as this is to celebrate each day as a special event. And Sacramento abounds with celebrations. Whether it is the spectacular Railfair with its puffing, colossal vintage locomotives or the beautiful Camellia Festival with its fragile, exquisite display of flowers, the community revels. Whether it is the pulsing excitement of the Dixieland Jubilee or the sweeping melodies of the Sacramento Philharmonic, the community rejoices. Whether it is the casual fellowship of friends at a picnic in the park or the private joy of a family together at Sunday dinner, the community celebrates.

The Junior League of Sacramento proudly dedicates this book to all families and friends who gather together to share good food and to celebrate the spirit of community.

Section I
CELEBRATE
FAMILY & FRIENDS

Section II
CELEBRATE
FABULOUS FOOD

Section III
CELEBRATE
STYLE

Section IV
CELEBRATE
SUCCESS

CELEBRATE!

Family & Friends

Romantic Interludes

You awaken and realize that it is Saturday and the kids are at Grandma's, and you two are deliciously ALONE.

In the middle of a busy morning at work you find yourself dreaming about her and that spot in the park. And suddenly you're writing poetry and planning a picnic for two.

It's Friday night and you're both all dressed up to go out, but suddenly you realize that on this particular Friday night you'd much rather stay IN.

Romantics don't need a special day or reason to celebrate. All they need is a little imagination, a little time, and each other!

Morning Glory

Breakfast in bed for two

Saturday morning.
The kids are away, and the lawn is mowed.
No early tee-off time, or cartoons blaring in the den.
Just the two of you,
Tucked in that warm cocoon
of fluffy down and soft cotton.
Just the two of you,
Traveling together in the drowsy paradise
between asleep and awake.
Just the two of you,
Lazy and cozy in leisure festivity.

Was that the morning paper hitting the porch?
Let it wait!!

Saturday morning.
There's a warm and sunny kitchen down the hall,
Where two lovers can summon up a breakfast feast-
To Go. . .
Then scurry back to where it all began.
Just the two of you,
And one plate piled high,
And two forks.
Lazy and cozy in perfect tranquility.

Is that a knock at the front door?
I didn't hear a thing.

Raspberry Ricotta Crêpes

Banana Fizz

Coffee with Whipped Cream
and Chocolate Shavings

Blueberry Scones

Afternoon Delight

A Romantic Picnic

Chicken in Parchment with
Wild Rice and Raspberry
Papaya Salsa

Marinated Broccoli and
Cauliflower in Champagne
Vinaigrette

Cantaloupe and
Strawberries with Brown
Sugar Cream

Dear One, meet me later in the park,
Where white gardenias lightly scent the air
And where the dappled sunlight filters
Softly all day through.
And we will steal a moment, me with you.

Dear One, meet me later in the park,
Where only birds and butterflies will spy,
And we will talk of times gone by,
When we were first together.
And we will share a feast and balmy weather.

Dear One, meet me later in the park,
Where time is just a signal for the blooming,
And we can sit in silence with the leisure of the flower
As we celebrate each other in one splendid stolen hour.

Moonlight
Madness   *A Romantic Dinner for Two*

Nice fire.

Care to dance?

There's no music.

I've been known to hum
a wild waltz.

In that case I'd love to dance.

Nice little bistro. Come
here often?

Oh, I spend a lot of time here.

What a coincidence.
So do I.

So I've noticed.

You noticed me, huh.

Mostly that tie.

My mother gave
me this tie.

Keep humming.

Maybe we should waltz
into the kitchen and
check on things.

*Good idea, those two chefs are
probably out . . . dancing.*

Smells terrific, if I do
say so myself.

They are quite a team.

It's a little dark. I'll
get the light.

*No problem, I'll just follow the
glow from your tie.*

Cute, very cute. Shall I pour?

Everything is ready.

Yes, this is quite a nice bistro
we have here.

Well . . . we call it home.

Shrimp Foil Packets with
Red Pepper
Snow Peas and Caviar

Baked Asparagus
with Parmesan
and Almonds

Honeydew Sorbet

Salmon Mousseline
en Croûte

Angela Pia

15

Checkerboard of Smoked
Salmon and Caviar

Caribbean Shrimp with
Island Salsa

Bora Bora Chicken Rolls

Parmesan Chicken Bites

Pheasant Galantine

Fresh Crudités with Thai
Peanut Dip

Avocado Croustades

Spanakopita

Delicious Débuts

The cocktail party is one of the most popular forms of home entertaining.

They usually fall into two basic categories—the cocktail party and the

cocktail buffet. Both offer a range of versatility which invites imagination.

A cocktail party may be a short affair which serves as a prelude to some

other evening activity, or it may be offered as a full evening's entertain-

ment with a light supper buffet. Elegant or casual, it is a wonderful way to

celebrate almost any occasion.

Savory Soirée

A great

beginning

to a great

evening

Guests will delight in the delicious fare of 'Savory Soirée'. This affair is planned in the style of the traditional cocktail party, meaning simply that it will serve as a prelude to the evening's activities. The beginning and ending times of the gathering will be stated on the invitation, and many of the guests will be going on after the party to dinner, the theatre or other activities. The food

offerings are scrumptious and passed elegantly, but are light, since in this situation they are not meant to serve as the evening's meal. Celebrating with 'Savory Soirée' is a wonderful way to welcome larger numbers of guests into one's home, since seating for all is not necessary. A 'Savory Soirée' is a great beginning which will make any great evening more memorable.

Ceviche with
Avocado Salsa

Caviar Torte

California Curried
Salmon Mousse

Clams Casino

Tartlettes aux
Champignon

Cajun Shrimp

Beef Satay with
Peanut Sauce

Crostini

Carpaccio

Variety is truly the spice of this party! A cocktail buffet featuring foods from

around the world is a feast for both the eye and the palate. Imagine tables set

Continental Cravings

up around the home or the garden, gayly dec-

*A cocktail
buffet with
international
flavor*

orated and loaded with tempting international treats. Unlike the traditional

cocktail party, guests may linger on into the evening enjoying the company.

The heartier fare of the buffet may serve as a light supper, and a wise host

will want to supply some extra seating for those who wish to sit and chat. An

international buffet offers tremendous possibilities and is a delightful chal-

lenge to the imagination. No matter what the occasion, this celebration of

ethnic cuisine will certainly satisfy those "continental cravings."

Elegant Events

A splendid dinner served on fine china and silver in the intimate atmosphere of a candle lit dining room is a memorable event. A beautiful luncheon in the garden with flowers, fine linen and sparkling crystal enhancing the delicious fare is an occasion to remember. While fine china, silver and linen napery are not prerequisites to successful entertaining, it is fun now and again to serve our guests at a magnificent formal table. This is the time to be dramatic and daring with food—a time to surprise your guests with a little something that you have been keeping up your sleeve for just the right occasion. This is a time to be lavish in planning for the delight of those invited. Celebrate with elegance and then get ready for the applause!

A splendid evening with family and dear friends commemorating a special event—a promotion, graduation or engagement—is surely the most personal of celebrations. For it is here that we bring together the very best in service from our cupboards, the finest in culinary talents from our kitchen, and from our hearts the most exceptional hospitality. A formal dinner requires a tireless effort dedicated to tradition and a sense of gracious living. To be invited is to share an occasion to remember.

Cream of Red Pepper Soup

Pasta with Lobster, White Corn, Peppers and Basil

Pineapple Lime Thyme Sorbet

Crown of Lamb with Whole Grain Mustard, Spinach and Couscous

Carrot Bundles

Baby Lettuce and Brie with Walnut Port Wine Vinaigrette

Chocolate Fudge Terrine

Candles á la Carte

Friendly Formality at Dinner

DINING ON A DREAM

Midnight Supper

Steamed Crab Vermouth

Caesar Salad

Capellini with Chicken and Cucumbers

Raspberry Grand Marnier Soufflé

The end of the final act shouldn't necessarily mean the end of an exciting evening at the theatre. Have a curtain call at your home with a dramatic midnight supper. Guests will welcome the opportunity to linger over a simply elegant dinner while reviewing the evening's entertainment. Keep the menu light and do most of the work ahead of-time. Celebrate with a late night supper, whenever a special evening calls for an encore.

LINENS
LACE &
LUNCHEON

Springtime luncheon in the garden

Toast the bride. Welcome the new neighbor. Honor the mother-to-be. Celebrate

any happy occasion with a fabulous luncheon in the dappled sunshine of the gar-

den. Marvelous food served on crisp linen amid the loveliness of spring flowers is

a particularly beautiful way to say congratulations!

Kir Champagne Punch

Mushroom Paté

Shiitake Mushrooms with
Asparagus and Greens

Chicken en Croûte

Lemon Tea Bread

Bavarian Apple Torte

English Wassail Tea

Grandpa's Eggnog

Garden Sandwiches

Curry Tea Sandwiches

Tomato Basil Brie

Persimmon Orange
Raisin Bread

Cranberry Scones

Cranberry Tarts

Croquembouche

Afternoon Appointments

If the popularity of the afternoon tea party seems to have diminished in the past few years, it can only be that our hectic schedules often leave little time for this loveliest of all "afternoon appointments." Certainly the custom of taking a few moments during the afternoon for tea and a light repast is one of the most civilized traditions in existence. A tea party need not be a stuffy affair, but rather a comfortable gathering of friends. And though these events do lend themselves to a certain elegance, imagination and planning, not linen and silver service, are the key ingredients to an enjoyable afternoon tea. Children, too, enjoy these events, and a children's tea is an excellent after school gathering. Whether the traditional small sandwiches and cakes are served or something more adventuresome such as delicious dim sum, guests will be pleased and delighted. For what could be more enjoyable than having an "afternoon appointment" to share tea, treats and conversation with treasured friends near the end of a busy day.

The Holiday Season has traditionally been a time for celebration in our society. Those busy weeks which begin with the Thanksgiving feast in late November and end as we welcome a New Year on January first are filled with days of cultural and religious significance, such as Christmas and Hanukkah. This is a season of sharing, where acts of kindness and charity lighten our hearts. It is a season of festivity, where family and friends gather together to share memories of the past and hopes for the future. We exchange tokens of love and pause to reflect the beauty and happiness in our lives. What could be more welcome during these weeks than a friendly invitation to drop in for afternoon tea. This is a pleasant and relaxing opportunity to offer one of the nicest holiday gifts — warm and sincere hospitality. The Holiday Season is a very special time of year—a time to celebrate with family, friends, community and church, as we prepare for a new year of sharing one with another.

Share the Season

Holiday Tea for Family & Friends

In Old China centuries ago special tea houses served a variety of delightful appetizers known as dim sum, which literally means "touch the heart." These delicious little dumplings were not served as a prelude to a meal but as a treat to be enjoyed with tea whenever the heart desired. There is a wide variety of dim sum delicacies, and dim sum restaurants are very popular throughout Northern California. In these restaurants diners sit at small tables as carts laden with the wonderful dim sum delights are wheeled around the room so that they may choose. Dim sum makes a hearty brunch or lunch, and many of the dim sum dishes make terrific hors d'oeuvres.

Touch The Heart
an afternoon dim sum tea

We admit to taking some liberties with the dim sum tradition in that we suggest serving dim sum at an afternoon tea. As in the Chinese tea houses, friends can gather and enjoy refreshing tea and these delightful appetizers as they relax and chat to their hearts' delight.

Minty Melon Punch

Chive Har Gow

Oriental Meatballs with Ginger Sherry Glaze

Steamed Pork Dumplings

Vegetable Wonton

Hoisin Chicken Drummettes

Cha Siu Bow

Happy New Year Cookies

StaY and PLaY

An afternoon tea for children

Children are fascinated by the idea of the tea party. It seems that long before they are able to get through a family meal with a semblance of acceptable table behavior, they can arrange any number of dolls and Teddy bears around the playroom table and quite successfully mimic the gracious stylings of the traditional adult tea party. They love the ceremony, especially if there is no adult pressure to "act accordingly."

We have set our children's tea table for those after-school hours, when children, tired from their long day, are still hungry for the company of their friends and always anxious for special treats from the kitchen. Surely, if today's adult tea party is an event which invites relaxed enjoyment, then a children's tea should also be an opportunity for young friends to gather and enjoy each other's company— perhaps where we can ease the dictates of etiquette a bit with only a few ground rules concerning common courtesy. Children will love the simple elegance of the gathering, and you may find that their early experience at the Teddy Bear teas of their playrooms will serve them well as they celebrate the end of their busy day in the cozy atmosphere of a friendly home.

Orange Pineapple Punch

Peruvian Hot Chocolate

Armenian Kids' Delight

Pacific Melon Berry Salad

Gobblers

Frozen Bourbon Slush

Clam Loaf

Smoked Salmon Salad with
Dijon Vinaigrette

Lobster Salad with Creamy
Orange Dressing

French Baguettes with
Sweet Butter

Raspberry Kiwi Tart

Traveling Tables

The picnic has long been one of our most popular celebration gatherings. Who among us cannot remember fried chicken and potato salad served from a wicker basket at a wood slat table in the country. Today, innovations in food storage and serveware have made it possible for a traveling table to offer an amazing variety of scrumptious offerings. With a little creativity, planning, and minimal equipment we can prepare almost any kind of food and transport it to be served in any setting.

We have set the traveling table for three delightful gatherings—a dinner served elegantly on the deck of a boat, a pregame tailgate luncheon, with hearty fare for all the fans, and an all day teen party, featuring that old favorite, pizza, in three tasty variations. So away we go for a day of great company and tantalizing food. And with the traveling table, we can celebrate anywhere!

DINNER ON DECK

An elegant dinner served dockside

All hands stand ready to cast off for a scrumptious dinner at the captain's table. Served aboard ship or dockside, there is little to compare with this festive nautical banquet. Guests will go overboard with praise for this elegant evening at water's edge—a celebration of calm seas, fair weather, and smooth sailing.

Bleacher Brew

Green Chile Chili
with Condiments

Muffuletta

Roast Beef and
Tomato Lavosh

Northern French
Potato Salad

Carmelitas

Car Fare   *a tailgate picnic*

Come to the party in the parking lot! A tailgate
picnic, served right out of the trunk of the car, is a
delicious and unique way to rendezvous with those
friends who live miles away. Plan to meet at dear
old Alma Mater for Homecoming, or simply choose
a date and a central spot on the map—a beach,
park, or picnic ground beside the highway. Any-
time, anywhere, if the gang can get together, then
it's time to celebrate!

Pizza to the Third Power

Teenagers off

on a tangent

with their

favorite food

Teenagers love pizza—any time, any kind, any-where. Many think they could eat it three times a day. So let them. Pizza is the ultimate solution to the problem of hungry teens no matter when they appear. There is no better way to serve the whole group than with a delicious crusty pizza, drizzling with cheese and mouth-watering toppings. Serve pizza to the slumber party for breakfast, or to the football squad for lunch. It is hearty and nutritious and its variations are infinite. Here's a whole day of pizza. Just add some teenagers, their friends, some favorite music and a few activities, and cook up a party from morning till night.

Morning
Berry Banana Smoothie
Apple Brie and Walnut Breakfast Pizza

Noon
Tomato Mozzarella and Basil Pizza
St. Helena Summer Salad
Kahlua Pecan Cakes

Night
Calzone with Westphalian Ham
Toasted Walnut Spinach Salad
Butterscotch Crunch Ice Cream Pie

Bountiful Offerings

A beautiful buffet table laden with scrumptious looking food is truly a tempting sight. Good food and a "serve yourself and enjoy" atmosphere can transform almost any situation into a party. A neighborhood barbecue can be a refreshing treat during an August heat wave. The drudgery of working late at the office turns to festivity when piping hot soups are brought in to warm those weary souls. And who can resist pure indulgence at the sight of a spectacular selection of desserts offered after the opera. The bountiful offerings of the buffet table invite enjoyment and conviviality no matter what the group, no matter what the circumstance.

Just Desserts

an elegant dessert buffet

You are invited to get your Just Desserts a celebration Where All Sweet Dreams Come True — This party is icing on the cake!

Lemon Cheesecake

Chocolate Pearls

Meringues with Pastry Cream
and Fresh Fruit

Rum Chocolate Mousse

Luscious Lemon Tarts

Black and White Truffles

Marinated Turkey Legs
with Fresh Herbs

Oven Roasted Red Potatoes
with Rosemary

Pomodori Amore

Creamed Spinach with
Fresh Parmesan

Crème de Menthe Squares

Brandy Apple Soused Cake

DOG DAYS DINNER

DOG DAYS DINNER...

The best doggone barbecue under the sun

Who: The whole pack, pups too.

What: Food and play on a hot summer day.

Where: A shady spot with lots of grass;
room to roam or just sit.

Dress: Collar loose, coat shaggy.

After
Five
and
Still
Alive

a soup potluck

at the office

Working late at the office doesn't have to be torture. Take a few moments and treat yourselves to some relaxing conversation and some delicious food before diving into the evening's work.

To: All Staff

From: The Big Cheese

Subject: Food for Thought

MESSAGE: All staff will meet in the conference room at 5:30 p.m. for a "briefing" (nourishing and delicious) before commencing with the projects for the evening.

DRESS: Sleeves up, heels down, coats and ties -- on the rack!

Herb Bread

Parmesan Cheese Sticks

White Chili

Tortellini Soup

Beer Cheese Soup

Moroccan Lentil Soup

Lemon Carrot Soup

Delta Kiwi Bars

Sour Cream Brownies

CELEBRATE!

Fabulous Food

APPETIZERS

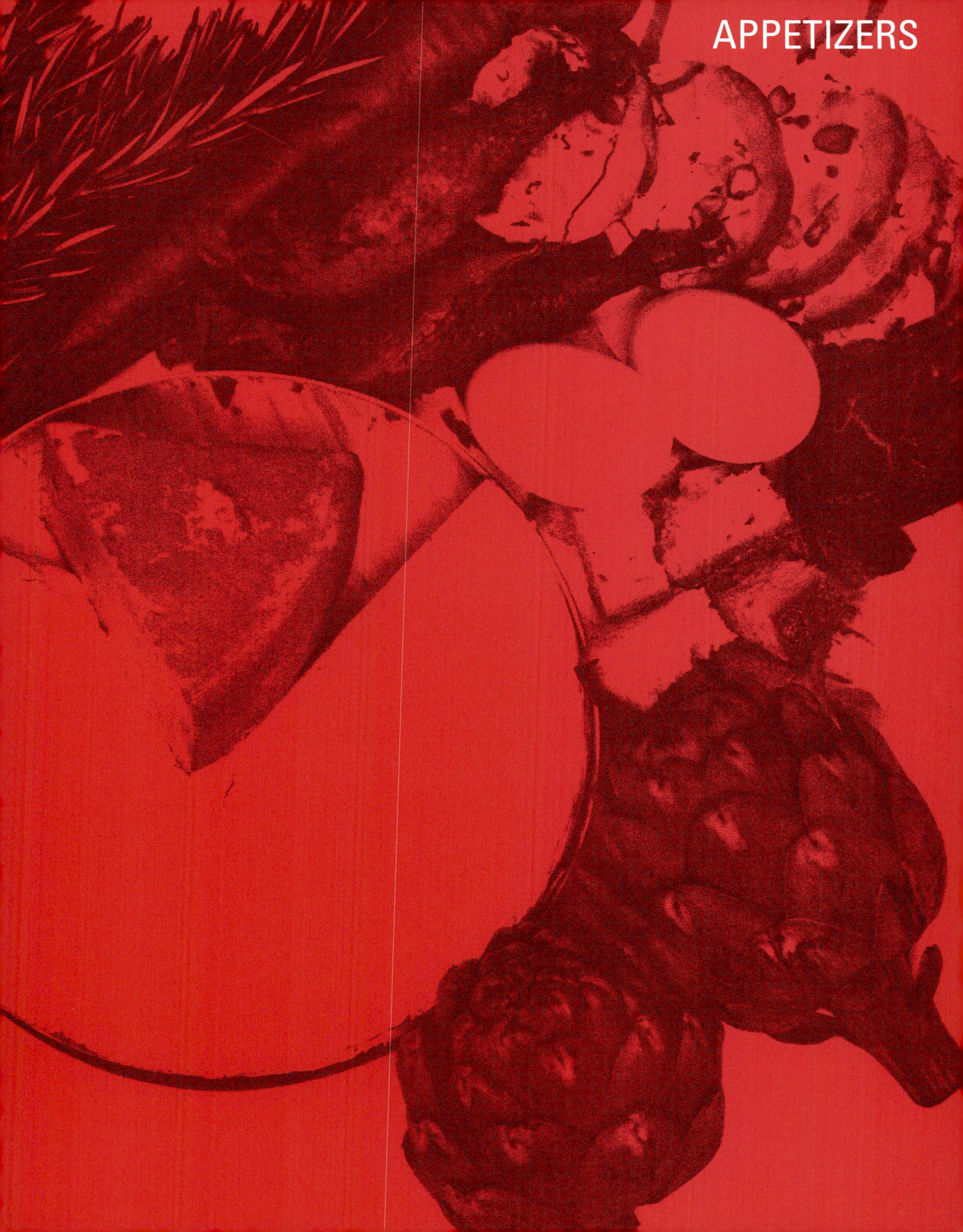

FRESH SALSA VERA CRUZ

1 large garlic clove

Juice and zest of 1 lime

1/4 cup chopped
red onions

1 pound fresh tomatoes,
peeled, seeded and
coarsely chopped

1 tablespoon sugar

1 cup loosely packed
cilantro leaves

1 jalapeño
pepper, minced

Salt and pepper

Drop garlic into food processor bowl while processor is running to finely mince garlic. Add lime zest, lime juice, onions, tomatoes and sugar and pulse to blend. Add cilantro and jalapeño. Process by pulsing, up to 1 minute or until salsa is the desired texture. Season with salt and pepper. Serve immediately or refrigerate up to 1 week. As a variation, substitute orange juice and orange zest for lime.

Makes 2 cups.

AVOCADO SALSA

3 garlic cloves, minced

2 avocados, mashed

1/2 small onion,
finely chopped

1 medium tomato, diced

Juice of 1 lemon

4 dashes Tabasco sauce

3 tablespoons diced
green chiles

1 teaspoon
Worcestershire sauce

1 teaspoon chili powder

1 teaspoon garlic salt

Freshly ground pepper

Combine all ingredients and mix well. This can be prepared in advance, but place an avocado pit into the salsa so that it does not turn brown. Serve with tortilla chips or as a condiment for grilled fish or chicken.

Makes 2 cups.

CLAM LOAF

16 ounces cream
cheese, softened

16 ounces clams,
minced, reserve juice

1 tablespoon clam juice

1/2 teaspoon salt

2 teaspoons lemon juice

2 teaspoons
Worcestershire sauce

5 drops Tabasco sauce

2 tablespoons
chopped parsley

2 to 3 green
onions, minced

1 round sourdough
loaf, unsliced

1 baguette, cubed

Mix all ingredients thoroughly except sourdough loaf and baguette. Add more clam juice if mixture is very thick. Cut a thin slice from top of sourdough loaf and hollow out center with fingers. Reserve bread to be used, in addition to the baguette cubes, for dipping. Fill loaf with clam mixture and replace top. Wrap tightly in 2 to 3 layers of foil. Bake at 250 degrees for 3 hours or 350 degrees for 2 hours. Check 1 hour before baking time is completed. The clam mixture should have the consistency of heavy cream. If it is too thick, add additional clam juice. Return to oven to complete baking. Serve with bread cubes. The bread shell, when empty, can be cut and served.

Serves 12.

ARTICHOKE FLAN

4 tablespoons
butter, softened

3 tablespoons fine, dry
bread crumbs

1 pound cream
cheese, softened

1 1/3 cups sour cream

1/4 cup crumbled
blue cheese,
room temperature

3 eggs

2 tablespoons
chopped parsley

1 tablespoon chopped
fresh dill

Pinch fresh thyme

Pinch fresh marjoram

Freshly ground pepper

1 cup quartered
artichoke hearts

6 to 12 artichoke
hearts, quartered,
for garnish

Spread a 9-inch pie plate with 1 tablespoon of the butter. Coat evenly with bread crumbs, shaking out excess. Chill. Combine cream cheese, 2/3 cup of the sour cream, blue cheese and 3 tablespoons of the butter in food processor or large bowl and blend well. Mix in eggs, herbs and seasonings. Gently fold in 1 cup quartered artichoke hearts. Spread mixture in prepared pie plate, distributing artichokes evenly. Bake at 375 degrees until puffed and lightly browned, about 30 to 35 minutes. Cool. The flan will settle. Spread top of cooled flan with remaining 2/3 cup sour cream. Garnish with quartered artichoke hearts. Cut into wedges and serve at room temperature. This can also be made in a springform pan.

Serves 12.

WARM GORGONZOLA DIP

7 slices bacon, diced

2 garlic cloves, minced

8 ounces cream
cheese, softened

1/4 cup half and half

4 ounces Gorgonzola
cheese, crumbled

2 tablespoons
chopped parsley

3 tablespoons
chopped almonds,
regular or smoked

Cook bacon in heavy skillet until almost crisp and drain excess fat. Add garlic and cook until bacon is crisp. Using a food processor or electric mixer, beat cream cheese until smooth. Add half and half and beat until combined. Stir in bacon mixture, Gorgonzola and parsley. Transfer to 2-cup ovenproof dish. Cover with foil. Prepare 1 day ahead, if desired, and refrigerate. Bring to room temperature before heating. Bake at 350 degrees until heated through, about 30 minutes. Sprinkle with almonds. Serve with crackers, bread and/or vegetables.

Serves 8 to 10.

CHUTNEY CHEESE SPREAD

6 ounces cream
cheese, softened

1/4 pound sharp Cheddar
cheese, shredded

1/4 cup chopped
green onions

2 tablespoons
dry sherry

1/2 to 3/4 teaspoon
curry powder

1/4 teaspoon salt

Pinch of cayenne pepper

1/3 to 1/2 cup
mango chutney

Slivered or sliced
almonds, toasted

Blend cream cheese, Cheddar cheese, onions, sherry, curry powder, salt and cayenne pepper until smooth. Shape on a serving plate to form a 1/2 inch thick layer or spread in a springform pan. Chill until firm. Before serving, spread chutney over top and sprinkle with toasted almonds. Serve with sesame or wheat crackers.

Serves 12.

FRESH CRUDITÉS WITH THAI PEANUT DIP

THAI PEANUT DIP

1 tablespoon minced shallots	1/4 cup water
3/4 tablespoon sesame oil	1 teaspoon red pepper flakes
6 ounces creamy peanut butter	1 teaspoon minced garlic
1/4 cup lemon juice	2 tablespoons shredded coconut
1/4 cup soy sauce	2 tablespoons brown sugar

Slice lengthwise and arrange on a large serving platter any combination of the following raw, fresh vegetables: celery, carrots, zucchini, cucumbers, red, green or yellow bell peppers, jicama, broccoli, cauliflower, Japanese eggplant, Brussels sprouts, turnips, green beans, green onions, daikon radishes, radishes, mushrooms, asparagus.

In a medium saucepan sauté shallots in oil until transparent. Add all other ingredients except brown sugar and cook over medium-low heat about 4 minutes, stirring constantly. Add sugar, cover pan and simmer 10 minutes, stirring frequently. If sauce thickens, add more water. Serve warm with fresh crudités.

Makes 2 cups.

PARMESAN CHEESE STICKS

8 ounces puff pastry, page 234	1/4 cup minced chives
1 egg beaten with 1 tablespoon of milk	1/2 cup freshly grated Parmesan cheese

Dust a work surface with flour and roll out the puff pastry into a 12 x 18-inch rectangle, 1/8 inch thick. Transfer to a 12 x 18-inch cookie sheet and trim the edges so that they are straight. Brush surface with egg wash, covering completely. Sprinkle evenly with chives. Sprinkle Parmesan over the entire surface, and gently pat it into the pastry. With a knife or pizza cutter, cut into strips 1/4 inch wide down the length of the sheet, and cut across at 3 inch intervals. Bake at 350 degrees for 10 minutes or until golden brown. Cool for 10 minutes until cheese sticks dry slightly.

Makes 60.

CROSTINI

2 baguettes, thinly sliced	5 oil-packed sun-dried tomatoes, chopped
4 tablespoons melted butter	3 tablespoons capers, drained
7 tablespoons olive oil	3 tablespoons minced parsley
8 large tomatoes, peeled, seeded and chopped	Freshly ground pepper
3 garlic cloves, minced	
3 anchovy fillets	

Heat butter with 4 tablespoons of the olive oil in a saucepan. Brush baguette slices on 1 side with the butter/oil mixture and toast at 400 degrees until lightly browned. Combine the remaining ingredients, including the 3 tablespoons olive oil. Season with pepper. Serve on toasted baguette slices.

Makes 48.

SPANAKOPITA

1 large onion, chopped

8 green onions, chopped

1 cup melted butter

1/2 teaspoon dried dill

2 tablespoons minced parsley

1 teaspoon chopped fresh mint

2 bunches spinach, rinsed, dried and chopped

Pinch of salt

1/4 pound feta cheese, crumbled

1 tablespoon grated Parmesan cheese

2 eggs, beaten

1 pound phyllo dough

In a large skillet sauté onion and green onions in 1/4 cup of the butter until translucent. Add dill, parsley and mint and sauté for 5 more minutes. Add spinach and pinch of salt. Continue cooking for 5 minutes. Remove mixture from heat, place in bowl and cool. Stir in feta and Parmesan cheeses. Fold in beaten eggs. Layer 5 sheets of phyllo, buttering between each. Spread some of the spinach mixture along the length of phyllo layers. Roll phyllo over once, tuck in the sides and roll to the end. Seal edges with melted butter and place seam side down on buttered baking sheet. Brush tops lightly with butter. Bake at 350 degrees for 30 minutes. Serve warm or cooled, cutting slices diagonally with a serrated knife.

Makes 36.

AVOCADO CROUSTADES

2 avocados, mashed

Salt

2 tablespoons lemon juice

1 baguette, cut into 1/2-inch slices and buttered

4 slices bacon, cooked until crisp and cut into 1/2-inch pieces

3/4 cup mayonnaise

1 teaspoon grated lemon rind

1 teaspoon onion flakes

Mix avocados with salt and lemon juice. Toast bread slices on both sides under broiler until lightly browned. Spread with avocado mixture and top with a bacon piece. Combine mayonnaise, lemon rind and onion flakes. Place a dab of this mixture on top of bacon. Broil until bubbly. Serve immediately.

Makes 24.

MUSHROOM BRIE EN CROÛTE

1/2 pound mushrooms, diced

2 garlic cloves, minced

1 tablespoon minced fresh ginger

1/2 to 1 teaspoon dried thyme

1/2 to 1 teaspoon beau monde seasoning

Dash of white pepper

1/4 cup dry sherry

8 ounces puff pastry, page 234

1 round Brie cheese, 8 ounces, rind removed, room temperature

1 egg white, beaten

Poppy seeds

Sauté mushrooms, garlic, ginger and seasonings in sherry until liquid evaporates. Remove from heat and set aside. Roll out pastry into 2 circles slightly larger than the Brie. Place Brie in the center of 1 circle and cover with mushroom mixture. Place the second circle on top and crimp edges to seal. Brush with egg white and sprinkle with poppy seeds. Place on an ungreased cookie sheet. Bake in a preheated oven at 375 degrees for 25 to 30 minutes, or until pastry is evenly browned. Serve with sliced baguette and apples.

Serves 12.

ASPARAGUS FRITTATA

4 to 6 green onions, thinly sliced, include tops

2 tablespoons butter

1 pound asparagus, cut into ½-inch pieces

6 eggs, beaten

½ teaspoon crumbled dried tarragon

2 tablespoons chopped parsley

¼ cup grated Parmesan cheese

1 teaspoon Dijon mustard

Salt and pepper

Sauté onions in butter until translucent. Add asparagus and sauté for 1 minute. In a bowl mix eggs, tarragon, parsley, Parmesan cheese, mustard, salt and pepper. Place butter and asparagus mixture into 10-inch square baking pan and top with egg mixture. Bake at 350 degrees for 20 minutes or until set. Cool and cut into 1-inch squares. Serve warm or cold. As a variation, these may be made in mini muffin pans.

Makes 100 1-inch squares.

CAPONATA

1 large eggplant, cut into ½-inch cubes

½ cup olive oil

½ green bell pepper, chopped

1 red bell pepper, chopped

2 stalks celery, chopped

½ red onion, chopped

1 large garlic clove, minced

2 tomatoes, seeded and chopped

Freshly ground pepper

6 ounces sliced black olives

¾ cup capers

1 tablespoon caper juice

2 tablespoons minced parsley for garnish

In a large, shallow pan cook eggplant in olive oil until tender. Add green pepper, red pepper, celery, onion and garlic and cook for 10 minutes, stirring constantly. Add tomatoes and ground pepper and cook until vegetables are blended. Remove from heat and add olives, capers and caper juice. Chill. Before serving, sprinkle with parsley. Serve with melba toast.

Serves 8 to 10.

CLAMS CASINO

2 tablespoons unsalted butter

1 teaspoon anchovy paste

24 medium-sized clams

1 red bell pepper, finely diced

1 green bell pepper, finely diced

2 slices bacon, cut into small pieces

Watercress for garnish

Cream butter and anchovy paste together. Soak clams in salted water and scrub with a brush to remove sand. Place clams on a baking pan and heat at 400 degrees for 3 to 5 minutes or until clams just begin to open. Remove and cover with cold water to cool. Open clams and remove meat, reserving shells. Place a small amount of anchovy butter in the bottom of each shell and replace the clam meat. Sprinkle with several pieces of red and green peppers. Top with a piece of bacon. Broil for 4 minutes or until bacon is cooked. Serve clams on a bed of rock salt, garnished with watercress.

Makes 24.

CHIVE HAR GOW

DUMPLING WRAPPERS

6 tablespoons wheat starch	1/2 cup plus 2 tablespoons boiling water
2 tablespoons cornstarch	

FILLING

1/2 cup finely chopped chives	Salt
3/4 pound fresh large shrimp, peeled, deveined and finely diced	Sugar
	1 teaspoon chicken broth
	1 teaspoon sesame oil
1/4 cup finely diced bamboo shoots	Pepper

A wonderful Chinese dim sum recipe.

Mix wheat starch and cornstarch together. Add boiling water and mix well. Cover with a damp towel and set aside.

Combine chives, shrimp, bamboo shoots and seasonings and mix well. Divide wrapper dough and roll into 30 equal balls. Flatten each to a circle of 2 3/4 inches in diameter. Place filling in center of wrapper, moisten edge to be sealed, and fold into half moon shape. Place dumplings on an oiled steamer rack and steam for 5 minutes. Serve hot.

Makes 30.

CAJUN SHRIMP

2 pounds jumbo shrimp, shelled and deveined, tails left on	1 tablespoon chopped fresh thyme
1 cup dry white wine	3 garlic cloves, minced
1 teaspoon mustard seeds	1 1/2 tablespoons herb or Dijon mustard
1 teaspoon red pepper flakes	5 tablespoons lemon juice
2 bay leaves	1 cup olive oil
1 lemon half	Salt and freshly ground black pepper
3 tablespoons chopped fresh basil	1 small red bell pepper, cored, seeded and diced
3 tablespoons chopped fresh dill	1 small yellow bell pepper, cored, seeded and diced
1 tablespoon chopped fresh rosemary	
1 tablespoon chopped fresh tarragon	

Combine wine, mustard seeds, red pepper flakes, bay leaves and lemon half in a 4-quart pan. Add water so that the pan is three-quarters filled and heat to boiling. Add the shrimp and cook over high heat until shrimp are opaque in the center, 3 to 4 minutes. Drain and cool. Combine the basil, dill, rosemary, tarragon, thyme, garlic, mustard and lemon juice in a large bowl. Whisk in the oil and season with salt, pepper and additional red pepper flakes, if desired. Stir in the red and yellow peppers. Add shrimp and marinate in the oil for at least 3 hours. Serve at room temperature with selected, decorative greens.

Serves 8 to 10.

CARIBBEAN SHRIMP
WITH ISLAND SALSA

40 medium shrimp, peeled and deveined	2 tablespoons pickling spices
1/2 cup water	1 tablespoon whole black peppercorns
1/3 cup dark rum	1 teaspoon red pepper flakes
2 tablespoons lemon juice	1 teaspoon salt

In a large pan combine all ingredients except shrimp. Heat over medium high until liquid begins to steam. Add shrimp and stir until light pink and opaque, just firm to the touch. Remove with a slotted spoon to a bowl of crushed ice. Toss with the ice to quickly stop the cooking. Chill shrimp with ice until ready to serve. Drain and arrange on serving platter with Island Salsa.

Serves 10 to 12.

ISLAND SALSA

5 Roma tomatoes, peeled, seeded and diced	Zest and juice of 2 limes
1 papaya, peeled, seeded and diced	2 tablespoons dark brown sugar
1 small red onion, diced	Dash cumin
1/2 cup sliced black olives	Dash chili powder
2 tablespoons finely chopped fresh mint	Dash red pepper flakes
	Dash salt
	2 shakes Worcestershire sauce

Combine tomatoes, papaya and onions in a bowl. Place half in a food processor or blender to purée. Return purée to other half. Add remaining ingredients and blend well. Set aside for 1 hour or more. Salsa is best when served at room temperature.

CHECKERBOARD OF SMOKED
SALMON AND CAVIAR

White bread, crusts removed and trimmed to 2-inch squares	Unsalted butter, softened
Sour cream	Smoked salmon, very thinly sliced
Black caviar	Golden caviar for garnish
Brown bread, crusts removed and trimmed to 2-inch squares	Dill sprigs for garnish

Photograph, page 16. No amounts for the ingredients are given because checkerboard can be any size.

Slightly moisten white bread squares with sour cream and spread evenly with black caviar. Spread the brown bread with butter and layer with smoked salmon. Place squares on a serving plate or board alternating salmon and caviar to form a checkerboard. Garnish caviar squares with a dab of sour cream and one golden caviar. Garnish salmon squares with a small sprig of dill.

SCALLOPS MACADAMIA

2 pounds sea scallops, rinsed, drained and dried

Salt and pepper

1/2 cup finely chopped macadamia nuts

1/2 cup seasoned bread crumbs

1 egg

1/2 cup milk

1/2 cup flour

Juice of 1 lemon

Oil

Lightly salt and pepper the scallops. Combine nuts and bread crumbs and set aside. Beat egg with milk. Add flour and 1/2 teaspoon salt and beat until smooth. Dip scallops into batter and roll in nut/bread crumb mixture. Fry until golden brown in hot oil, approximately 3 minutes. Drain on paper towels. Squeeze lemon juice over the top and serve hot. The scallops also can be served with ranch dressing for dipping.

Serves 16 to 20.

CRAB WONTON

1/2 pound fresh crabmeat, flaked

12 ounces cream cheese, softened

5 green onions, chopped

4 ounces water chestnuts, drained and chopped

Salt and pepper

1 package wonton wrappers

Oil

Blend crabmeat, cream cheese, onions and water chestnuts. Add salt and pepper. Place a rounded teaspoon of this mixture in the center of each wonton wrapper and fold into a triangle. To seal, moisten fingers with water and run lightly along edges. Fry in hot oil until brown on both sides, about 1 1/2 minutes. To prepare in advance, assemble and chill or freeze on a floured cookie sheet. Fry and serve warm.

Makes 3 1/2 dozen.

VEGETABLE WONTON

2 carrots, shredded

1/2 cup shredded daikon radish

1/4 cup diced white onions

1/4 cup diced celery

3/4 cup shredded Napa cabbage

1 ounce black mushrooms, soaked and slivered

1/4 teaspoon sesame oil

3/4 teaspoon salt

1 1/2 teaspoons sugar

1/4 cup oyster sauce

1/4 teaspoon white pepper

1/4 pound bean sprouts, ends trimmed

1/2 teaspoon cornstarch mixed with 1 tablespoon water

1/4 cup minced Chinese or regular chives

1 package wonton wrappers

Oil

Briefly blanch carrots, radish, onions, celery, cabbage and black mushrooms. Drain. Stir fry vegetables with sesame oil until limp. Add salt, sugar, oyster sauce, white pepper and bean sprouts. Add cornstarch mixture and chives. Remove from heat and drain completely. Put a little less than 1 teaspoon of filling in the center of the wonton wrapper and wrap it into a flower or half moon shape. Seal edges with a small amount of water. Do not overstuff wrappers. Deep fry in hot oil until crisp and golden. Drain on paper towels and serve immediately with hot mustard or a sweet and sour sauce.

Makes 50 to 60.

GINGER FRIED WONTON WITH SWEET AND SOUR SAUCE

1 pound ground pork

6 water chestnuts, minced

6 Chinese black mushrooms, soaked and minced

3 green onions, finely sliced

$^{1}/_{2}$ teaspoon white pepper

2 tablespoon minced fresh ginger

1 tablespoon soy sauce

1 teaspoon sesame oil

1 pound wonton wrappers

Oil

Combine pork and all other wonton ingredients except the wrappers and oil. This can be done a day in advance. To assemble, place 1 teaspoon of filling in center of wonton wrapper. Fold square wrapper in half to form triangle, moistening to seal. Bring 2 corners together to form a "bonnet". Repeat until all wrappers and filling are used. Deep fry wontons in hot oil a few at a time for 5 minutes or until golden brown. Serve with Sweet and Sour Sauce.

Makes 48.

SWEET AND SOUR SAUCE

1 yellow onion, chopped

1 bell pepper, chopped

1 tablespoon oil

20 ounces pineapple chunks, reserve juice

1 cup pineapple juice, add water, if necessary, to make 1 cup

$^{1}/_{3}$ cup white vinegar

$^{3}/_{4}$ cup sugar, may use $^{1}/_{2}$ brown and $^{1}/_{4}$ white

$1^{1}/_{2}$ cups water

1 teaspoon salt

8 ounces tomato sauce

4 tablespoons cornstarch dissolved in 2 tablespoons cold water

Stir fry onion and bell pepper in oil for 1 minute. Remove and set aside. Combine pineapple liquid, vinegar, sugar, water, salt and tomato sauce. Bring to a boil, stirring constantly. Reduce heat to low. Add cornstarch mixture to sauce, stirring constantly until sauce reaches a desired thickness. Add vegetables and pineapple.

BEGGARS' POUCHES WITH MACADAMIA NUTS, BACON AND PINEAPPLE

4 ounces puff pastry, page 234

16 macadamia nuts, roasted

4 ounces lean smoked bacon, cut into $^{1}/_{2}$-inch squares

$^{1}/_{2}$ cup chopped pineapple

16 chives, wilted in hot water

Technique, page 237.

Dust a counter top with flour and roll the puff pastry into a 6 x 6-inch square, $^{1}/_{16}$ inch thick. Trim the edges so that they are straight. Cut into 16 squares, $1^{1}/_{2}$ x $1^{1}/_{2}$ inches. In the center of each square place a piece of bacon, chopped pineapple and 1 macadamia nut. Lift up the corners of the pastry square and pinch together just below the points of each corner to form a pouch. Tie with a chive. Deep fry in hot oil for 4 minutes or until pouches are golden. Serve warm.

Makes 16.

BEGGARS' POUCHES WITH LAMB SAUSAGE

4 ounces puff pastry, page 234	1 tablespoon chopped fresh rosemary or basil
8 ounces lean lamb trimmings	1 egg, slightly beaten
1½ ounces bacon or lamb back fat	1 teaspoon flour
3 garlic cloves, minced	2 teaspoons salt
1 shallot, chopped	Pepper

Technique, page 237.

In a meat grinder grind lamb and bacon together or place them in a food processor and pulse until they are coarsely chopped. Transfer to a bowl and mix in the garlic, shallots and herbs. Add the egg, flour, salt and pepper. Prepare pouches as directed in the recipe for Beggars' Pouches with Macadamia Nuts, Bacon and Pineapple.

Makes 16.

ARTICHOKE IN PHYLLO

⅓ cup finely chopped carrots	2 eggs, beaten
½ cup finely chopped green onions	½ cup grated Parmesan or Romano cheese
2 tablespoons olive oil	¾ cup ricotta cheese
⅓ cup finely chopped parsley	Coarsely ground pepper
8½ ounces artichokes, drained and thinly sliced lengthwise	Phyllo dough
	4 to 5 tablespoons melted butter

Sauté the carrots and onions in olive oil just until the onion is clear. Add the parsley and artichokes and toss all together in the sauté pan. Cool. In a large bowl mix the eggs with the cheeses and add pepper. Mix in the cooled mixture from the sauté pan and blend together gently. Unroll the phyllo sheets so that they lay in a flat stack. With a sharp knife or kitchen shears, cut the stack into strips that are about 2½ inches wide. Keep phyllo covered with plastic wrap. Using 2 strips of phyllo at a time, stack 1 on the other. Place 1 teaspoon of filling at the bottom of the strip and fold into a triangle, as one folds a flag. When entire strip has been folded, brush the filled triangle with melted butter. Repeat with remaining phyllo and filling. Bake at 425 degrees for 8 to 10 minutes.

Makes 3 dozen.

BRUSCHETTA

½ pound Roma tomatoes, cored and diced	1 tablespoon chopped fresh basil
½ cup finely diced celery	Feta cheese, crumbled
2 tablespoons minced Italian parsley	½ cup olive oil
¼ cup minced red onion	4 cloves garlic, minced
2 tablespoons balsamic vinegar	1 baguette, sliced
Salt and pepper	Chopped fresh basil for garnish

Combine all of the ingredients, except ¼ cup of the olive oil, 1 minced garlic clove and baguette. Set aside. Combine remaining ¼ cup olive oil with 1 minced garlic clove and brush over baguette slices. Bake at 350 degrees until toasted, about 10 minutes. Top baguette with bruschetta mixture and arrange on a platter garnished with fresh basil. Serve warm or cold. The baguette may be replaced by toasted focaccia.

Makes 24.

ITALIAN SAUSAGE IN PHYLLO

4 Italian hot sausages, about 12 ounces

1 medium red bell pepper, finely chopped

1/4 cup minced onions

1/4 cup finely chopped hazelnuts

2 tablespoons butter

4 large mushrooms, finely chopped

1/2 teaspoon salt

1/4 teaspoon pepper

1 teaspoon crushed celery seed

1 teaspoon crushed anise seed

1 teaspoon dark brown sugar

Phyllo dough

1/2 cup melted butter

Simmer sausages in water for 10 minutes, prick with a fork, drain and cool. Remove casings, cut into 1-inch pieces and chill. Sauté bell pepper, onions and hazelnuts in 1 tablespoon of the butter until tender. Add mushrooms, seasonings, celery and anise seeds and 1 more tablespoon of butter, if necessary. Sauté until all liquid is absorbed. Add brown sugar, mix well and cool. Place sausages in a food processor and pulse until chopped. Add vegetable mixture and process until blended. Unroll phyllo sheets so that they lie flat in a stack. With a sharp knife cut the stack lengthwise into 2 1/2-inch wide strips. Keep phyllo covered with a damp tea towel or plastic wrap. Take 2 strips of phyllo and place 1 on the other. Brush with melted butter. Place 1 tablespoon of filling at the bottom of the strip and fold diagonally, over filling, into a triangle, as one folds a flag. Continue folding side over side until entire strip has been folded into the triangle. Brush with butter and place triangle on a cookie sheet. Continue process until all filling is used. Bake at 400 degrees for 10 minutes. Phyllo triangles can be frozen on cookie sheets, then stored in freezer bags. Thaw slightly before baking.

Makes 24.

ORIENTAL MEATBALLS WITH GINGER SHERRY GLAZE

6 tablespoons minced yellow onions

1 1/2 pounds ground sirloin

1 pound lean ground pork

1 1/2 cups herb-seasoned bread crumbs

2 large eggs, slightly beaten

1/4 cup plus 1 tablespoon soy sauce

2 tablespoons cream sherry

1/2 teaspoon minced fresh ginger

1/2 teaspoon salt

1/4 teaspoon white pepper

1/2 cup cornstarch

Sesame oil

Thoroughly mix the minced onions with the ground sirloin and pork. Stir in bread crumbs, 1/2 cup at a time, until well combined. Toss together with the eggs. Add soy sauce, which has been mixed with the sherry, ginger, salt and pepper. Mix thoroughly by hand and chill. When ready to use, form into small meatballs and roll in cornstarch. Add enough oil to coat the bottom of a large skillet. Sauté meatballs in batches, gently turning, until they are well browned, and adding additional oil, if needed. Meatballs can be refrigerated at this point and reheated in a small amount of cream sherry over low heat.

Makes 96.

GINGER SHERRY GLAZE

1 1/2 cups pineapple juice

1/4 cup cornstarch

1 cup beef consommé

1 tablespoon soy sauce

1 tablespoon honey

1 tablespoon grated fresh ginger

3 tablespoons cream sherry

1 each small red, yellow and green bell pepper, cut into 1-inch squares

Mix 1/2 cup of the pineapple juice with the cornstarch and set aside. In a 2-quart saucepan heat the remaining pineapple juice with the consommé, soy sauce, honey and ginger. Gradually stir in the cornstarch/pineapple juice mixture and heat gently until thickened. Add sherry and bell pepper chunks and simmer an additional 3 minutes. Pour over meatballs and serve in a chafing dish.

CARPACCIO

1½-pound filet mignon, uncooked and sliced paper thin, can be done by the butcher

⅓ cup olive oil

½ teaspoon salt

Freshly cracked pepper

½ cup thinly sliced green onions

1 medium onion, chopped

1 cup finely chopped parsley

2 tablespoons lemon zest

½ cup capers, drained and rinsed

3 garlic cloves, finely chopped

1 hard-boiled egg, chopped

Arrange meat in a circular fashion on a platter. Slowly drizzle with olive oil. Layer all other ingredients, except the egg, on top of meat. Serve immediately, or chill for up to 2 hours. Just before serving, add chopped eggs. Serve with thinly sliced baguette.

Serves 12.

BEEF SATAY WITH PEANUT SAUCE

MARINADE

2½ pounds beef tenderloin, cut into ½-inch wide strips

1¼ cups white wine

¼ cup sherry

¼ cup plus 2 tablespoons soy sauce

1½ teaspoons minced garlic

1¼ teaspoons minced fresh ginger

¼ teaspoon salt

¼ teaspoon pepper

Thread beef strips onto skewers, 2 per skewer. Combine remaining ingredients and pour over beef. Marinate for at least 12 hours. Remove beef from marinade and wipe dry. Bake at 375 degrees for 5 minutes or until done. Serve with warm Peanut Sauce.

Makes 25.

PEANUT SAUCE

1 teaspoon oil

2 teaspoons sesame oil

½ cup minced red onions

2 tablespoons minced garlic

1 teaspoon minced fresh ginger

1 tablespoon red wine vinegar

1 tablespoon sugar

⅓ cup chunky peanut butter

¼ teaspoon coriander

⅔ cup hot water

3 tablespoons catsup

In a skillet heat oil and sesame oil. Add onions, garlic and ginger and sauté for 5 to 7 minutes. Add vinegar and sugar and cook until sauce caramelizes. Remove from heat and stir in peanut butter, coriander, water and catsup.

CHA SIU BOW

DOUGH

1 package dry yeast	2 teaspoons baking powder
1¼ cups warm water	3 tablespoons shortening
6 cups flour	½ cup milk
½ cup sugar	

Dissolve yeast in water. Add flour, sugar, baking powder, shortening and milk. Knead for 15 to 20 minutes. Place in large mixing bowl. Cover and allow to rise in a warm place until dough doubles, about 1½ hours. Punch down and knead again. Divide into 24 dough balls of equal size.

FILLING

2 pounds pork butt, sliced into strips	4 tablespoons catsup
1 tablespoon minced fresh ginger	2 tablespoons hoisin sauce
1 tablespoon minced garlic	1 tablespoon ground bean sauce
1 tablespoon soy sauce	4 tablespoons sugar
1 teaspoon salt	1 teaspoon five spice powder
2 tablespoons white wine or sherry	

Combine ingredients except pork. Pour mixture over meat and marinate overnight. Remove meat from marinade and place on a roasting rack. Roast at 375 degrees for 45 minutes, turning occasionally. When cooled, dice meat into very small pieces. Mix with Seasoning Sauce. At this point filling may be made ahead, wrapped tightly and frozen. To make bows, flatten ball of dough into a circle. Place 1 tablespoon of filling in middle of dough. Gather sides around filling and twist dough to seal. Place on piece of waxed paper. Repeat. Allow bows to rise 1 hour. Steam in large, oiled steamer for 15 minutes. For baked bows brush tops with an egg wash and bake at 350 degrees for 15 minutes or until golden.

Makes 24.

SEASONING SAUCE

2 teaspoons hoisin sauce	1 cup chicken stock
1 tablespoon catsup	2 tablespoons cornstarch mixed with 1 tablespoon water
3 tablespoons oyster sauce	2 teaspoons sherry
1 teaspoon sugar	
⅛ teaspoon white pepper	

Mix ingredients except cornstarch and water. Cook over medium high heat for 5 minutes. Bring to a boil and add cornstarch mixture. Stir until mixture thickens.

STEAMED PORK DUMPLINGS

1/2 pound medium shrimp, minced	Pinch of salt
1 pound ground pork, use pork butt, remove all fat and grind in food processor, if possible	1/4 teaspoon sugar
	1/2 teaspoon sesame oil
	3 teaspoons soy sauce
3 green onions, diced	1 package round wonton wrappers
2 large bamboo shoots, chopped	1 carrot, diced, for garnish

Combine shrimp, pork, onions and bamboo shoots. Add salt, sugar, sesame oil and soy sauce. Mix thoroughly. Place a small amount of filling in the center of each wonton wrapper, bringing the sides up without closing. Flatten out the bottom by pressing down gently so that it stands up. With a knife smooth the meat mixture on the top to flatten. Crimp in the center "waistline" and place a small piece of diced carrot on the top for garnish. Repeat until all ingredients are used. Steam, over boiling water, in an oiled steamer for 20 minutes. Serve with Garlic Soy Dipping Sauce. These can be made ahead and frozen. Steam them just before serving.

Makes 75.

GARLIC SOY DIPPING SAUCE

1 tablespoon soy sauce	1 garlic clove, smashed
1 tablespoon rice wine vinegar	1 piece fresh ginger, smashed
1 teaspoon sesame oil	

Combine ingredients and mix well.

BORA BORA CHICKEN ROLLS

2 whole chicken breasts, halved, skinned and boned	24 to 32 small butter lettuce leaves
2 cups chicken broth	
4 teaspoons curry powder	

Place chicken, chicken broth and curry powder in a medium saucepan. Bring to a boil and simmer for 25 minutes or until chicken is tender. Remove from pan and chill. Cut each half breast lengthwise into 6 to 8 strips. Place a strip of chicken in each lettuce leaf and fold the sides of the lettuce leaf over the ends of the chicken. Roll and secure with a toothpick. Chill for at least 1 hour.

Makes 24.

DIPPING SAUCE

1 cup sour cream or yogurt	1/4 cup finely chopped chutney
4 tablespoons finely chopped peanuts	1 cup coconut, toasted

Place sour cream, peanuts and chutney in a small bowl and mix. Arrange lettuce-wrapped chicken on a large, round platter with a bowl of Dipping Sauce in the center. Surround the bowl with the coconut. When serving, dip chicken rolls into sauce and then into coconut.

MANDARIN POT STICKERS

DOUGH

3 cups flour

³/₄ cup warm water

FILLING

1¹/₂ pounds ground pork

¹/₂ cup finely chopped cabbage

3 tablespoons finely chopped bok choy, white part only

2 tablespoons finely chopped green onions

1 teaspoon salt

¹/₂ teaspoon garlic powder

¹/₂ teaspoon ginger

1 teaspoon sugar

¹/₂ teaspoon pepper

2 tablespoons sesame oil

1 tablespoon oyster sauce

1 cup chicken stock

Mix water and flour together. The mixture will be stiff. Knead for 10 minutes. Wrap in plastic and let rest for at least 30 minutes. Flour a work surface and roll dough into a rectangle ³/₄ inch thick. Cut into 4 equal strips. Roll 1 strip at a time to make a log. Cut each strip into 9 ¹/₂-inch pieces. Roll each piece into a circle 2¹/₂ inches in diameter. Add flour to the work surface as needed.

Mix all of the filling ingredients, except chicken stock, together. Chill for 1 hour. Place 1 tablespoon of filling in the middle of each circle of dough. Fold dough over filling to make a half circle. Tuck in each corner of dough and make 5 pleats on flat side, pressing to seal. The top should be smooth and the pot sticker slightly crescent-shaped. Repeat with remaining dough circles and filling. At this time, pot stickers can be frozen. Heat 1 tablespoon oil in a 12-inch non-stick frying pan. Place pot stickers flat side down and fry on medium-high heat for 2 minutes or until golden brown on bottom. Add chicken stock, cover and simmer 10 to 15 minutes, or until liquid evaporates Serve with Dipping Sauce.

Makes 36.

DIPPING SAUCE

¹/₂ teaspoon chili oil

5 tablespoons vinegar

3 tablespoons soy sauce

Combine all ingredients.

PARMESAN CHICKEN BITES

3 whole chicken breasts, halved, skinned and boned

¹/₂ cup crushed herb-seasoned stuffing mix or seasoned bread crumbs

¹/₂ cup grated Parmesan cheese

2 tablespoons finely minced parsley

¹/₃ cup melted butter

2 garlic cloves, mashed

Cut each breast half into 4 or 5 pieces, 1¹/₂-inches square. Combine stuffing, Parmesan and parsley until blended. Dip chicken in butter mixed with garlic and roll in crumb mixture. Place on non-stick baking sheets. Bake at 400 degrees for 10 minutes, or until tender. Serve hot or cold.

Makes 30.

FOIL-BAKED CHICKEN

$3^1/_2$ pounds chicken, skinned, boned and cut into $1^1/_2$ x 2-inch pieces

3 green onions, slivered

3 thin slices fresh ginger, slivered

MARINADE

1 teaspoon catsup

1 tablespoon oil

1 tablespoon hoisin sauce

1 tablespoon white wine or dry sherry

$^1/_2$ teaspoon salt

1 teaspoon cornstarch

1 tablespoon oyster sauce

1 tablespoon soy sauce

Dash of pepper

$^1/_2$ teaspoon sugar

$^1/_2$ teaspoon sesame oil

Combine marinade ingredients and mix well. Add chicken, green onions and ginger. Marinate 30 minutes to 2 hours. Place each chicken piece in the center of a 4 x 4-inch foil square. Fold foil over chicken to form a triangle. Double fold the open edges to seal packet. Place packets in a single layer on a baking sheet. Bake at 450 degrees for 15 minutes or until packets puff up. Foil packets may be made ahead and stored in refrigerator or freezer. Bring to room temperature before cooking.

Makes 40 to 45.

HOISIN CHICKEN DRUMETTES

12 chicken drumettes

3 tablespoons hoisin sauce

$1^1/_2$ tablespoons honey

1 tablespoon sugar

Pinch of salt

1 garlic clove, minced

1 tablespoon minced fresh ginger

1 tablespoon oil

Combine hoisin sauce, honey, sugar, salt, garlic, ginger and oil and blend well. Coat drumettes with sauce. Place in an ovenproof dish and bake at 350 degrees for 45 minutes. Serve hot or cold.

Serves 4.

MAH-FRY CHICKEN

2 whole chicken breasts, halved, skinned, boned and cut into bite-sized pieces

1/2 cup sugar

1 teaspoon ginger

1 teaspoon garlic salt

1 egg, beaten

1/2 cup soy sauce

1/3 cup flour

Oil

Combine sugar, ginger, garlic salt, egg and soy sauce. Add chicken pieces and marinate overnight. Remove chicken from marinade, dip in flour and deep fry in oil. Serve warm. As a variation, use giblets or asparagus instead of chicken.

Makes 24.

GORGONZOLA PISTACHIO LOAF

1 pound cream cheese, room temperature

1/2 pound Gorgonzola cheese, crumbled, room temperature

1/2 cup unsalted butter, room temperature

1/2 cup parsley

1/2 cup fresh basil leaves

1 cup pistachios, shelled

Parsley sprigs for garnish

Combine cream cheese, Gorgonzola and butter in a bowl and mix until well blended. In a food processor pulse the parsley, basil and pistachios until they are finely chopped. Line a 3 to 4-cup mold with plastic wrap. Spread a layer of cheese mixture in the bottom. Top with a layer of nut mixture. Continue layering until both mixtures have been used, finishing with the cheese. Cover with plastic wrap and chill several hours. Allow loaf to come to room temperature before serving. Unmold onto a plate, garnish with parsley and serve with crackers.

Serves 12.

CAVIAR TORTE

6 hard-boiled eggs, chopped

3 tablespoons mayonnaise

1 onion, finely chopped

8 ounces cream cheese, softened

1/2 cup sour cream

4 ounces black lumpfish caviar, drained

1 lemon, thinly sliced, for garnish

Dill sprigs for garnish

Blend eggs and mayonnaise together. Place on bottom of an 8-inch springform pan. Add onions as the next layer. In a food processor blend cream cheese and sour cream until smooth. Gently "frost" the top of the torte. Chill 4 hours or overnight. Just before serving, top with caviar. Garnish with lemon and sprigs of dill. Serve with water crackers.

Serves 12.

COUNTRY PÂTÉ

1/4 pound back fat or bacon, sliced

1/2 pound veal, cleaned of sinew and fat, coarsely chopped

1/2 pound veal, chicken or pork liver, coarsely chopped

1/2 pound pork back fat or bacon, boiled and chopped

1/4 cup crushed garlic

1/4 cup finely chopped shallots

1/2 cup chopped mixed fresh herbs, rosemary, thyme and basil

1 tablespoon salt

1 teaspoon pepper

1 teaspoon nutmeg

1 teaspoon celery seed

1/2 cup port wine

2 eggs, slightly beaten

1/4 cup flour

Line a terrine with the back fat or bacon. Place all of the remaining ingredients in a large bowl and mix thoroughly. Place the mixture into the lined terrine. Place in a water bath and bake at 350 degrees for 45 minutes. Cool to room temperature with 2 pounds of weight over pâté . Pour off any fat which rises to the top. Remove weight and pour Aspic into the terrine. Chill overnight. The pâté will be best on the second day.

Makes 1 1/2 pounds.

ASPIC

2 cups consommé

2 cups port wine

1 envelope unflavored gelatin

Bring consommé and wine to a boil. Gradually add the gelatin and stir until completely dissolved. Strain through a fine sieve to remove any gelatin lumps.

MUSHROOM PÂTÉ

1 medium onion, quartered

2 tablespoons butter

1/2 pound mushrooms

1 1/2 tablespoons lemon juice

1 teaspoon Worcestershire sauce

1/2 teaspoon salt

1/8 teaspoon pepper

2 tablespoons mayonnaise

Place onions in a food processor and pulse until finely chopped. Melt butter in a skillet over medium heat and add onions. Place mushrooms, in 2 batches, in food processor. Pulse until finely chopped and add to onions. Stir in lemon juice, Worcestershire, salt and pepper. Cook, stirring constantly, over medium heat, about 15 minutes, or until mixture becomes a grey paste and juices have evaporated. The mixture should not brown. Remove from heat and cool. Add mayonnaise and additional pepper, if desired. Pack into small soufflé dishes or a crockery pot and chill. Serve with sliced baguette or crackers.

Makes 1 cup.

TOMATO BASIL BRIE

1 pound Brie cheese, rind removed

1/2 cup packed fresh basil leaves

2 tablespoons pine nuts

1 tablespoon olive oil

1/2 teaspoon garlic salt

1/4 teaspoon white pepper

1/2 teaspoon minced onions

1/4 cup freshly grated Parmesan cheese

3 medium tomatoes, peeled, seeded and diced

Fresh basil leaves for garnish

Chill Brie, split in half crosswise and set aside. Mince basil leaves in processor or blender. Brown pine nuts in olive oil. Add garlic salt, pepper and onions. Combine basil, Parmesan cheese and tomatoes with pine nut mixture until well blended. Place half of this mixture on bottom half of Brie. Top with other Brie half. Spread remaining tomato/basil mixture on top. Wrap lightly in plastic wrap. Chill up to 4 hours to allow blending of flavors. Serve at room temperature, garnished with whole basil leaves. Serve with crackers or thinly sliced baguette.

Serves 12.

JALAPEÑO PÂTÉ

2 tablespoons oil

1 pound chicken livers, rinsed and drained

3/4 teaspoon salt

2 teaspoons minced garlic

1/4 cup gold tequila

1 tablespoon New Mexico chili powder

2 tablespoons ancho chili powder

1/2 cup minced green onions

2 teaspoons minced fresh jalapeño peppers

1/2 pound unsalted butter, chilled

1/2 cup heavy cream

Heat the oil in a skillet over high heat. Add the chicken livers, salt and garlic. Cook for 1 minute, stirring. Reduce heat and add tequila. Flame mixture with a match, shaking the pan over medium heat for 15 seconds. Add the chili powders, green onions and peppers. Cook for 2 minutes more on low heat, or until livers are done. Transfer to a food processor and pulse the mixture until smooth. Cool for 10 minutes. With the machine running, add the butter in slices. Pâté should be warm when the butter is added. Pulse until smooth. Remove pâté to a bowl and cool to room temperature. Whip the cream to soft peaks. Fold into pâté. Pour into a mold or individual serving dishes. Chill for at least 3 hours before serving. The pâté will keep well, chilled and covered, for up to 3 days. Bring to room temperature before serving. Surround with tortilla chips.

Serves 8 to 10.

CALIFORNIA CURRIED SALMON MOUSSE

2 salmon steaks, about 1 pound	3 chicken bouillon cubes
8 ounces cream cheese	1/2 cup finely chopped celery
1 cup sour cream	1/2 cup finely chopped green onions
2 envelopes unflavored gelatin	1 cup mayonnaise
1/4 cup plus 3 tablespoons water	1 teaspoon curry powder

Heat 2 cups salted water in an 8-inch skillet to boiling. Add salmon steaks, cover and simmer 8 minutes or until fish flakes easily with a fork. Remove steaks, cool and flake, discarding the bones. Set aside. Combine cream cheese and sour cream in double boiler. Stir over medium heat until blended. Remove from heat. Soften gelatin in 1/4 cup cold water and add to cream cheese mixture. Dissolve bouillon in 3 tablespoons hot water. Fold in bouillon and remaining ingredients, including the flaked salmon. Pour into 5-cup mold and chill until set. To serve, unmold mousse onto lettuce- or parsley-lined plate. Garnish with unsalted crackers. If you use a fish mold, add an eye to the salmon by using a black peppercorn or a slice of pimento-stuffed green olive. Add a mouth with red pimento or red pepper slice. Add fins or scales with tiny cooked shrimp. The mousse may be made ahead and kept, chilled, for up to 2 days. Unmold just before serving.

Serves 20.

SALMON PÂTÉ

1/3 cup non-fat cottage cheese	1 teaspoon Dijon mustard
1 pound fresh salmon, cooked	1 tablespoon lemon juice
3 artichoke hearts, rinsed, drained and coarsely chopped	1 tablespoon capers, rinsed and drained
1 green onion, coarsely chopped	1/4 cup pimentos, drained
3 tablespoons chopped fresh dill	Cucumber slices for garnish
6 drops Tabasco sauce	Fresh dill, chopped, for garnish

Blend cottage cheese in a food processor until smooth. Add salmon, artichokes, green onions, dill, Tabasco, Dijon, lemon juice and capers. Blend until well mixed and smooth. Add pimentos and blend, leaving specks of red color visible. Pour into a 2 1/2-cup mold and chill for several hours or overnight. Garnish with cucumber and fresh chopped dill. Serve cold with crackers or cucumber slices.

Serves 10 to 12.

PHEASANT GALANTINE

1 pheasant,
2 to 3 pounds

1 whole egg

1/4 cup heavy cream

1 teaspoon salt

1/2 teaspoon
white pepper

1 tablespoon
fresh herbs, basil,
tarragon and thyme

1/2 cup finely chopped
pistachio nuts

1 teaspoon finely
chopped shallots

1 teaspoon
crushed garlic

2 nectarines, thinly
sliced, for garnish

1/4 pound, 1/2 inch thick
prosciutto, julienned,
for garnish

1/4 pound, 1/2 inch wide,
Port Salut cheese,
julienned, for garnish

ASPIC

2 teaspoons
unflavored gelatin

2 cups pheasant or
chicken stock,
clarified, page 246

Photograph, page 228. Technique, page 233. The combination of game, sweetness of fruit, smokiness of cheese and saltiness of prosciutto makes for a wonderful mouthful.

Completely bone the pheasant and cut away any excess fat. Lay the pheasant flat and remove half the breast by cutting across the breast and leaving some breast meat still attached to the skin. Cut away any excess fat that may be attached. Remove all the thigh meat and cut the leg off to be used as garnish. Chop half the thigh and breast meat that has been removed and purée the remaining meat in a food processor. To the purée, add the egg and cream and continue to mix until smooth. Add salt and pepper. Place this mixture in a bowl and fold in the herbs, pistachio nuts, shallots and garlic until fully incorporated. Place the pheasant flat on a 12-inch square piece of cheesecloth and spoon the purée (forcemeat) down the center, lengthwise. Lift the edge and gently roll the pheasant and cheesecloth over, lay the cheesecloth back down and continue to roll the pheasant into a cylindrical shape and complete rolling. Secure by twisting the ends and tying them. Bake in a water bath (bain marie) at 350 degrees for 45 minutes. Remove from oven and cool. Once cooled, remove from cheesecloth and rewrap with plastic. Chill. To serve, slice glazed galantine 1/4 inch thick and garnish each slice with fruit, prosciutto and cheese. If a whole pheasant is not available, recipe can be made using 3 whole breasts. Purée half and dice half.

Serves 12.

Bring stock to a medium boil. While stirring, add gelatin and continue to stir until all is dissolved. Cool to room temperature. Spoon aspic over chilled galantine to desired thickness.

SPINACH IN PUFF PASTRY

1 onion, chopped

1 tablespoon butter

1 tablespoon oil

10 ounces frozen
spinach, drained
and chopped

10 to 16 ounces Gruyère
or Swiss cheese, grated

2 eggs, beaten

1/2 teaspoon
dried oregano

16 ounces puff pastry,
page 234

Sauté onions in butter and oil. Combine spinach, grated cheese, onions, 1 egg and oregano in a bowl. Roll out puff pastry into a large rectangle. Spoon filling along center of left half of pastry. Fold over remaining half and pinch sides and ends together to seal. Make egg wash with remaining egg and a little water. Brush top of pastry and slit diagonally with a serrated knife. Bake at 350 degrees for 15 to 20 minutes. This may be prepared ahead and frozen, wrapped loosely in foil. When ready to bake, remove from freezer, open foil and bake.

Serves 4.

SHRIMP FOIL PACKETS WITH RED PEPPER, SNOW PEAS AND CAVIAR

40 medium shrimp, rinsed and dried

1 cup butter

1 red bell pepper, finely chopped

1 can straw mushrooms, rinsed and drained

1/2 cup finely chopped green onions

1/2 cup chopped parsley

1 teaspoon garlic salt

2 tablespoons soy sauce

1 1/2 teaspoons Worcestershire sauce

1/2 teaspoon ginger

Dash Tabasco sauce

Caviar

1/4 pound snow peas, sliced into thin strips

Cut 8 squares of aluminum foil, approximately 12 x 12 inches. Place 5 shrimp on half of each foil square. Melt butter in a saucepan over medium heat and add remaining ingredients, except caviar and snow peas. Stir for 2 minutes. Divide mixture evenly and pour over each shrimp portion. Sprinkle with caviar and top with snow peas. Fold foil over shrimp and seal all edges, forming a square packet. Put packets on a baking sheet and bake for 20 minutes at 350 degrees. Snip an X on the top of each with scissors. Serve as individual appetizers or a first course.

Makes 8.

TOMATO, BASIL AND CHEESE TART

CRUST

1 1/4 cups flour

6 tablespoons unsalted butter, chilled and cut into pieces

2 tablespoons shortening

1/4 pound bacon, cooked, drained and crumbled

1/4 teaspoon salt

3 to 4 tablespoons ice water

In a food processor pulse flour, butter, shortening, bacon and salt until it resembles coarse meal. Add ice water and pulse until dough forms a ball. Chill for 1 hour. On a lightly floured surface roll out dough to 1/8 inch thick and 10 inches in diameter. Line a 9-inch springform pan with the dough and trim edges to fit. Prick shell with a fork and bake at 425 degrees for 20 minutes. Cool.

FILLING

4 ripe tomatoes, sliced

1 cup firmly packed fresh basil leaves

1 cup ricotta cheese

2 eggs, slightly beaten

1/4 pound mozzarella cheese, grated

1/2 cup grated Parmesan cheese

Salt and pepper

Oil

Sprinkle tomatoes with salt on both sides and drain on paper towels. In a food processor combine basil and ricotta. Pulse to purée. Add eggs and pulse until blended. Stir in mozzarella and Parmesan cheeses, salt and pepper. Pat tomatoes dry. Line bottom of tart shell with half of the tomatoes. Spread with cheese mixture. Top with remaining tomato slices, overlapping them slightly. Brush top with oil. Bake at 350 degrees for 40 to 50 minutes. Cool for 10 minutes. Serve hot or at room temperature.

Serves 6 to 8.

EGGPLANT PEPPERONI TART

CRUST

1³/₄ cups flour	3 tablespoons shortening, chilled
³/₄ teaspoon salt	¹/₄ cup ice water
¹/₂ teaspoon sugar	
6 tablespoons unsalted butter, chilled	

Pulse flour, salt, sugar, butter and shortening in a food processor until the mixture is crumbly. Add ice water and pulse until the mixture forms a ball. Remove and let rest at room temperature for 30 minutes. On a lightly floured board roll out dough to fit an 11-inch tart pan. Place in the pan and trim edges. Prick all over with a fork, line with parchment and fill with pie weights. Bake at 375 degrees for 8 minutes. Remove parchment and weights and bake an additional 7 minutes or until lightly browned. Cool to room temperature.

FILLING

¹/₃ cup olive oil	1 teaspoon salt
10 cups peeled and diced eggplant	¹/₄ teaspoon pepper
1 tablespoon minced garlic	6 ounces pepperoni, very thinly sliced
³/₄ teaspoon dried rosemary, crumbled	³/₄ pound mozzarella cheese, grated
1 teaspoon dried thyme	

Heat olive oil in a large skillet. Add eggplant, garlic and herbs. Sauté over medium-low heat 15 minutes or until tender. Season to taste with salt and pepper. Drain if necessary. Spread eggplant in tart shell. Arrange pepperoni slices on top. Bake at 375 degrees for 15 minutes. Remove and sprinkle mozzarella on the top. Return to oven and bake an additional 10 to 15 minutes or until cheese is bubbly. Let sit for 5 minutes before slicing. Serve in wedges as a first course or small squares as an appetizer.

Serves 8.

ZUCCHINI AND SAUSAGE TART

1 9-inch pie shell, baked and cooled	2 eggs
2 cups shredded zucchini	1 cup half and half
2 tablespoons butter	¹/₂ cup heavy cream
2 large sweet or hot Italian sausages, crumbled	¹/₄ cup grated Parmesan cheese
¹/₄ cup grated Cheddar cheese	Salt and pepper

Sauté zucchini in butter for 5 minutes. Drain thoroughly and set aside. Cook sausage for 5 minutes and drain. Layer zucchini, sausage and Cheddar cheese in pie shell. Beat eggs, half and half, cream, Parmesan cheese, salt and pepper until blended. Pour egg/cheese mixture over the top of the zucchini and sausage. Bake at 450 degrees for 15 minutes. Reduce heat to 350 degrees and bake an additional 15 minutes. Let stand for 15 minutes before serving.

Serves 6.

HERB TART

1 unbaked 9-inch
tart shell

3 tablespoons
minced onions

2 garlic cloves, minced

1 cup peeled, diced
and salted eggplant

2 cups sliced
oyster mushrooms

2 cups stemmed and
diced shiitake
mushrooms

2 tablespoons diced
sun-dried tomatoes

1/2 cup pancetta,
diced and fried

1 red bell pepper,
roasted and diced

1/4 cup heavy cream

1 egg

2 tablespoons minced
fresh thyme

1/2 tablespoon minced
fresh oregano

1 teaspoon minced
fresh marjoram

Salt and pepper

2 ounces goat cheese,
cut in chunks

Line a 9-inch tart pan with pastry and prick with a fork. Sauté onions, garlic and eggplant in butter until onions are translucent. Add mushrooms and sun-dried tomatoes. Sauté for an additional 3 minutes. Add all other ingredients, except goat cheese, and fold together. Place ingredients into prepared tart pan and bake at 350 degrees until firm, about 30 minutes. Sprinkle goat cheese on top during the last 10 minutes of baking. Remove and cool for at least 5 minutes before serving.

Serves 6 to 8.

TARTLETS AUX CHAMPIGNON

Pastry dough, page 238

1/2 cup butter

1 cup minced onions

1/4 cup minced shallots

2 pounds mushrooms,
thinly sliced

3 tablespoons
lemon juice

3 cups heavy cream

Salt and white pepper

Gruyère cheese, grated

Roll out pastry to 1/8 inch on a floured surface. Cut into rounds and press into 4-inch tartlet pans or mini muffin tins. Prick bottoms with a fork. Chill for 1 hour. Line with parchment and fill with pie weights. Bake at 400 degrees for 15 minutes or until golden brown. Cool. Melt butter in a saucepan and sauté onions and shallots until translucent. Add mushrooms and lemon juice. Sauté until liquid evaporates. Add cream and cook until reduced by half. Season with salt and white pepper. Fill shells with mushroom mixture and sprinkle with cheese. Bake at 425 degrees for 10 to 12 minutes.

Makes 12 4-inch tarts or 24 mini tarts.

HAM, MUSHROOM AND ONION QUICHE

CRUST

2 cups flour	1 teaspoon salt
1/4 pound butter, chilled and cut into 1/2-inch pieces	1/3 cup ice water
1/4 pound margarine, cut into 1/2-inch pieces	

FILLING

2 cups diced smoked ham	3 cups heavy cream
2 cups diced onions	1 teaspoon salt
2 cups sliced fresh mushrooms	1/2 teaspoon white pepper
2 tablespoons oil	3/4 cup grated Swiss cheese
1 tablespoon butter	3/4 cup grated Parmesan cheese
4 large eggs	
4 extra large egg yolks	

For one deep dish recipe use a 3-inch deep springform or flan pan with removable bottom, 10 inches in diameter.

In a food processor with the steel blade, put flour, butter, margarine and salt. Blend until dough resembles coarse meal. Add ice water all at once. Blend until dough forms a ball. Remove, wrap in plastic wrap and chill for at least 30 minutes. Grease pan with butter. Roll out the dough and line bottom and sides of pan. Trim edges and prick bottom with fork. Chill again for at least 1 hour.

Sauté ham in non-stick pan and set aside. Sauté onions and mushrooms in butter and oil until lightly browned and all liquid evaporates. Mix thoroughly with ham and drain excess liquid. Beat eggs, egg yolks, cream, salt and white pepper together. Stir in grated cheeses until evenly mixed. Set aside. Fill the unbaked shell with the ham mixture. Ladle egg mixture over the meat. Bake at 300 degrees for 1 1/2 hours. Quiche is done when a knife blade inserted in the center comes out clean.

Serves 6 to 8.

BREADS
AND
BREAKFASTS

GINGERBREAD WAFFLES

1 egg

1 cup molasses

3/4 cup buttermilk

1/3 cup melted butter

2 cups flour

1 1/2 teaspoons
baking soda

1 1/2 teaspoons ginger

1/2 teaspoon cinnamon

1/2 teaspoon salt

Whipped cream

Sliced fresh peaches

Beat egg until foamy and light in color. Add molasses, buttermilk and butter and blend well. Add dry ingredients and mix until just moistened. Bake in a well-greased waffle iron. Serve with whipped cream and sliced peaches.

Serves 6.

BLUEBERRY BUTTERMILK HOT CAKES

2/3 cup flour

3 teaspoons
baking powder

2 tablespoons sugar

1/2 teaspoon
baking soda

1/2 teaspoon salt

2 cups sour milk or 1 1/3
cups buttermilk plus
2/3 cup milk

2 egg yolks

4 tablespoons
melted butter

2 egg whites, beaten
to soft peaks

2 cups blueberries

Combine flour, baking powder, sugar, baking soda and salt. Add milk, egg yolks and butter. Fold in egg whites. Gently stir in blueberries. Cook on hot griddle. Because of the thickness, about 1/2 inch, these hot cakes need to cook longer than regular pancakes.

Serves 6.

PRALINE BRUNCH TOAST

8 eggs

1 1/2 cups half and half

3/4 cup plus 1 tablespoon
packed brown sugar

2 teaspoons vanilla

8 slices sourdough
bread, 3/4 inch thick

1/2 cup butter

1/2 cup maple syrup

3/4 cup coarsely
chopped pecans

In a bowl thoroughly blend eggs, half and half, 1 tablespoon of the brown sugar and vanilla. Pour half of the egg mixture into a 9 x 13-inch baking dish. Place bread slices in mixture, trimming to fit, if necessary. Pour remaining egg mixture over bread. Cover and chill several hours or overnight. Melt butter in another 9 x 13-inch baking dish. Stir in remaining 3/4 cup brown sugar and syrup. Sprinkle with pecans. Carefully place soaked bread slices on top of nuts. Pour any remaining egg mixture over bread. Bake at 350 degrees for 30 to 35 minutes. To serve, invert onto plates and sprinkle with any nuts that remain in baking dish.

Serves 6 to 8.

RASPBERRY RICOTTA CRÊPES

CRÊPES

1 egg	1 teaspoon vanilla
1 cup milk	1/4 teaspoon salt
1 tablespoon sugar	1 cup flour
1 tablespoon brandy	Oil

RASPBERRY FILLING

1 pint raspberries	1 tablespoon butter
3/4 cup sugar	1 cup ricotta cheese
3/4 cup water	

Whisk egg with milk. While whisking, add sugar, brandy, vanilla and salt. Blend well. Add flour slowly, beating constantly. Chill 15 minutes or longer. Heat an 8-inch crêpe pan or skillet. Oil pan, pouring off excess oil. Tilting the pan, coat evenly with 2 to 3 tablespoons batter. Bubbles should appear right away. Cook until sides peel away from pan, approximately 30 seconds. Turn and cook briefly on other side.

Makes 8 crêpes.

Bring half pint of the raspberries, sugar and water to a boil in a small saucepan. Reduce until sauce coats the back of the spoon. Add remaining raspberries and butter. Turn off heat when butter is melted, stirring carefully to keep the remaining raspberries whole. Reserve half of the raspberry mixture for the sauce and set aside. Add ricotta cheese to the remaining sauce and blend carefully. Fill crêpes, rolling gently. Top with reserved Raspberry Filling.

CHILE PUFF

5 eggs	1/4 teaspoon salt
1 cup cottage cheese	8 ounces Monterey Jack cheese, grated
2 tablespoons melted butter	4 ounces mild green chiles, diced
1/4 cup flour	
1/2 teaspoon baking powder	

This recipe can be doubled nicely, but increase baking time 10 to 15 minutes. It also can be prepared and chilled overnight before baking.

Mix eggs, cottage cheese and butter. Add flour, baking powder and salt. Add Monterey Jack cheese and chiles and mix well. Pour into a greased 8-inch square pan. Bake at 350 degrees for 35 minutes. Let stand 5 to 10 minutes before serving.

Serves 6.

SOUR CREAM CRUNCH COFFEE CAKE

2 cups flour	1/2 cup butter, cut into small pieces
1/2 teaspoon salt	1 teaspoon baking soda
1 teaspoon cinnamon	1 cup sour cream
Dash of nutmeg	1 egg, beaten
Dash of cloves	1 1/2 cup chopped walnuts or pecans
1 2/3 cups brown sugar	

In a food processor blend flour, salt, spices and brown sugar. Cut in butter to resemble coarse meal. Press half of mixture into bottom of a greased 9-inch square pan. Stir baking soda into the sour cream and mix into remaining flour mixture. Add the egg. Pour batter over bottom layer and spread evenly. Sprinkle nuts over batter. Bake at 350 degrees for 40 to 50 minutes.

Serves 12.

RASPBERRY CREAM CHEESE COFFEE CAKE

8 ounces cream cheese, softened

1 cup sugar

$^1/_2$ cup butter, softened

1$^3/_4$ cups flour

2 eggs

$^1/_4$ cup milk

1 teaspoon baking powder

$^1/_2$ teaspoon baking soda

$^1/_2$ teaspoon vanilla

$^1/_4$ teaspoon salt

$^1/_2$ cup raspberry preserves

Powdered sugar

In a large bowl beat cream cheese, sugar and butter until fluffy. Add 1 cup of the flour, eggs, milk, baking powder, baking soda, vanilla and salt. Beat 2 minutes. Beat in remaining flour on low speed until well mixed. Spread evenly in a greased and floured 9 x 13-inch baking pan. Spoon preserves onto top of batter. Cut through batter with a knife to create a marbled appearance. Bake at 350 degrees for 30 to 35 minutes. Cool slightly on a wire rack. Sift powdered sugar over top.

Serves 12.

ORANGE CINNAMON COFFEE CAKE

1 cup butter, softened

4 tablespoons shortening

2$^1/_2$ cups sugar

4 eggs, separated

3$^1/_2$ cups flour, sifted 6 times

4 teaspoons baking powder

$^3/_4$ teaspoon salt

1$^1/_2$ cups orange juice

1 teaspoon vanilla

2 tablespoons cocoa

1 cup chopped nuts

1 teaspoon cinnamon

Butter

1 cup powdered sugar

Grated rind of 1 orange

Cream butter and shortening with 2 cups of the sugar. Add egg yolks, 1 at a time, mixing well after each addition. Remove $^1/_2$ cup of the sifted flour and to it add the baking powder and salt. Sift and add to batter and beat 4 minutes. Add the remaining flour alternately with 1$^1/_4$ cups of the orange juice and vanilla. Beat and fold in the egg whites. Mix the remaining $^1/_2$ cup sugar with cocoa, nuts and cinnamon. Alternate layers of dough with the cocoa/ cinnamon mixture and dot with butter. Bake in a greased angel food cake pan for 1 hour at 350 degrees. Test for doneness and bake an additional 15 minutes if necessary. Ice with the mixture of powdered sugar, remaining $^1/_4$ cup orange juice and orange rind.

Serves 12.

CHOCOLATE CHIP BANANA COFFEE CAKE

1/2 cup butter, softened

8 ounces cream cheese, softened

3/4 cup plus 2 tablespoons granulated sugar

1/2 cup light brown sugar

2 eggs

1 cup puréed bananas

1 teaspoon vanilla

2 1/4 cups flour

1 1/2 teaspoons baking powder

6 ounces semisweet chocolate chips

3/4 teaspoon cinnamon

3/4 teaspoon nutmeg

1 cup sifted powdered sugar

1 tablespoon milk

1/4 teaspoon vanilla

Cream butter and cream cheese. Gradually beat in 3/4 cup granulated sugar and brown sugar. Beat in eggs, 1 at a time. Stir in banana purée and vanilla. Sift together flour and baking powder and add to the banana mixture. In a separate bowl, combine chocolate chips, remaining 2 tablespoons granulated sugar, cinnamon and nutmeg. Stir half into batter. Spread half of the batter into a greased 9 x 13-inch pan. Sprinkle with remaining chocolate mixture. Spread remaining batter on top. Bake at 350 degrees for 25 to 30 minutes or until a toothpick inserted in center comes out clean. For glaze stir powdered sugar, milk and vanilla until smooth. Glaze cake while slightly warm.

Serves 12 to 16.

ORANGE NUT COFFEE CAKE

2 cups flour

1 teaspoon baking powder

1 teaspoon baking soda

Dash of salt

1 teaspoon cinnamon

1/4 teaspoon nutmeg

1 cup sugar

1 egg

3/4 to 1 cup milk

1/2 cup oil

Juice of 1 orange

1 to 2 tablespoons grated orange rind

3/4 cup powdered sugar

1 tablespoon half and half

1/2 teaspoon vanilla

Sift dry ingredients together. Add egg, milk, oil, orange juice and rind. Beat at medium speed until just mixed. Pour into a greased and floured 9 x 13-inch pan or 2 8-inch round pans. Sprinkle with Topping. Bake at 350 degrees for 30 minutes. Combine powdered sugar, half and half and vanilla. Drizzle over partially cooled cake and spread with spoon until smooth.

Serves 12 to 16.

TOPPING

1 cup brown sugar

1/4 cup butter

1 cup chopped nuts

Combine sugar, butter and nuts. Mix well.

CHOCOLATE STREUSEL COFFEE CAKE

1/2 cup shortening

1 1/4 cups sugar

3/4 cup packed brown sugar

2 eggs

3 cups flour

4 teaspoons baking powder

3/4 teaspoon salt

1 1/2 cups milk

6 ounces semisweet chocolate chips, melted

2/3 cup coconut

1/2 cup chopped nuts

1 teaspoon cinnamon

1/4 teaspoon nutmeg

Cream shortening, 3/4 cup of the sugar and brown sugar together. Beat in eggs. Sift flour, baking powder and salt together. Add alternately with milk to sugar mixture, blending well after each addition. Spread evenly in a greased 9 x 13-inch pan. Spoon melted chocolate over batter. Cut through batter with a knife to create a marbled appearance. Combine coconut, nuts, remaining 1/2 cup sugar, cinnamon and nutmeg. Sprinkle over batter. Bake at 375 degrees for 35 to 45 minutes, or until a toothpick inserted in center comes out clean. Serve warm.

Serves 12 to 16.

APPLE STREUSEL MUFFINS

1 1/2 cups flour

1/2 cup sugar

2 teaspoons baking powder

1 teaspoon cinnamon

1/4 teaspoon allspice

1/4 teaspoon baking soda

1/4 teaspoon salt

2 large eggs

1 cup sour cream

1/2 cup melted butter

1 cup peeled and diced apple

Mix 1 1/2 cups flour, 1/2 cup sugar, baking powder, cinnamon, allspice, baking soda and salt in a large bowl until thoroughly blended. In a separate bowl beat eggs and add sour cream and butter. Stir in apple. Pour egg mixture over flour mixture until dry ingredients are moistened. Spoon batter into greased muffin cups. Top each muffin with a generous sprinkling of Streusel Topping . Bake at 375 degrees for 20 minutes or until browned and a wooden pick inserted in center comes out clean. Cool at least 1 hour.

Makes 18 regular or 12 large muffins.

STREUSEL TOPPING

1/2 cup chopped walnuts

1/4 cup flour

3 tablespoons sugar

2 tablespoons butter, softened

1/4 teaspoon cinnamon

Mix all topping ingredients with a fork until crumbly.

VIENNA COFFEE CAKE

1 cup butter, softened	15$\frac{1}{2}$ ounces condensed milk
1$\frac{3}{4}$ cups sugar	1 teaspoon vanilla
4 eggs	1 tablespoon unsweetened cocoa
3$\frac{1}{4}$ cups flour	1 teaspoon cinnamon
$\frac{1}{2}$ teaspoon salt	Butter
1 tablespoon baking powder	

Cream together butter and 1$\frac{1}{2}$ cups of the sugar until fluffy. Add the eggs, 1 at a time, beating well after each addition. Sift together flour, salt and baking powder. Mix the milk and vanilla together. Add the dry ingredients alternately with the milk, mixing just until blended after each addition. Combine the remaining $\frac{1}{4}$ cup sugar, cocoa and cinnamon. Place a layer of batter and a layer of cocoa/cinnamon into a well-greased bundt pan. Repeat layering once and end with batter. Bake at 350 degrees for 60 minutes or until a toothpick inserted into the center comes out clean. Cool thoroughly on a rack before removing from the pan. Before serving, slice into serving-size pieces and butter each slice lightly. Reform into the original shape and reheat in a slow oven.

Makes 1 cake.

CRANBERRY ORANGE MUFFINS WITH CRANBERRY RAISIN PRESERVES

1 egg	1 teaspoon salt
$\frac{3}{4}$ cup sugar	3 tablespoons orange rind
1 cup sour cream	$\frac{1}{2}$ cup chopped nuts
2$\frac{1}{2}$ cups flour	1 cup sliced cranberries
1 teaspoon baking soda	
1 teaspoon baking powder	

Beat egg and sugar together. Add sour cream, flour, baking soda, baking powder and salt. Stir until moist. Add orange rind, nuts and cranberries. Spoon into greased muffin cups. Bake at 350 degrees for 20 to 25 minutes. Serve with Cranberry Raisin Preserves.

Makes 24.

CRANBERRY RAISIN PRESERVES

1 cup whole cranberries	1 cup sugar
1 cup raisins	$\frac{3}{4}$ cup water

Cook cranberries, raisins and sugar in water in a small saucepan until cranberries are soft and preserves are thickened. Cool.

RICE BRAN MUFFINS WITH WALNUT TOPPING

1¼ cups whole wheat flour

1 cup rice bran

½ cup sugar

2 teaspoons baking powder

½ teaspoon salt

1 cup milk

⅓ cup oil

2 egg whites, lightly beaten

¼ cup firmly packed brown sugar

¼ cup chopped walnuts

½ teaspoon cinnamon

Combine flour, rice bran, sugar, baking powder and salt in a large bowl. Combine milk, oil and egg whites in a small bowl. Add to dry ingredients and stir just until dry ingredients are moistened. Spoon batter into muffin cups. Combine brown sugar, walnuts and cinnamon in a small bowl. Sprinkle over batter. Bake at 400 degrees for 15 to 17 minutes. Remove from cups and cool for a few minutes on a wire rack. Serve warm. Muffins may be frozen and reheated. For best results do not substitute oat bran for rice bran in this recipe.

Makes 12.

JACK-O'-LANTERN MUFFINS

½ cup melted butter

¾ cup brown sugar

2 eggs

1 cup puréed pumpkin

½ cup buttermilk

2 cups flour

1 teaspoon baking soda

2 teaspoons baking powder

½ teaspoon salt

1 teaspoon allspice

1½ teaspoons cinnamon

½ teaspoon cloves

½ teaspoon mace

½ cup raisins

1 cup chopped nuts

Beat butter, brown sugar, eggs, pumpkin and buttermilk together. Sift dry ingredients together and add to mixture. Add raisins and nuts, stirring just enough to moisten. Spoon into greased muffin cups. Bake at 400 degrees for 25 to 30 minutes.

Makes 18.

BUTTERMILK BRAN MUFFINS

3 cups bran buds

1 cup boiling water

1½ cups sugar

1 teaspoon salt

½ cup butter, softened

2 eggs, well beaten

2 cups buttermilk

2½ teaspoons baking soda

2½ cups flour

Pour boiling water over bran buds in large bowl. Let stand to moisten. Add sugar, salt, butter and eggs. Mix well. Combine buttermilk and baking soda. Stir into batter with flour until mixture is moistened. Pour batter into well greased muffin cups. Store in the refrigerator, covered, for up to 2 weeks. Bake at 400 degrees for 20 minutes.

Makes 24.

ORANGE ROLLS

2 packages active dry yeast	3 eggs, beaten
1 1/4 cups warm water	4 1/2 cups flour
1 cup sugar	Grated rind of 1 orange
1/2 cup shortening	1/2 cup butter, softened
1 teaspoon salt	

Dissolve yeast in 1/2 cup of the warm water. Mix 1/2 cup of the sugar, shortening, salt, the remaining 3/4 cup warm water and eggs. Add to yeast. Beat in flour. Let rise until it doubles in size. Punch down. Cover well and chill. On a floured surface, roll dough into a rectangle 1/4 inch thick. Mix orange rind, remaining 1/2 cup of sugar and butter and spread over dough. Roll up like a jelly roll and slice into 1-inch slices. Place in well greased muffin cups. Bake at 400 degrees for 10 minutes or until lightly browned. Remove immediately and serve with Orange Butter.

Makes 18 to 24.

ORANGE BUTTER

1/2 cup butter, softened	1/4 teaspoon orange extract
3 tablespoons powdered sugar	2 teaspoons orange rind

In a food processor or mixing bowl, cream butter and sugar. Add extract and orange rind. Blend to a fluffy consistency.

CINNAMON STICKY ROLLS

1 cup brown sugar	1 cup hot water
1 cup heavy cream	1 package active dry yeast
3 to 3 1/2 cups flour	1 teaspoon salt
3/4 cup sugar	1 egg
1/2 cup plus 2 tablespoons butter, softened	2 teaspoons cinnamon

Mix brown sugar and cream in an ungreased 9 x 13-inch pan. In a large mixing bowl blend 1 1/2 cups of the flour, 1/4 cup of the sugar, 2 tablespoons of the butter, water, yeast, salt and egg. Beat for 3 minutes at medium speed. Stir in remaining flour and knead on floured surface for 1 minute. Press or roll dough into a 7 x 15-inch rectangle. Combine the remaining 1/2 cup sugar, 1/2 cup butter with cinnamon and spread over dough. Starting at long side, roll tightly and seal edges. Cut dough into 16 to 20 rolls. Place cut side down on cream mixture. Cover and let rise until doubled, about 35 to 45 minutes. Bake at 400 degrees for 20 to 25 minutes. Cool 10 to 15 minutes before inverting onto a tray.

Makes 16 to 20.

PERSIMMON ORANGE RAISIN BREAD

3½ cups puréed persimmon pulp, 4 to 6 large persimmons

3 eggs

4 cups sugar

4 teaspoons baking soda

1 teaspoon salt

1 teaspoon cinnamon

1 teaspoon cloves

1 teaspoon nutmeg

5 cups flour

1 cup oil

Grated rind of 1 orange

2 cups chopped nuts

2 cups raisins

In a large mixing bowl combine persimmon pulp, eggs and sugar. Mix thoroughly. Add soda, salt and spices. With mixer on low speed add flour, 1 cup at a time, to the pulp mixture. When all the flour is blended, add oil and mix into batter. Fold in orange rind, nuts and raisins. Divide batter among 3 greased loaf pans. Bake at 350 degrees for 60 to 75 minutes or until a toothpick inserted in the center comes out clean. Cool 5 minutes. Remove from pans and tightly wrap in plastic while still warm. Cool to room temperature and chill overnight to allow loaves to darken and spices to blend. Serve at room temperature or slightly warmed.

Makes 3 loaves.

CHOCOLATE TEA BREAD

1½ cups flour

1⅓ cups sugar

⅓ cup cocoa

1 teaspoon baking soda

¾ teaspoon salt

¼ teaspoon baking powder

⅓ cup shortening

2 eggs

½ cup applesauce

⅓ cup water

⅓ cup chopped nuts

½ cup semisweet chocolate chips

Combine all ingredients, except nuts and chocolate chips, in a large mixing bowl. Beat on low speed to blend for 30 seconds. Beat on high speed for 3 minutes. Stir in nuts and chips. Grease and flour a 9 x 5 x 3-inch loaf pan. Pour mixture into pan and bake at 350 degrees for 60 minutes or until a toothpick inserted in center comes out clean. Cool slightly and remove from pan. Cool thoroughly before slicing.

Makes 1 loaf.

PINEAPPLE NUT BREAD

1 egg, beaten

⅓ cup milk

⅓ cup melted butter

1 cup undrained crushed pineapple

1 cup chopped walnuts

8 ounces dates, chopped

2¾ cups flour

¾ cup sugar

1 tablespoon baking powder

¼ teaspoon baking soda

½ teaspoon salt

Combine egg, milk, butter, pineapple, walnuts and dates. Sift dry ingredients and combine the two mixtures. Stir to blend. Place mixture in a greased and floured loaf pan and bake at 350 degrees for 45 minutes or until a toothpick inserted in the center comes out clean.

Makes 1 loaf.

ZUCCHINI WHEAT BREAD

3 eggs, beaten

1 cup oil

2 cups sugar

2 cups grated
raw zucchini

3 teaspoons vanilla

3 cups whole wheat flour

1 teaspoon salt

1 teaspoon baking soda

1/2 teaspoon
baking powder

3 teaspoons cinnamon

1 cup chopped walnuts

1 cup chopped dates

1/2 cup raisins

Beat eggs until light and foamy. Add oil, sugar, zucchini and vanilla. Gently mix until well blended. Sift together the dry ingredients. Add to the egg mixture and blend. Add nuts, dates and raisins. Pour batter into 2 greased loaf pans. Bake at 325 degrees for 1 hour. Let stand for 15 minutes before removing from pans. Cool on a rack.

Makes 2 loaves.

LEMON TEA BREAD

1 cup butter, softened

3 cups sugar

4 eggs, beaten

1 cup milk

3 cups flour

2 teaspoons
baking powder

1 teapsoon salt

Grated rind of 2 lemons

1 cup chopped nuts

1 cup lemon juice

A marvelous way to use those wonderful California lemons!

Cream butter and 2 cups of the sugar. Beat in eggs and gradually stir in milk. Combine dry ingredients and stir into egg mixture. Add lemon rind and stir until mixture is well blended. Stir in nuts. Pour batter into 2 well-greased loaf pans. Bake at 325 degrees for 1 hour. Combine remaining 1 cup sugar and lemon juice. Remove bread from oven and evenly prick tops of loaves with a fork. Pour the sugar and lemon juice mixture over the loaves. Cool slightly and remove from pans.

Makes 2 loaves.

APRICOT BREAD

1 pound dried apricots,
cut into small pieces

2 cups water

2 cups sugar

3/4 cup butter

1 teaspoon cinnamon

1 teaspoon cloves

1/2 teaspoon nutmeg

1 teaspoon salt

2 eggs, beaten

4 cups flour

2 teaspoon baking soda

In a large saucepan cook apricots, water, sugar, butter, spices and salt for 5 minutes. Cool. Add eggs and flour which has been sifted with baking soda. Stir until everything is moistened. Pour into 2 greased 9 x 5-inch loaf pans and bake at 350 degrees for 1 hour. Cool before slicing.

Makes 2 loaves.

APRICOT CHOCOLATE LOAVES

DOUGH

1 cup warm water	1 tablespoon oil
1 package active dry yeast	1 teaspoon salt
1 tablespoon sugar	
2$\frac{1}{2}$ cups flour	

Combine water, yeast and sugar. Stir in 1 cup of the flour. Add oil and salt. Add remaining flour. Knead for a few minutes until smooth and elastic. Let rise in covered bowl for 45 minutes. On a lightly floured surface roll half of the dough into an 8-inch square. Place on a greased cookie sheet. Spread half of the filling in a 4-inch wide strip down the center of the dough, leaving 2 inches on either side. Slit dough at 1-inch intervals along each side of the filling. Fold strips, 1 at a time, diagonally over filling, alternating from side to side. Repeat with remaining dough and filling. Cover and let rise in a warm place until double, about 1 hour. Bake at 350 degrees for 30 minutes or until golden brown. Cool on wire rack. Top with icing.

Makes 2 loaves.

FILLING

1 cup dried apricots, chopped	1 teaspoon cinnamon
$\frac{3}{4}$ cup water	$\frac{1}{2}$ cup semisweet chocolate chips
$\frac{1}{3}$ cup brown sugar	

In a small saucepan combine apricots and water. Bring to boil, reduce heat and simmer, uncovered, about 10 minutes or until the water is absorbed. Stir in the brown sugar until dissolved. Add the cinnamon. Stir in the chocolate chips until melted. Cool.

ICING

$\frac{1}{2}$ cup sifted powdered sugar	1 tablespoon milk
$\frac{1}{4}$ teaspoon vanilla	

In a small bowl combine powdered sugar, vanilla and enough of the milk to make an icing thin enough to drizzle over the loaves.

CRANBERRY APPLESAUCE BREAD

$\frac{1}{2}$ cup butter, softened	1 teaspoon cinnamon
$\frac{3}{4}$ cup sugar	$\frac{1}{2}$ teaspoon cloves
2 eggs	$\frac{1}{4}$ teaspoon nutmeg
1 cup applesauce	1 cup quick cooking oatmeal
1$\frac{1}{2}$ cups flour	$\frac{3}{4}$ cups whole cranberry sauce
$\frac{3}{4}$ teaspoon baking soda	
$\frac{1}{4}$ teaspoon salt	

Raisins and walnuts may be added to this batter.

Cream butter and sugar together. Add eggs and mix well. Stir in applesauce. Sift together flour, baking soda, salt and spices and blend into egg mixture. Stir in oatmeal and cranberry sauce. Mix well. Pour into a greased 9 x 5-inch loaf pan. Bake at 350 degrees for 60 minutes or until a toothpick inserted in the center comes out clean.

Makes 1 loaf.

ORANGE PUMPKIN BREAD

2/3 cup butter

2 1/2 cups sugar

4 eggs

16 ounces pumpkin

2/3 cup water

3 1/3 cups flour

2 teaspoons baking soda

1 1/2 teaspoons salt

1 teaspoon cinnamon

1 teaspoon cloves

1/2 teaspoon baking powder

1 orange

2/3 cup chopped nuts

2/3 cup raisins

Cream butter and sugar thoroughly. Add eggs, pumpkin and water. Sift together flour, soda, salt, cinnamon, cloves and baking powder. Add to pumpkin mixture. Remove seeds from orange. Using a blender, grind orange, including rind and add to pumpkin. Stir in nuts and raisins. Pour into a well greased 9 x 5 x 3-inch loaf pan. Bake at 350 degrees for 60 minutes or until a toothpick inserted in the center comes out clean.

Makes 1 loaf.

SAVORY BREAD

2 cups boiling water

1 cup old fashioned oats

1/2 cup honey

1/2 cup molasses

2 packages active dry yeast, softened in a small amount of warm water

1/2 teaspoon dried basil

1/2 teaspoon dried oregano

1/2 teaspoon dried parsley

1/2 teaspoon anise seed

1/2 teaspoon dried savory

6 cups flour

Pour boiling water over oats and stir in honey and molasses. Cool to lukewarm and add dissolved yeast. Mix herbs together and add to oats. Stir in 4 cups of flour and then knead in the remaining 2 cups. Let dough rise in a warm place until doubled, about 1 1/2 to 2 hours. Divide dough in half. Put into 2 greased loaf pans. Let rise until doubled again, about 1 hour. Place in a cold oven, set temperature to 325 degrees and bake for 50 to 60 minutes or until bread pulls away from sides of pan. Cool on a wire rack.

Makes 2 loaves.

HERB BREAD

1/4 teaspoon salt

1/4 teaspoon dried savory

1/2 teaspoon dried thyme

Dash of cayenne pepper

Dash of paprika

3/4 cup butter, softened

1 unsliced loaf white bread

Blend salt, savory, thyme, cayenne and paprika with butter. Cut all but the bottom crust from bread. Make 1-inch cuts across the bread but not through bottom and spread the herbed butter between slits. Make 1 lengthwise cut down the center but not through the bottom. Spread herbed butter down long cut and also on the sides and top of loaf. Place on cookie sheet and bake at 350 degrees for 20 to 25 minutes.

Serves 10.

ONION HERB BREAD

1 tablespoon butter

1½ tablespoons sugar

1 teaspoon salt

½ cup milk, scalded

1 package active
dry yeast

½ cup warm water

2¼ cups whole
wheat flour

1 tablespoon dried
onions

1 teaspoon dried herbs,
dill, thyme
and rosemary

Butter

Combine butter, sugar and salt with milk. Cool to lukewarm. Dissolve yeast in water and add to milk mixture. Add flour, onions and herbs and mix for 2 minutes. Let rise for 45 minutes. Pour into an 8-inch greased pie pan. Bake at 350 degrees for 60 minutes. Butter top of bread when it is removed from the oven.

Serves 8.

HONEY CORN MUFFINS

¾ cup flour

1¼ teaspoons
baking powder

½ teaspoon salt

⅓ cup
yellow cornmeal

1 egg

⅓ cup milk

¼ cup honey

3 tablespoons oil

¼ cup unpeeled
diced apple

Mix flour, baking powder and salt. Stir in cornmeal. Combine egg, milk, honey and oil. Add to dry ingredients, stirring just enough to moisten flour mixture. Fold in apple. Spoon batter into greased muffin cups. Bake at 400 degrees for 20 minutes.

Makes 12.

SOUTHERN CORNBREAD STICKS

1 cup yellow cornmeal

½ cup flour

2 teaspoons
baking powder

¼ teaspoon salt

1 cup buttermilk

½ teaspoon baking soda

2 eggs

2 tablespoons
bacon drippings

This can be baked in a square pan and used for cornbread stuffing.

In a small bowl mix together the cornmeal, flour, baking powder, salt and set aside. Beat the buttermilk with the baking soda and add it with the eggs to the cornmeal mixture. Stir until blended. Place a small amount of bacon drippings into each corn stick mold. Place the pans for 5 minutes into an oven which has been preheated to 450 degrees. Remove the pans and tip to thoroughly coat each mold with the drippings. Pour any excess drippings into the batter and stir. Spoon batter into each mold to three-quarters full. Bake for 20 to 30 minutes or until the sticks are golden brown and have come away slightly from the sides. Serve hot with butter.

Makes 14 sticks.

CREAM TEA SCONES WITH CLOTTED DEVONSHIRE CREAM

2 cups flour	1 teaspoon grated orange rind
1/4 cup sugar	
	1 egg, separated
1 tablespoon baking powder	1 egg, beaten
1/2 teaspoon salt	3/4 cup heavy cream, room temperature
4 tablespoons butter, chilled and cut into pieces	Sugar
1/2 cup currants or raisins	

Combine flour, sugar, baking powder and salt. Cut butter into dry ingredients until the mixture resembles coarse meal. Stir in currants or raisins and orange rind. Add egg yolk to beaten egg. Blend into the cream. Stir cream mixture into dry ingredients with a fork until the dough pulls away from the bowl. Gently knead about 15 times on a floured surface. Roll out the dough to 1 inch thickness. Cut with a biscuit cutter. Place 1 inch apart on a cookie sheet. Brush tops with egg white. Sprinkle with additional sugar. Bake at 400 degrees for 12 to 15 minutes or until nicely browned. Serve with Clotted Devonshire Cream.

Makes 6 to 8.

CLOTTED DEVONSHIRE CREAM

1 cup heavy cream	1 1/2 cups sour cream
3 tablespoons powdered sugar	

In a chilled bowl beat cream and sugar together until soft peaks form. Gently fold in sour cream until blended.

BLUEBERRY SCONES

2 cups flour	1/4 cup buttermilk
1/4 cup sugar	1/4 cup milk
1 tablespoon baking powder	1 egg
6 tablespoons butter, chilled and cut into pieces	1/2 cup blueberries
	Sugar

Mix together flour, sugar and baking powder. Cut butter into dry ingredients until the mixture resembles coarse meal. Combine buttermilk, milk and egg. Stir into dry ingredients until moistened. Gently knead 15 times on a floured surface. Add blueberries and mix gently. Shape dough into a round, 1/2 inch thick. Cut into 6 wedges. Sprinkle with additional sugar. Bake on a lightly greased baking sheet at 350 degrees for 15 minutes or until golden brown.

Makes 6.

CRANBERRY SCONES

3¹/₃ cups bran or whole wheat flour

2 tablespoons sugar

Pinch of salt

1¹/₂ teaspoons baking powder

¹/₂ cup butter, chilled and cut into pieces

1¹/₂ cups dried cranberries

Grated rind of ¹/₂ orange

Grated rind of ¹/₂ lemon

1 cup cold milk

Sugar

Combine flour, sugar, salt and baking powder in a large bowl. Cut in butter and mix until mixture resembles coarse meal. Stir in cranberries, orange and lemon rind. Slowly add milk and mix until dough begins to form a ball. Roll out to ¹/₂ inch thickness. Using a 2 or 3-inch cutter, cut into circles. Place on a baking sheet and sprinkle with additional sugar. Bake at 375 degrees for 12 to 15 minutes or until golden brown.

Makes 12.

APRICOT POCKETS

2 cups dried apricots

2 cups water

¹/₂ cup plus 1 tablespoon sugar

3 cups flour

¹/₂ teaspoon salt

1 cup shortening

1 package active dry yeast

¹/₂ cup milk, scalded and cooled to warm

1 egg, slightly beaten

¹/₂ teaspoon vanilla

Powdered sugar

These also can be made with puff pastry, page 234.

Simmer apricots, water and ¹/₂ cup of the sugar until tender. Drain, chop and set aside. Sift flour, remaining 1 tablespoon sugar and the salt together. Cut in shortening until mixture resembles coarse meal. Add dry yeast to warm milk and combine with egg and vanilla. Add egg mixture to flour mixture and blend well. Divide dough into 4 parts. Roll 1 part at a time on a surface dusted with powdered sugar into a 9-inch square. Cut into 3-inch squares. Place a teaspoon of chopped apricots on the center of each square. Pinch opposite corners together over the filling, pinching along edges to seal. Repeat with remaining dough and place pastries 2 inches apart on a cookie sheet. Let stand 10 minutes, then bake at 350 degrees for 12 to 15 minutes. Remove from pan immediately and roll in powdered sugar.

Makes 36.

SANDWICHES
AND
SOUPS

HOT CHICKEN SANDWICHES

4 cups cooked,
diced chicken

1/2 cup mayonnaise

1/2 cup chopped
green onions

1/2 cup chopped celery

2 tablespoons
Dijon mustard

1 teaspoon
Worcestershire sauce

Salt and pepper

1 loaf French bread

1/4 pound grated
Monterey Jack cheese

Combine filling ingredients in a bowl and mix well. Season with salt and pepper. Remove the top crust from the bread and scoop out, leaving the crust intact. Fill with chicken mixture. Top with grated cheese and broil until cheese is melted.

Serves 8.

SUMMER BREAD

1 round loaf
sourdough bread

3/4 cup butter, softened

1/8 teaspoon salt

1 tablespoon
chopped parsley

1 tablespoon
poppy seeds

1 tablespoon
chopped onions

Swiss cheese,
thinly sliced

Ham, thinly sliced

Slice the bread vertically 5 to 6 times but not all the way through the bottom crust. Cream together the butter, salt, parsley, poppy seed and onions. Spread approximately three-quarters of the creamed mixture between the slices, and place ham and cheese between them. Frost the top and sides of the loaf with remaining butter mixture. Bake at 350 degrees for 15 to 20 minutes.

Serves 8 to 10.

TAILGATE BEEF SANDWICHES

2 1/2 to 3-pound
boneless beef pot roast

3 tablespoons oil

Salt

Freshly ground pepper

1 onion, sliced

2 garlic cloves, minced

1 bay leaf

3/4 cup water

1 cup chili sauce

4 teaspoons
Worcestershire sauce

1 bay leaf,
finely crumbled

2 teaspoons mustard

6 tablespoons garlic
wine vinegar

2 tablespoons
chopped parsley

2 tablespoon chopped
green onions

4 tablespoons diced
green bell pepper

8 to 10 buttered French
rolls, potato rolls or
flour tortillas

Brown beef on all sides in 1 tablespoon of the oil. Add salt, pepper, onions, garlic, bay leaf and water. Cover tightly and simmer 2 to 2 1/2 hours until tender. Cool. Cut beef into strips and combine with marinade made by combining chili sauce, Worcestershire sauce, bay leaf, mustard, vinegar, remaining 2 tablespoons oil, parsley, green onions and green pepper. Cover and chill until ready to use. Place marinated beef in rolls and serve. Tortilla beef rolls may be reheated or served at room temperature.

Serves 8 to 10.

MUFFULETTA

1 9-inch round
sourdough bread,
unsliced

1 1/2 cups chopped green
pimento olives

1 cup chopped
kalamata olives

2/3 cup olive oil

1/3 cup minced parsley

4 ounces pimentos,
drained and chopped

2 to 3 tablespoons
capers

2 teaspoons
minced garlic

1 tablespoon chopped
fresh oregano

1/4 teaspoon pepper

1/4 pound Italian salami,
thinly sliced

1/4 pound provolone
cheese, thinly sliced

1/4 pound mortadella,
thinly sliced

In a bowl mix olives, oil, parsley, pimentos, capers, garlic, oregano and pepper. Let stand, covered, overnight. Drain and reserve leftover marinade. Split the bread horizontally and remove some of the bread top and bottom leaving the shell 1/2 inch thick. Brush insides with reserved marinade. Mound half of the olive mixture in bottom shell. Add meats and cheese in alternating layers. Top with remaining half of the olive mixture. Wrap in foil, weight with plates and chill. Cut into wedges to serve. This may also be prepared using a long loaf of sourdough bread.

Serves 16.

GARDEN SANDWICHES

8 ounces cream
cheese, softened

1/4 teaspoon salt

2 tablespoons
lemon juice

1 garlic clove, minced

1 1/2 teaspoons chopped
fresh basil

1 1/2 tablespoons
mayonnaise

2/3 cup grated carrots

1/2 cup minced
red bell pepper

1/4 cup minced onions

1/4 cup chopped
cucumber

1/4 cup chopped celery

Small rye rounds or
assorted breads

Great with soup or use to spread on small rye rounds as cocktail sandwiches.

Combine cream cheese, salt, lemon juice, garlic, basil and mayonnaise. Beat until fluffy. Fold vegetables into cheese mixture and chill for several hours or overnight. Serve on assorted breads.

Makes 2 cups.

TURKEY ARTICHOKE LAVOSH

1 large Armenian lavosh cracker bread, about 16 inches across

1 pound cream cheese, softened

1/2 cup chopped chives

1 red bell pepper, finely diced

4 artichoke hearts, marinated and thinly sliced

3/4 pound turkey breast, sliced

To soften the lavosh, run cold water over both sides, lay on top of a wet towel and cover with another wet towel. Let it soak for 1 hour or until it can be folded without cracking. In a bowl or food processor place the cream cheese, add chives, mix thoroughly, and spread evenly over the lavosh. Sprinkle with red bell pepper and artichoke hearts. Cover with turkey slices. To roll the lavosh, start by folding over the first 3 inches, then continue to roll the entire length. Once rolled, wrap tightly in plastic wrap and chill for at least 1 hour, preferably longer. When ready to serve, slice into ovals 1 inch thick.

Makes 12 1-inch slices.

ARMENIAN KIDS' DELIGHT

1 large Armenian lavosh cracker bread, about 16 inches across, softened

1/4 cup honey

3/4 cup chunky peanut butter

1 cup raisins

1/2 cup coconut

1 banana, thinly sliced

Follow instructions for softening, preparing and serving lavosh as described with Turkey Artichoke Lavosh. Mix the honey and peanut butter until well blended. Spread evenly on three-quarters of the cracker bread. Sprinkle raisins, coconut and banana slices on the peanut butter mixture.

Makes 12 1-inch slices.

ROAST BEEF AND TOMATO LAVOSH

2 large Armenian lavosh cracker breads, about 16 inches across, softened

8 ounces cream cheese, softened

1/4 cup ranch-style dressing

1 tablespoon Dijon mustard

1 1/2 cups alfalfa sprouts

12 ounces roast beef, thinly sliced

1 tomato, thinly sliced

1 small red onion, thinly sliced

1 1/2 cups shredded mozzarella cheese

1/2 cup chopped black olives

2 tablespoons chopped cilantro

Pepper

Follow instructions for softening, preparing and serving lavosh as described with Turkey Artichoke Lavosh. Spread the cream cheese over the entire cracker bread. Mix the ranch dressing and Dijon mustard together and spread on cracker bread. Sprinkle alfalfa sprouts and layer the roast beef on upper three-quarters. Arrange the tomatoes, onions, cheese and black olives on top. Sprinkle with cilantro and pepper.

Makes 12 1-inch slices.

CURRY TEA SANDWICHES

8 ounces cream cheese, softened

1/4 cup orange marmalade

1/3 cup finely chopped walnuts

2 teaspoons curry powder

Combine ingredients and mix well. Cover and chill for at least 1 hour. Spread on cocktail bread or crackers.

Serves 8 to 10.

AVOCADO TEA SANDWICHES

1 avocado

1/2 teaspoon lemon juice

2 tablespoons chopped, toasted almonds

2 tablespoons cooked, crumbled bacon

Salt and pepper

1/8 teaspoon cayenne pepper

1/8 teaspoon chili powder

1/4 teaspoon garlic salt

6 slices thinly sliced bread

Mash avocado and add lemon juice. Stir in almonds and bacon and add seasonings. Mix until creamy and spread between slices of bread. Cut into fourths, diagonally.

Makes 12 tea sandwiches.

STUFFED HARD ROLLS

12 small sourdough French rolls

1 1/2 pounds ground beef

1 large onion, chopped

1/2 pound jack cheese, grated

1/2 pound Cheddar cheese, grated

1/2 cup diced green chiles

1 teaspoon garlic salt

1/2 teaspoon white pepper

Brown beef and onions. Strain fat and return meat and onions to pan. Mix cheeses, chiles and seasonings. Cut ends off rolls and remove most of the bread, leaving only the crust. Stuff rolls with meat mixture. Wrap in foil and freeze or bake at 350 degrees for 30 minutes.

Makes 12.

MOROCCAN LENTIL SOUP

2 tablespoons olive oil

1 medium
onion, chopped

2 garlic cloves, minced

1 medium carrot, sliced

6 cups chicken stock

1 cup tomatoes, peeled,
seeded and chopped

4 green onions, sliced,
tops included

1 cup red lentils

1/2 teaspoon pepper

1/4 cup chopped parsley

1/4 cup chopped cilantro

2 teaspoons ginger

2 teaspoons turmeric

2 teaspoons paprika

1 teaspoon cinnamon

1 teaspoon cumin

1 bay leaf

Salt

1/2 cup fine noodles

5 to 6 spinach leaves,
cut into thin strips

1/2 cup plain yogurt
for garnish

Heat a large saucepan. Add the olive oil and heat until it ripples. Add onions and sauté over high heat, stirring frequently, until translucent. Add the garlic and carrots and sauté briefly. Add all remaining ingredients except noodles, spinach and yogurt and bring to a boil. Lower heat to simmer. Cover partially and cook 15 to 20 minutes or until lentils are cooked and carrots are slightly tender. Add the noodles and spinach and cook, partially covered, until noodles are tender, about 7 minutes more. Remove the bay leaf. If soup is too thick, add a small amount of boiling water or additional stock. Garnish each bowl with a spoonful of yogurt.

Serves 6.

FIVE BEAN SOUP

2 1/2 cups dried beans, 1/2
cup each pinto, kidney,
navy, lima, white or
any combination

1 ham hock

3 leeks, chopped

6 carrots, chopped

2 onions, chopped

5 tomatoes, chopped

1/2 cup chopped parsley

24 ounces tomato juice

1 1/2 cups chicken broth

1 cup beef broth

3 cups water

1 tablespoon
Worcestershire sauce

2 1/2 teaspoons
seasoned salt

Boil the beans in 4 quarts of water for 10 minutes. Set aside for 1 hour. Drain well. Combine with the remaining ingredients and simmer for 3 hours or more. Remove meat from the ham hock, shred and return to the soup. Reheat before serving.

Serves 6.

MINESTRONE

4 slices bacon, diced

1 large onion, chopped

1 stalk celery, chopped

3 tomatoes, peeled
and chopped

1 leek, chopped

3 cups beef broth

1 cup tomato sauce

4 cups water

2 vegetable
bouillon cubes

2 beef bouillon cubes

1/2 cup dried pink beans,
soaked overnight

3/4 cup dried split peas

1/2 cup dried barley

2 garlic cloves, minced

1/4 cup chopped
parsley

1 teaspoon dried basil

1 large zucchini,
chopped

2 carrots, sliced

1/2 pound green beans,
cut into 1/4-inch slices

1 stalk celery, sliced

1/2 pound spinach,
thinly sliced

1/2 cup Burgundy wine

1 cup pasta

Grated Parmesan cheese

Sauté bacon, onions and chopped celery until clear and slightly browned. Add tomatoes, leeks, broth, tomato sauce, water, boullion, beans, peas, barley, garlic, parsley and basil. Simmer for 1 1/2 hours. Bring to a boil and add zucchini, carrots, green beans, sliced celery, spinach, wine and pasta. Cook until pasta is tender, 8 to 10 minutes. Serve with grated Parmesan cheese.

Serves 8.

RUMMAGE SALE SOUP

1 cup sliced celery

Butter

2 pounds stewed
tomatoes

28 ounces beef
consommé

1 cup dry white wine,
sherry or Madeira

2 tablespoons
minced onions

1/4 cup chopped parsley

2 tablespoons
lemon juice

2 tablespoons cornstarch
mixed
with 1/2 cup water

Curry powder

Croutons

Freshly grated
Parmesan cheese

For years this has been the family dinner for Junior League members who work on this week-long, annual event. It's quick, tasty and can be eaten several days in a row!

Sauté celery in butter for about 5 minutes. Add tomatoes, consomme, wine, onions, parsley and lemon juice. Heat until soup comes to a boil. While boiling, slowly add cornstarch mixture. Stir until thickened. Season with curry powder. Serve with croutons and Parmesan cheese.

Serves 6 to 8.

LA CRÈME DE TOMATO EN CROÛTE

1 cup coarsely chopped
yellow onions

6 garlic cloves, minced

4 tablespoons
unsalted butter

3 pounds tomatoes,
quartered

1 bay leaf

3 cups heavy cream

Salt and white pepper

2 tablespoons
tomato paste

1 carrot, julienned,
for garnish

1 green onion, slivered,
for garnish

Cook onions and garlic in butter until soft. Add tomatoes and seasonings and heat slowly, uncovered, until tomatoes are soft. Run through a blender or food processor and strain. Add the cream and tomato paste. Cool slightly. Pour the soup into individual crocks and garnish with a few carrots and onion slivers. Lay a circle of prepared puff pastry, egg wash side down, on top of each crock and stretch it tightly, as for a drum head, and down the sides. Repeat with remaining crocks. The wash helps form a seal between the sides of the bowl and the pastry. Chill the crocks for 3 hours to set the pastry. They may be held for up to 2 days if the pastry is covered. Put additional egg wash on the top side of the pastry and bake in an oven preheated to 450 degrees for 20 minutes or until golden brown. Do not open the oven during baking as this will cause the pastry to fall. Serve immediately.

Serves 6 to 8.

CROÛTE

2 pounds puff pastry,
page 234

2 eggs, beaten

1 tablespoon milk

Roll out puff pastry to $1/8$ inch thick. Paint the surface with egg wash made by combining eggs and milk. Cut 6 to 8 circles of pastry that are 2 inches larger in diameter than the soup crocks.

BEER CHEESE SOUP

$1/2$ cup finely diced celery

$1/2$ cup finely
diced carrots

$1/2$ cup diced onions

$3/4$ cup butter

$1/2$ cup flour

$1/2$ teaspoon dry mustard

5 cups chicken stock

2 tablespoons grated
Parmesan cheese

$1^1/2$ cups grated
Cheddar cheese

11 ounces beer

Salt and pepper

Sauté vegetables in butter until soft but not browned. Sprinkle with flour and dry mustard, stirring to coat vegetables completely. Slowly add chicken stock and simmer for 5 minutes. Blend in cheeses and beer. Bring to a boil and simmer for 10 minutes. Season with salt and pepper.

Serves 6.

BLACK BEAN SOUP

1 pound dried black beans, rinsed

3 cups chopped tomatoes

1 1/2 cups chicken broth

2 medium red onions, chopped

2 carrots, chopped

2 green chiles, roasted, peeled, seeded and chopped

2 jalapeño peppers, roasted, peeled, seeded and chopped

1 tablespoon minced garlic

2 tablespoons olive oil

1 1/2 tablespoons cumin

1 1/2 teaspoons coriander

1 teaspoon red pepper flakes

Salt

2 tablespoons tequila

2 tablespoons red wine vinegar

Sour cream

Chopped cilantro

10 flour tortillas, warmed

Place beans in a stock pot and cover with water. Bring to a boil, cover, reduce heat and simmer for 1 hour. Add tomatoes and chicken broth and continue to simmer. Sauté onions, carrots, chiles, peppers and garlic in oil until soft. Add this mixture to the beans. Season with cumin, coriander, pepper flakes and salt. Cover beans and simmer for 4 to 5 hours, stirring often to prevent sticking. Add more chicken broth if mixture seems too thick. Remove from heat and cool. When cooled, place one-quarter to one-half of the beans in a food processor and process until puréed. Return purée to pot and reheat. Just before serving add tequila and vinegar. Ladle soup into bowls and garnish with sour cream and a sprinkle of cilantro. Serve with warm tortillas.

Serves 10.

BROCCOLI VEGETABLE SOUP

4 slices lean bacon, cut into 1-inch pieces

4 cups sliced mushrooms

1 cup chopped onions

1 tablespoon minced garlic

1 tablespoon minced parsley

6 cups chicken broth

3 cups chopped broccoli flowerettes and stems

1 cup chopped tomatoes, peeled and seeded

1/2 teaspoon dried thyme

1/2 teaspoon salt

1/4 teaspoon freshly ground pepper

1 cup trimmed coarsely chopped spinach

1/4 cup freshly grated Parmesan cheese

In a stainless steel or enameled pot, cook bacon over moderate heat until it begins to turn crisp. Add mushrooms, onions, garlic and parsley. Cook until onions are translucent, about 5 minutes. Add chicken broth, broccoli, tomatoes, thyme, salt and pepper. Simmer over moderately low heat for 25 minutes. Add spinach and Parmesan and continue cooking for 5 minutes. Serve hot. This soup freezes well.

Serves 6.

TORTELLINI SOUP

1 onion, chopped

1 shallot, chopped

2 garlic cloves, minced

2 tablespoons olive oil

1/2 teaspoon
dried oregano

1 cup sliced mushrooms

1 cup sliced carrots

2 stalks celery, sliced

8 cups chicken broth

1 cup chicken,
cooked and slivered

1/2 pound mild Italian
sausage, cooked
and crumbled

2 tablespoons pesto

1/2 pound fresh
or frozen tortellini

1/2 cup dry vermouth

1 cup broccoli
flowerettes or 1 cup
slivered zucchini

Freshly grated
Parmesan cheese

This can be made days ahead; however, the tortellini, vermouth and green vegetables must not be added until just before serving.

Sauté onions, shallots and garlic in olive oil until translucent. Add the oregano, mushrooms, carrots, celery and sauté about 4 minutes. Add broth, chicken, sausage and pesto. Bring to a boil, reduce heat and simmer, uncovered, 10 minutes. Add the tortellini and cook 10 minutes. Add more broth, if needed. Add the vermouth and the broccoli or zucchini and cook an additional 5 minutes. Top with Parmesan cheese.

Serves 8.

CREAM OF MUSHROOM SOUP

3 cups chicken broth

1 cup chopped onions

2 cups sliced,
fresh mushrooms

1/4 teaspoon nutmeg

4 tablespoons butter

4 tablespoons flour

1 teaspoon salt

Few dashes
white pepper

2 cups milk

In a saucepan combine chicken broth, onions, mushrooms and nutmeg. Bring mixture to boil. Reduce heat and simmer for 7 minutes. Place one-third of the mixture in a blender or food processor. Cover and blend 30 to 60 seconds or until smooth. Pour into a bowl and continue to purée remaining vegetable mixture. In the same saucepan melt butter, blend in flour, salt and pepper. Add milk all at once. Cook and stir until mixture is thickened and bubbly. Stir in blended vegetable mixture and stir until soup is heated thoroughly.

Serves 6 to 8.

CREAM OF RED PEPPER SOUP

3 large red bell peppers

1 medium
onion, chopped

1 garlic clove, minced

2 tablespoons butter

2 tablespoons olive oil

2 cups chicken broth

2 cups half and half

Salt

Freshly ground pepper

Wash peppers and place on broiler pan. Broil until blackened, turning to broil all sides. Place in a paper bag to cool. When cool, peel, seed and dice. Sauté onions and garlic in butter and olive oil until tender. Add peppers and chicken broth. Cover and simmer 25 to 30 minutes or until vegetables are very tender. Pour mixture into blender or food processor and process until smooth. Return to pan and stir in cream. Cook over low heat until soup is heated throughly. Season with salt and freshly ground pepper.

Serves 4.

TERRIFIC TOMATO SOUP

5 large tomatoes, chopped

1 large carrot, chopped

1 1/2 large onions, chopped

2 small potatoes, peeled and chopped

1 bay leaf

3 sprigs of parsley

1 stalk celery, sliced

5 cups chicken broth

4 chicken bouillon cubes

1 large ham hock

1/4 cup sugar

6 ounces tomato paste

1 teaspoon dried basil

Salt and pepper

1 1/2 cups heavy cream

Chopped chives for garnish

Seasoned croutons for garnish

In a large soup pot, place the vegetables. Add the bay leaf, parsley, celery, broth, bouillon cubes, ham hock, sugar, tomato paste, basil, salt and pepper. Bring to a boil over medium heat and simmer for 1 hour. Remove from heat. Remove the ham hock and bay leaf. Purée the soup in a food processor and force the soup through a sieve. Return the purée to the soup pot. Over medium heat stir until it boils. Skim off any fat. Add the cream and reheat. Do not let it boil. Serve hot, garnished with chives and croutons.

Serves 6 to 8.

PURÉE OF BANANA SQUASH SOUP

2 tablespoons unsalted butter

1 cup chopped yellow onions

1/2 cup grated carrot

1/2 cup chopped red bell pepper

1/2 teaspoon grated lemon rind

1 teaspoon chopped parsley

1/4 teaspoon celery seed

1/4 teaspoon crushed dried basil

1/4 teaspoon crushed dried marjoram

1/8 teaspoon crushed dried thyme

1 pinch each crushed dried rosemary and dry mustard

1/2 teaspoon ginger

1 1/2 pounds banana squash, split and seeded

2 1/2 cups chicken stock

1 tablespoon honey

5 tablespoons cream sherry

Salt and pepper

Heavy cream for garnish

Melt butter in stock pot or large saucepan. Add onions, carrots, red pepper, lemon rind, parsley and seasonings. Mix well. Cover tightly and braise gently over low heat for 20 minutes. Rub surface of squash with butter and place in a foil lined pan. Bake at 375 degrees for 30 minutes or until tender. Add stock to onion mixture and heat. Scoop pulp from squash and purée in a food processor. Add stock mixture to squash purée and return soup to pot. Stir in honey and cream sherry. Add salt and pepper. Serve garnished with 1 tablespoon cream swirled to create a marbled effect.

Serves 4.

CHICKEN VEGETABLE BISQUE

1½ to 2 cups cooked chicken, puréed

1 medium yellow onion, chopped

4 tablespoons butter

2 cups water

4 cups chicken broth

1½ cups chopped summer squash

1½ cups chopped cauliflower

1 teaspoon lemon pepper

3 tablespoons flour

1 cup milk

Juice of 1 lemon

½ cup grated Parmesan cheese

This is a very hearty soup. Served with a salad or selection of fresh fruit and a loaf of crusty bread, it makes an inviting winter meal.

Brown the onions in 2 tablespoons of the butter in the bottom of a 6-quart stock cooking pot. Add water, chicken broth, chicken, squash, cauliflower and lemon pepper. Sauté until vegetables are soft. Remove from heat and transfer to a food processor or blender. Purée until smooth. Return to stock pot. In a small saucepan melt the remaining 2 tablespoons butter. Add the flour and mix together thoroughly into a paste consistency. Warm the milk slightly, and slowly add it, stirring constantly over medium heat to avoid lumps. When the mixture is creamy add it to the soup and blend thoroughly. Add lemon juice and continue to cook for another 10 to 15 minutes. Do not boil. Just before serving, stir in the Parmesan cheese.

Serves 6 to 8.

ARTICHOKE SOUP

2 onions, chopped

2 garlic cloves, minced

2 stalks celery, chopped

6 tablespoons butter

14 ounces artichoke hearts, rinsed, drained and chopped

¼ teaspoon dried thyme

Salt and pepper

4 cups chicken broth

1 cup water

1 cup sauvignon blanc

3 tablespoons flour

1 tablespoon snipped fresh dill

1 tablespoon minced green onions

1 tablespoon lemon juice

Sauté onions, garlic and celery in 3 tablespoons of the butter for 10 minutes until softened. Add artichokes, thyme, salt and pepper and continue to sauté for another 6 minutes. Add broth, water and wine. Bring to a boil and simmer for 20 minutes. Purée mixture, small amounts at a time, in a blender or food processor and return to the saucepan. Knead the flour and remaining 3 tablespoons of butter to make a paste. Bring the soup to a boil and gradually whisk in small balls of butter/flour paste and simmer until slightly thickened. Stir in the dill, green onions and lemon juice.

Serves 6.

MEATBALL SOUP

½ pound ground beef

¼ pound bulk pork sausage

¾ cup fine dry bread crumbs

1 egg, beaten

¾ cup milk

1 small onion, minced

½ teaspoon salt

¼ teaspoon pepper

¼ teaspoon allspice

10 cups chicken or beef broth or a combination

Combine all ingredients except broth. Chill 1 or more hours to blend flavors. Shape into walnut-sized balls. Bring broth to a boil in a large pot. Gently drop meatballs into broth. Cover and simmer 15 to 20 minutes. Spoon meatballs into soup bowls. Pour the hot broth over them.

Serves 8.

LEMON CARROT SOUP

6 tablespoons unsalted butter	1½ teaspoons salt
1 large onion, chopped	¼ teaspoon white pepper
1 large garlic clove, sliced	1 teaspoon dried thyme
1½ pounds carrots, sliced	1 cup sour cream or créme fraîche, page 249
1 potato, sliced	¼ teaspoon Tabasco sauce
3 large tomatoes, chopped	¼ cup lemon juice
¼ cup chopped parsley	Lemon slices for garnish
4 cups chicken stock	Carrot curls for garnish

Melt 4 tablespoons of the butter in a large saucepan. Add onions and garlic. Cover and cook over low heat until softened, about 5 minutes. Add carrots, potatoes, tomatoes, parsley, stock, salt, pepper, thyme and remaining butter. Bring to a boil, reduce heat to low and simmer, covered, 1 hour. Strain and reserve broth and vegetables. Purée vegetables in food processor until smooth. Return broth and purée to the pan. Add crème fraîche and Tabasco. Bring to a boil and simmer for 15 minutes. Stir in lemon juice. Garnish with lemon slices and carrot curls.

Serves 6.

TORTILLA SOUP

1 pound ground beef	Salt and pepper
3 garlic cloves, minced	4 teaspoons Worcestershire sauce
1 medium onion, chopped	2 tablespoons soy sauce
1 cup diced green chiles	Dash of Tabasco sauce
2 tablespoons oil	10 ounces frozen corn
1¼ cups beef broth	1 cup shredded Cheddar cheese
5½ cups chicken broth	6 corn tortillas, cut into strips and fried in oil
6 cups water	1 avocado, peeled and diced
1 teaspoon cumin	
2 teaspoons chili powder	

Make miniature meatballs out of ground beef and set aside, uncooked. Cook garlic, onions and green chiles in oil until soft. In large saucepan add broths, water, cumin, chili powder, salt, pepper, Worcestershire sauce, soy sauce, Tabasco, corn and meatballs. Add onion/green chile mixture. Bring to a boil, lower heat, cover and simmer 1 hour. To serve, place 2 to 3 tablespoons shredded cheese in a bowl and cover with hot soup. Float tortilla strips and diced avocado on top.

Serves 8 to 10.

CALIFORNIA CHOWDER

1 cup butter

1/2 pound slab bacon, cut into 1/2-inch squares

1 large onion, diced

4 stalks celery, sliced

3 carrots, diced

3/4 cup flour

2 tablespoons chopped parsley

2 tablespoons chopped fresh thyme

2 large potatoes, diced

3/4 pound geoduck, horseneck or razorneck clams or 3/4 pound abalone, julienned

6 cups milk

1/2 pound fresh Dungeness crabmeat

1/2 pound California white sea bass, cut into large chunks

12 fresh oysters, shucked

1 bay leaf

Salt and pepper

In a large stock pot, melt 1/2 cup of the butter. On medium heat, sauté bacon, onions, celery and carrots until onions are translucent. Sprinkle the flour over the vegetables and stir. Add the herbs, potatoes and clams or abalone. Slowly, while stirring, add the milk. Gently bring to a slow boil and add remaining seafood, bay leaf, remaining 1/2 cup butter and salt and pepper. Simmer for 5 minutes or until fish is done. Serve immediately.

Serve 6 to 8.

CAJUN FISH CHOWDER

1 3/4 pounds red snapper fillets

2 tablespoons olive oil

1 cup chopped yellow onions

2 garlic cloves, minced

2 cups diced red bell peppers

1 1/2 cups thinly sliced green onions, including tops

1 teaspoon crushed red pepper

1/2 teaspoon dried thyme

1 bay leaf

28 ounces whole tomatoes, drained and chopped, liquid reserved

1 cup dry white wine

1 1/2 cups cubed potatoes

4 cups liquid, juice from tomatoes plus water or clam juice

1/2 cup evaporated skim milk

Salt and pepper

1/4 cup minced parsley for garnish

Heat oil in large stock pot. Sauté onions until transparent and stir in the garlic, peppers and green onions. Cook for 1 minute. Add a little wine if it gets dry. Stir in red pepper, thyme and bay leaf. Cover and cook 3 to 5 minutes. Add tomatoes and stir for 1 minute. Add wine and potatoes. Cover and simmer 10 minutes. Add liquid. When potatoes are soft, add snapper fillets and simmer 5 minutes. Stir in milk, salt and pepper. Garnish with parsley.

Serves 6 to 8.

SEAFOOD CHEDDAR BISQUE

1/4 pound uncooked
scallops, chopped

1/4 pound uncooked
shrimp, peeled,
deveined and chopped

1/4 pound cooked
crabmeat, shredded

2 green onions, white
part only, chopped

1 stalk celery, chopped

2 tablespoons
chopped parsley

1 1/2 tablespoons
chopped pimentos

2 1/2 cups rich fish stock

1 cup plus 2 tablespoons
clam juice

3 tablespoons butter

5 tablespoons flour

3 tablespoons
dry vermouth

1/4 cup half and half

3/4 cup heavy cream

1 teaspoon dill weed

3/4 teaspoon dried thyme

1/2 teaspoon
seafood seasoning

1/2 teaspoon freshly
ground pepper

1/4 teaspoon nutmeg

Salt

1 1/2 cups grated
Cheddar cheese

Shrimp for garnish

Fresh dill for garnish

Place scallops, shrimp, crabmeat, onions, celery, parsley, and pimentos with fish stock and clam juice in a heavy, large saucepan and simmer 30 minutes. Cool and purée until smooth. Melt butter in heavy, small saucepan over low heat. Whisk in flour and stir 3 minutes. Blend in vermouth. Remove from heat. Whisk in half and half. Stir into seafood mixture. Blend in cream, dill weed, thyme, seafood seasoning, pepper and nutmeg. Season with salt. Add cheese and stir until melted. Simmer 10 minutes. Serve hot garnished with 1 whole shrimp and a sprig of dill.

Serve 4.

STEAMED CRAB VERMOUTH

1/2 cup butter

1 1/4 cups dry vermouth

2 cups chicken broth

2 tablespoons
chopped parsley

2 tablespoons
minced garlic

1 tablespoon soy sauce

1 tablespoon lemon juice

1 tablespoon sugar

4 pounds crab, cooked,
cracked and cleaned

Serve with French bread followed by cheese and fruit. This can be made also with clams.

In a large skillet melt butter. Gradually stir in 1 cup of the vermouth. Add the chicken broth, parsley, garlic, soy sauce, lemon juice and sugar. Bring to a boil, reduce heat, cover and simmer for 10 minutes. If desired, cool, cover and chill broth for up to 24 hours. To the hot or reheated broth, add crab. Cover and simmer until crab is heated through, about 10 to 15 minutes. Pour remaining 1/4 cup vermouth over crab. Ladle broth and crab into large, shallow bowls.

Serves 4.

HALIBUT STEW ITALIANO

2 pounds halibut,
cut into 1-inch pieces

3/4 cup chopped onions

1 garlic clove, minced

1 cup chopped celery

1 cup sliced mushrooms

1/2 cup chopped
green peppers

2 tablespoons olive oil

29 ounces peeled
tomatoes

1 cup tomato juice

2 cups white wine

1 beef bouillon cube

2 teaspoons salt

2 teaspoons pepper

1/2 teaspoon mixed
Italian seasonings

1/2 cup uncooked rice

10 ounces Italian
green beans

2 tablespoons
minced parsley

Grated Parmesan cheese

Sauté onions, garlic, celery, mushrooms and green peppers in oil. Add tomatoes, tomato juice, wine, bouillon and seasonings. Cover and simmer 5 minutes. Add rice. Cover and simmer 15 minutes. Add halibut, beans and parsley. Cover and simmer 5 to 10 minutes more or until fish is done. Do not overcook. Serve with cheese sprinkled on top.

Serves 8.

JAMBALAYA

8 ounces rock shrimp

8 ounces sausage

8 ounces smoked ham

1 onion, diced

1 red bell pepper, diced

1 green bell
pepper, diced

2 tablespoons butter

2 tomatoes, diced

1 teaspoon cayenne
pepper

3 jalapeño peppers,
roasted, seeded
and diced

1 tablespoon
minced garlic

2 bay leaves

2 tablespoons chopped
fresh thyme

10 whole cloves

2 tablespoons parsley

6 cups brown stock,
page 245

Salt and pepper

1/2 cup uncooked
white rice

1 cup water

Crayfish for garnish

Lobster for garnish

Parmesan cheese

In a 5-quart pot, sauté the sausage, ham, onions and bell peppers in butter until the vegetables are soft. Add tomatoes, cayenne, jalapeños, garlic, bay leaves, thyme, cloves and parsley. Stir and cook for a few minutes. Add brown stock and bring to a boil. Add salt and pepper. Add shrimp just before serving. The traditional method of thickening this soup is to cook the rice, adding it to the broth and simmering until thick. Or, the rice may be prepared separately, placed into bowls and the soup poured over. Garnish with crayfish and lobster. Serve with Parmesan cheese.

Serves 6.

MUSSELS AND SCALLOPS WITH HERBED BROTH AND VEGETABLES

1/4 cup olive oil	Pinch saffron threads
3 shallots, finely chopped	Freshly ground pepper
2 garlic cloves, finely chopped	1 1/2 pounds mussels, well scrubbed
6 ounces tomato paste	3/4 pound new potatoes, diced
6 tablespoons butter, cut into small pieces	1 medium zucchini, diced
6 tablespoons heavy cream	1 stalk celery, thinly sliced
1 tablespoon chopped fresh tarragon	1 medium eggplant, cut into 1-inch cubes
1 tablespoon chopped fresh basil	2 tomatoes, seeded and cut into 1-inch cubes
1 tablespoon chopped chives	20 scallops

In a large saucepan heat oil over low heat. Add shallots and garlic and cook until soft, about 5 minutes. Add tomato paste. Pour in 2 cups strained Court Bouillon. Bring to a boil and boil 10 minutes. Whisk in pieces of butter, 1 at a time. Stir in cream. Add herbs and saffron. Season with pepper. Remove from heat and set aside. Place mussels in large, non-aluminum saucepan with 1 to 2 cups Court Bouillon or enough to completely cover the bottom of the pan. Cover and cook over medium-high heat until mussels open, about 8 to 10 minutes. Remove with slotted spoon and keep warm. Strain liquid in which mussels were cooked through a fine mesh sieve lined with a double layer of dampened cheesecloth and add to herbed broth. Steam vegetables separately until almost done. Add vegetables to broth and simmer over low heat. Add scallops and continue simmering until they are done, about 10 minutes. Ladle into heated, shallow soup plates. Place mussels on top. Serve immediately.

Serves 4.

COURT BOUILLON

2 cups dry white wine	2 garlic cloves, chopped
2 cups water	2 sprigs of parsley
2 carrots, cut into 1-inch pieces	Pinch of fresh thyme
1 medium onion, quartered	1 teaspoon salt
1 stalk celery, cut into 1-inch slices	5 to 6 black peppercorns, crushed

Combine wine and water in a large, non-aluminum saucepan. Add vegetables and seasonings. Bring to a boil and simmer over medium heat 30 minutes. Strain and reserve for cooking shellfish.

GREEN CHILE CHILI

1 pound butterball steak, cut into small pieces

3 pounds ground round

1 large onion, minced

3 garlic cloves, minced

8 ounces diced green chiles

1 tablespoon cumin

1/2 cup beer

5 cups cooked small red beans

28 ounces whole tomatoes

8 ounces tomato sauce

2 tablespoons white vinegar

5 tablespoons sugar

Salt and pepper

1/4 cup grated Cheddar cheese

1 tablespoon flour

Sliced olives

Grated cheese

Sour cream

Chopped avocado

Cook steak and ground round with onions, stirring constantly. Drain off fat. Add all other ingredients except the cheese and flour. Simmer for 2 to 3 hours, stirring occasionally. Combine Cheddar cheese and flour with a little water to make a loose paste. Stir into chili until well blended. Serve with a selection of condiments.

Serves 8 to 10.

WHITE CHILI

2 whole chicken breasts, halved, skinned, boned and diced

2 tablespoons olive oil

3 shallots, minced

3 garlic cloves, minced

1 1/2 cups chicken broth

1 pound tomatillos, husks and stem ends removed, finely chopped

1/2 teaspoon cumin

1/2 teaspoon coriander

1/2 teaspoon dried oregano

1 teaspoon chili powder

4 ounces diced green chiles

Juice of 1 lime

30 ounces white kidney beans, rinsed and drained

Red onion, chopped

Monterey Jack cheese, shredded

Chopped avocado

Sour cream

Photograph, page 35.

Sauté diced chicken in olive oil and remove. Add shallots and garlic and brown. Add chicken broth, tomatillos and spices. Return chicken to pan and simmer for 20 minutes. Add chiles, lime juice and beans. Ladle into bowls and serve with red onions, cheese, avocado and sour cream as condiments.

Serves 4 to 6.

HOT AND SOUR SOUP

10 dried black mushrooms

1/2 cup dried cloud ears

1/4 cup tiger lily buds, or golden noodles

8 cups chicken stock or broth

1/4 pound lean pork butt, thinly sliced

1/2 cup bamboo shoots, sliced like matchsticks

1/2 cup sliced water chestnuts

1 teaspoon grated fresh ginger

12 ounces tofu, cubed

1 tablespoon soy sauce

1 tablespoon rice vinegar

1 tablespoon red wine vinegar

1 tablespoon sherry

2 tablespoons cornstarch

2 eggs, beaten

Salt

1/2 teaspoon white pepper

1 teaspoon sesame oil

1 teaspoon chile oil

2 green onions, sliced

You may serve extra sesame and chile oils, to be mixed in equal parts, on the table for the few brave souls who may dine there.

Soak mushrooms, cloud ears and lily buds in hot water for 20 minutes. Squeeze out extra water. Sliver the cloud ears and mushrooms. Bring stock to a boil. Add pork, mushrooms, cloud ears, lily buds, bamboo shoots, water chestnuts and ginger. Lower heat and simmer 15 minutes. Add tofu. Mix soy, vinegars and sherry with cornstarch until it forms a thin paste. Bring the soup to a boil again and drizzle cornstarch mixture into the soup, stirring constantly. Continue to boil and stir in a circular motion while drizzling the beaten egg into the soup. The egg should look like long threads in the soup. Add salt and pepper. Just before serving, add sesame and chile oils and green onions, reserving some green onion slices for garnish.

Serves 6 to 8.

SORREL SOUP

1 cup minced leeks, white part only

1/4 cup minced onions

3 cups chopped sorrel

1 pound mushrooms, chopped

1 garlic clove, minced

1 carrot, minced

6 tablespoons butter

2 tablespoons flour

8 cups chicken broth

2 potatoes, diced

3 egg yolks

3 cups half and half

Salt and white pepper

1/2 teaspoon beau monde seasoning

1 tablespoon lemon juice

Parsley for garnish

Lemon slices for garnish

Paprika for garnish

Sauté the leeks, onions, sorrel, mushrooms, garlic and carrot in butter until the sorrel is discolored and the vegetables are just soft. Sprinkle the flour over the vegetables and cook for 3 minutes. Add the broth and potatoes. Cover and simmer until the potatoes are tender. Cool slightly, and purée the mixture in a blender or food processor. Beat the egg yolks and half and half together. Add a small amount of hot soup to this and then stir it slowly into the hot soup. Add salt and pepper, beau monde and lemon juice. Heat, without boiling, before serving. Garnish with parsley, lemon and paprika.

Serves 8 to 10.

FOUR ONION SOUP

6 tablespoons butter

2 cups finely chopped
yellow onions

4 large leeks, white
part only, cleaned
and thinly sliced

1/2 cup chopped shallots

6 green onions, chopped

7 garlic cloves, minced

4 cups chicken stock

1 teaspoon dried thyme

Salt

White pepper

1 cup heavy cream

1/4 cup cream sherry

Chives for garnish

Melt butter, add onions, leeks, shallots, green onions and garlic. Simmer slowly, covered, until vegetables are tender, about 25 minutes. Add chicken stock, thyme, salt and pepper. Bring to a boil, reduce heat and simmer partially covered for 20 minutes. Strain the soup over a bowl and transfer the solids with 1 cup of the liquid to a food processor and purée. Return the purée and remaining liquid to the saucepan and simmer over moderate heat. Whisk in heavy cream and simmer. Add the cream sherry, ladle into heated bowls and garnish with chives.

Serves 6.

SUMMER GUACAMOLE SOUP

2 avocados

3 cups chicken stock

1 tablespoon lime juice

2/3 cup sour cream

1 tomato, peeled
quartered and seeded

1/4 to 1/2 cup
cilantro sprigs

1/4 teaspoon
Tabasco sauce

Salt and pepper

Tortilla chips, crumbled

Blue cheese

Bacon, cooked and
crumbled

Salsa

Chopped cilantro

1 lime, thinly sliced

In a food processor, mix 3 halves of avocado with chicken stock, lime juice and sour cream until smooth. Add tomato and cilantro, pulse until both are coarsely chopped. Add Tabasco. Chop remaining avocado and whisk into soup. Serve cold with tortilla chips, blue cheese, bacon, salsa, cilantro and lime.

Serves 6.

BRAZILIAN CHICKEN SALAD

1 cup diced avocado

1 cup diced papaya

4 cups chopped romaine
or iceberg lettuce

2 whole chicken breasts,
halved, skinned, boned
and cut into small pieces

1 tablespoon
orange juice

¼ cup red wine vinegar

1 teaspoon sesame
seeds

¼ cup oil

1 orange, cut in half and
sliced, for garnish

Toss the avocado, papaya and lettuce together and arrange on plates. In a skillet cook the chicken in the orange juice. Add vinegar and sesame seeds. Continue to cook until done. Gradually add the oil, but do not boil. Place the chicken over the salad and pour on juices from the skillet. Garnish with orange slices. Serve warm.

Serves 4.

AUTUMN SALAD

4 whole chicken breasts

2 quarts chicken stock
or water

2 celery stalks, julienned

½ cup sliced
water chestnuts

¾ cup halved seedless
grapes, red and green

½ cup golden raisins

½ cup dried pitted
prunes, cut crosswise
into ½-inch slices

1 bunch chives, snipped,
or ¼ cup sliced
green onions

½ cup coarsely chopped
macadamia nuts

1 head Boston lettuce

Lime, melon, peach or
pear slices for garnish

Salt and pepper

Poach the chicken breasts, covered, in simmering stock or water for 20 minutes. Remove from the stock and cool. Remove the bones and skin and cut the chicken into 1-inch cubes. Mix remaining salad ingredients except lettuce and fruit slices. Toss gently with Tarragon Mayonnaise to coat well. Serve the salad in cups of Boston lettuce and garnish with fruit slices.

Serves 6 to 8.

TARRAGON MAYONNAISE

2 large eggs, room
temperature

2 teaspoons lemon juice

2 teaspoons
tarragon vinegar

1 teaspoon dry mustard

2 teaspoons
fresh tarragon

¾ teaspoon
curry powder

1½ teaspoons salt

2 cups oil

Freshly ground
white pepper

Combine the eggs, lemon juice, vinegar, mustard and seasonings in a food processor fitted with the steel blade. With the machine running, drizzle the oil in a slow, steady stream until the mayonnaise begins to thicken. Add the pepper, blend and chill.

CHICKEN AND TORTELLINI SALAD WITH HONEY AND MUSTARD VINAIGRETTE

3 tablespoons olive oil	3 stalks celery, diced
2 garlic cloves, minced	1 small red onion, thinly sliced
2 whole chicken breasts, skinned, boned and cut into thin strips	$^1/_3$ pound Gouda cheese, julienned
$^1/_2$ pound fresh tortellini, cooked and drained	$^1/_4$ pound Canadian bacon, cooked and julienned
1 green bell pepper, diced	

Heat 1 tablespoon of the olive oil in a skillet. Add garlic and sauté until browned. Remove. Add chicken to hot oil and sauté for 3 to 4 minutes. Remove. Toss tortellini with 2 tablespoons of the olive oil and cool. In a large salad bowl combine chicken, tortellini, green pepper, celery, onion and cheese. Pour Honey and Mustard Vinaigrette over salad and toss well to combine. Top with Canadian bacon and serve.

Serves 6 to 8.

HONEY AND MUSTARD VINAIGRETTE

$^3/_4$ cup olive oil	$^3/_4$ cup cider vinegar
2 tablespoons Dijon mustard	$^1/_4$ cup honey
1 teaspoon dry mustard	

In a small bowl combine olive oil with mustards, vinegar and honey.

SMOKED TURKEY SALAD WITH MARINATED ARTICHOKES AND CORN

$^1/_2$ pound smoked turkey, julienned	$^1/_4$ cup mixed chopped fresh herbs, basil, tarragon, thyme and parsley
1 cup fresh corn	
12 baby artichokes	1 tablespoon minced garlic
$^1/_2$ lemon	
1 cup milk	1 tablespoon minced shallots
$^1/_2$ cup balsamic vinegar	Salt and pepper
$^1/_2$ cup olive oil	1 head romaine or iceberg lettuce

Boil the corn briefly and rinse with cold water. Set aside. Cut the stems and leaf tips off the artichokes and cook in water to which $^1/_2$ lemon and 1 cup milk has been added. Cool and remove outer green leaves. In a bowl place the vinegar, olive oil, herbs, garlic and shallots and beat with a whisk. Add the corn and artichokes. Break up artichokes and remove any bristles from the centers. Toss in the dressing and season with salt and pepper. Set aside for 1 hour. Arrange the lettuce on plates and form a well in the center. Place a mound of the corn/artichoke mixture in the center. Sprinkle the sliced smoked turkey over and around the salad.

Serves 4.

CHINESE CHICKEN SALAD

3 whole chicken breasts, skinned and boned

3 tablespoons soy sauce

2 tablespoons sherry

1 teaspoon sugar

1 garlic clove, minced

1 tablespoon minced fresh ginger

1 ounce rice sticks, found in Chinese grocery section

1/2 package wonton wrappers, sliced into long, thin strips

Light oil for frying

1 medium head lettuce, shredded

4 green onions, slivered

2 tablespoons toasted sesame seeds

1/2 cup whole unsalted cashews

HOT MUSTARD DRESSING

2 tablespoons dry mustard combined with 1/4 cup water

1 teaspoon white pepper

6 tablespoons soy sauce

3 tablespoons sesame oil

This recipe can be prepared ahead and assembled prior to serving.

Combine chicken breasts with soy sauce, sherry, sugar, garlic and ginger. Cover and chill for 2 hours or more. Bake at 350 degrees for 40 minutes. Remove from oven, cool and shred into long thin strips. Combine Hot Mustard Dressing ingredients and pour over chicken. Stir together to blend. Set aside. Fry rice sticks in very hot oil, a handful at a time. Hot oil is imperative. Rice sticks will sink to the bottom, rise to the top and pop like popcorn. They will be white in color when done. Remove rice sticks and drain on paper towels. Next, fry the wonton wrappers, using the same method. Their color should be golden brown when done. Remove and drain on paper towels. Just before serving, combine chicken with the dressing, lettuce, green onions, sesame seeds and cashews. Toss with rice sticks and wonton wrappers.

Serves 6 to 8.

Combine all ingredients . As mixture continues to be stirred, the pungency of the mustard intensifies. Watch out!

FLORENTINE SALAD WITH ROAST BEEF

3 cups cooked long grain and wild rice or couscous, cooled

3 cups thinly sliced roast beef

2 cups spinach, cut into strips

1 small zucchini, sliced

1/4 small red onion, sliced

1 large tomato, diced

1/2 cup sliced celery

1 cup grated Parmesan cheese

1/2 cup sunflower seeds

TARRAGON DRESSING

2 teaspoons dried tarragon

3 tablespoons tarragon vinegar

2 teaspoons Dijon mustard

Salt and pepper

1/2 cup olive oil

Mix 1/2 cup Tarragon Dressing with cooled rice or couscous and beef. When ready to serve, toss with remaining ingredients and remaining dressing.

Serves 4 as a main course.

In a food processor combine dressing ingredients except oil. Slowly add oil, processing until thick and well blended.

CHICKEN SALAD IN CRÊPE BASKETS

2 to 2½-pound whole chicken

1 tablespoon salt

1 carrot, chopped

1 stalk celery, cut in half

½ onion

Pinch of thyme

1 bay leaf

3 sprigs parsley

¼ cup mayonnaise

1 tablespoon white wine vinegar

2 tablespoons minced chives

1 teaspoon curry powder

½ cup minced apples

¼ cup halved grapes

½ teaspoon salt

⅛ teaspoon white pepper

Crêpe baskets

Lettuce leaves

Hard-boiled eggs, quartered, for garnish

Sliced tomatoes for garnish

Olives for garnish

Sliced almonds for garnish

Baskets and filling may be prepared early in the day and held separately until serving time.

Place chicken in a large kettle and cover with water. Add salt, carrot, celery, onion, thyme, bay leaf and parsley. Bring to a boil, reduce heat and simmer for 45 minutes until chicken is tender. Remove chicken and cool. When cool enough to handle, skin and remove meat from the bone. Dice chicken and add mayonnaise, vinegar, chives, curry powder, apples, grapes, salt and white pepper. Blend together and chill. Prepare crêpes according to any standard recipe. To make baskets, one at a time, fit each crêpe inside a large ladle. Dip ladle into hot oil in a deep fat fryer. Fry until lightly browned and crisp. Oil should be hot, but not smoking, so that crêpes will brown without burning. Set on paper towels to drain. To serve, prepare a bed of lettuce on each of 4 plates. Mound salad mixture gently in crêpe baskets and place on lettuce leaves. Garnish each plate with hard-boiled eggs, sliced tomatoes and olives. Top with sliced almonds.

Serves 4.

CAESAR SALAD

2 heads romaine lettuce

Garlic croutons

CAESAR DRESSING

3 garlic cloves, minced

2 ounces anchovies

4 tablespoons Worcestershire sauce

1 egg

¼ to ½ cup grated fresh Parmesan cheese

Juice of 2 lemons

6 tablespoons red wine vinegar

½ cup olive oil

Tear lettuce leaves gently and place in salad bowl. Sprinkle croutons and Parmesan cheese over lettuce. Add dressing slowly while tossing.

Serves 8 to 10.

Mix garlic, anchovies and Worcestershire sauce, continuously cutting through mixture with sharp knives. Add egg, lemon juice and vinegar. Gradually whisk in oil until emulsified.

FRESH TUNA SALAD

1 head radicchio	1½ teaspoons honey
3 cups assorted greens	2 tablespoons cider vinegar
2 tablespoons mixed chopped fresh herbs, rosemary, dill, thyme, and parsley	2 tablespoons balsamic vinegar
2½ pounds tuna, cut into 1-inch squares	4½ teaspoons soy sauce
1 tablespoon olive oil	1 tablespoon butter

Combine radicchio, assorted greens and 1 tablespoon of the herbs and toss with Sherry Vinaigrette. Divide among 6 plates. Over high heat sauté tuna in olive oil until just opaque, adding more oil if necessary. Place pieces of tuna on each plate with salad. Add honey to skillet and cook over high heat 15 seconds. Add cider and balsamic vinegars and soy sauce. Boil to reduce by half. Remove from heat and whisk in butter and the remaining herbs. Pour honey mixture over tuna and salad.

Serves 6.

SHERRY VINAIGARETTE

1½ teaspoons sherry vinegar	¼ cup olive oil
1 teaspoon red wine vinegar	Salt and pepper

Whisk together sherry and red wine vinegars, olive oil, salt and pepper.

CALAMARI AND SHRIMP SALAD WITH LEMON LIME MAYONNAISE

6 medium-sized calamari, cleaned	4 cups mixed greens
½ pound large fresh shrimp, peeled and deveined	½ cup vinaigrette dressing
1 cup white wine	Lemon zest for garnish
1 teaspoon minced shallots	

Cook the calamari and shrimp in white wine and shallots. Rinse with cold water and pat dry. In a bowl, toss the calamari and shrimp in the Lemon Lime Mayonnaise. Toss the greens with any vinaigrette dressing and arrange on serving plates. Top with calamari and shrimp mixture. Garnish with lemon zest.

Serves 4.

LEMON LIME MAYONNAISE

3 egg yolks	1½ cups oil
1 tablespoon Dijon mustard	1 tablespoon lime juice
2 tablespoons red wine vinegar	1 tablespoon lemon juice

Combine the egg yolks, mustard and vinegar in a food processor fitted with a steel blade. With the machine running, gradually add the oil. Continue processing until thick. Add the lime and lemon juices. Set aside, but do not refrigerate.

LOBSTER SALAD WITH CREAMY ORANGE DRESSING

2 lobsters,
about 1 1/2 pounds

Court bouillon, page 97

1 red bell pepper,
thinly sliced

1 yellow bell pepper,
thinly sliced

1/2 cup diced
yellow tomatoes

6 ounces shiitake
mushrooms, sliced

8 red radishes, sliced

Bed of red and green
leaf lettuces

Photograph, page 28.

Cook lobster in court bouillon. Cool and remove tail and claw meat. Combine lobster, peppers, tomatoes, mushrooms and radishes. Lightly toss with Creamy Orange Dressing and serve on a bed of lettuce.

Serves 2 as a main course, 4 as a side salad.

CREAMY ORANGE DRESSING

1 teaspoon
minced shallots

Zest of 2 oranges

Juice of 2 oranges

Juice of 1/2 lemon

1/2 cup mayonnaise

Salt and white pepper

Combine shallots, orange zest, juices and mayonnaise. Season with salt and white pepper.

SMOKED SALMON SALAD WITH DIJON VINAIGRETTE

12 new potatoes, cooked
and sliced

3 tablespoons
minced shallots

1 green bell
pepper, julienned

3 tablespoons
minced parsley

3 tablespoons
minced chives

Lettuce leaves, enough
for 4 plates

Radicchio, enough
for 4 plates

1/3 pound smoked
salmon, cut into strips

Crème fraîche
page 249

Toss potatoes, shallots, bell pepper, parsley and chives with Dijon Vinaigrette. Line 4 plates with lettuce and radicchio and place a spoonful of potato mixture on top. Lay several strips of salmon over potatoes and top with a dollop of crème fraîche. Drizzle any remaining dressing over the top and garnish with a few chopped chives.

Serves 4.

DIJON VINAIGRETTE

2 tablespoons red
wine vinegar

1/2 cup olive oil

1 tablespoon lemon juice

1 tablespoon
Dijon mustard

Combine dressing ingredients. Blend well.

ORZO SALAD WITH BELL PEPPERS

3/4 cup orzo	3 tablespoons chopped cilantro
2 cups chicken stock	3 tablespoons chopped parsley
4 1/2 tablespoons olive oil	1 green onion, chopped
1 1/2 tablespoons red wine vinegar	3 tablespoons capers
1 tablespoon Dijon mustard	2 garlic cloves, minced
1 red bell pepper	4 tablespoons feta cheese, crumbled
1 yellow bell pepper	Salt and pepper

Cook orzo in stock about 10 minutes. Drain if necessary. Transfer to a bowl and immediately add oil which has been mixed with vinegar and mustard. Bake peppers at 450 degrees for 25 minutes. Place peppers in a brown paper bag for 10 minutes to steam. Remove peppers from bag, peel, seed and cut into long, thin strips. Add peppers and all other remaining ingredients to orzo and toss to blend. Serve chilled or at room temperature.

Serves 4.

WILD RICE SALAD

1 cup wild rice, rinsed	1/4 cup sliced dried figs or prunes
2 cups chicken stock	1/4 cup chopped walnuts
2 cups water	4 green onions, chopped
1/2 pound mushrooms, sliced	2 tablespoons raspberry vinegar
1 tablespoon olive oil	1/4 cup oil
1/4 cup sliced dried apricots	Salt and pepper

Bring water and stock to a boil. Add rice, cover and reduce heat. Simmer for 1 hour. Remove from heat and cool. Sauté mushrooms in olive oil until lightly browned. Add mushrooms, apricots, figs, walnuts and onions to rice. Combine raspberry vinegar with oil. Pour over rice mixture and toss lightly. Season with salt and pepper. Serve warm or cold.

Serves 4.

BLACK BEAN SALAD

1 1/2 cups black beans	1/2 red onion, diced
3 cups water	1 red bell pepper, diced
3/4 cup whole kernel corn	1 tablespoon red wine vinegar
2 plum tomatoes, diced	3 tablespoons olive oil
4 tablespoons chopped parsley	1 teaspoon cumin

Soak beans in water overnight. Bring to a boil and simmer 2 hours. Remove from heat, drain and cool. Add corn, tomatoes, parsley, onions and pepper to beans. Blend vinegar, olive oil and cumin and pour over bean salad. Toss and serve warm or cold.

Serves 4.

ST. HELENA SUMMER SALAD

1 pound shell pasta, cooked and drained

8 cups seedless red grapes

8 ounces Roquefort cheese, crumbled

1 cup chopped green onions

1 teaspoon minced garlic

4 tablespoons lemon juice

1 1/2 cups mayonnaise

1 1/2 cups chopped Seasoned Toasted Walnuts

Salt and pepper

Combine slightly cooled pasta with grapes, cheese, green onions and garlic. Mix gently, trying not to crush the grapes. Combine lemon juice and mayonnaise and stir into the pasta mixture. Add chopped walnuts. Cover and chill several hours or overnight before serving.

Serves 10 to 12.

SEASONED TOASTED WALNUTS

1/4 to 1/2 cup butter

2 cups walnut halves

Garlic powder

Salt

Melt a small amount of butter in a small baking dish. Tip the dish to coat the bottom of the pan. Add walnut halves to pan and sprinkle with garlic powder and salt. Bake at 400 degrees for 15 minutes, occasionally stirring with a fork to coat with seasonings and butter.

BROWN RICE OLIVE SALAD

1 cup brown rice, cooked in chicken stock and cooled

1/2 cup sliced celery

1/2 cup sliced olives

1/4 cup minced onions

1/4 cup minced red bell pepper

2 tablespoons rice bran

Lettuce leaves

Combine rice, celery, olives, onions and red bell pepper and set aside. Combine 1/4 cup of the Herb Vinaigrette with the rice bran and blend well. Pour over rice mixture and toss lightly. Serve on a bed of lettuce. Serve with remaining vinaigrette.

Serves 4.

HERB VINAIGRETTE

1 tablespoon Dijon mustard

1 tablespoon vinegar

1 tablespoon white wine

1 1/2 cups oil

Salt and pepper

1 tablespoon fresh herbs

Combine mustard, vinegar and wine. Gradually whisk in oil until emulsified. Season with salt, pepper and herbs.

CRUNCHY BANANA SALAD

3 cups chopped
romaine lettuce

2 bananas, sliced

1 unpeeled apple, sliced

¹/₄ cup raisins

¹/₄ cup peanuts

Combine salad ingredients and toss gently/ Serve immediately with Yogurt Honey Dressing.

Serves 6.

YOGURT HONEY DRESSING

¹/₄ cup yogurt

¹/₄ cup peanut butter

¹/₄ cup honey

Mix all ingredients until smooth.

PACIFIC MELON BERRY SALAD

2 cups cubed cantaloupe

1¹/₂ cups
orange sections

1 pint strawberries,
quartered

³/₄ cup seedless grapes

10 dates, pitted and
sliced lengthwise
in sixths

³/₄ cup diced celery

¹/₂ cup chopped walnuts

3 ounces cream
cheese, softened

1¹/₂ tablespoons
lemon juice

3 tablespoons
currant jelly

¹/₂ cup heavy
cream, whipped

Toss fruit and celery together with walnuts and chill. Blend the cream cheese, lemon juice and currant jelly and beat until smooth. Fold in whipped cream and chill. Stir into fruit and serve.

Serves 12.

POMODORI AMORE

4 to 5 medium
tomatoes, sliced

¹/₂ cup olive oil

16 whole, small, fresh
basil leaves, or
8 large, halved

2 ounces anchovy fillets

¹/₂ cup finely diced
red onions

2 heaping
tablespoons capers

Coarsely ground
black pepper

Place tomato slices on small platter. Drizzle with olive oil. Place 1 basil leaf and an anchovy fillet on each. Sprinkle with onions. Top each slice with 3 or 4 capers and sprinkle with pepper.

Serves 8.

NORTHERN FRENCH POTATO SALAD

1 pound sliced bacon, cut into 1½-inch pieces

3 pounds small red potatoes, unpeeled and cut into ¼-inch slices

1 pound green beans, cut into 2 to 3-inch pieces

Cook bacon until lightly browned. Drain on paper towels. Boil potatoes in salted water until tender and drain. Cook green beans until tender crisp, 5 to 8 minutes. Combine potatoes and beans. Pour Tarragon Dressing over warm vegetables. Add bacon pieces and toss gently until well mixed. Serve immediately or cover and keep at room temperature.

Serves 8 to 10.

TARRAGON DRESSING

¼ cup tarragon vinegar

¼ cup beef consommé

½ cup chopped green onions

1 teaspoon chopped fresh sweet basil

1 teaspoon chopped fresh tarragon

¼ cup chopped parsley

1 garlic clove, minced

1 teaspoon dry mustard

1 teaspoon salt

Freshly ground pepper

Combine all ingredients and blend well.

GARDEN GREENS WITH BERRY SALSA AND GOAT CHEESE

4 cups mixed garden greens, such as arugula, watercress, kale and frisée

4 ounces goat cheese, crumbled

Arrange mixed greens on 4 plates, add Berry Salsa and sprinkle with goat cheese.

Serves 4.

BERRY SALSA

1 pint fresh raspberries

1 pint fresh blueberries

1 cup quartered strawberries

½ cup chopped cilantro

¼ cup diced red onions

1 cup diced red tomato

2 small jalapeño peppers, seeded and chopped

2 tablespoons orange juice

2 tablespoons lemon juice

1 tablespoon lime juice

1 teaspoon salt

1 teaspoon sugar

2 tablespoons oil

Combine all ingredients. Chill for 1 hour.

SPRING VEGETABLE SALAD WITH ALMOND VINAIGRETTE

8 heads baby lettuce

16 baby carrots

16 baby ears of corn

12 baby zucchini with blossoms

1/2 cup roasted, slivered almonds

ALMOND VINAIGRETTE

1 tablespoon Dijon mustard

2 tablespoons champagne vinegar

1/2 cup almond oil

Arrange the lettuce on plates. Toss the uncooked vegetables in the Almond Vinaigrette and arrange them over the greens. Sprinkle with almonds.

Serves 4.

Whisk together the mustard and vinegar. Gradually add the oil until emulsified.

BULGUR WHEAT SALAD

2 teaspoons butter

1 cup bulgur

2 large handfuls capellini fideo noodles, crushed

1 1/2 cups chicken broth

1 cup chopped celery with leaves

2 to 3 green onions, chopped

1/2 cup chopped parsley

1/2 pound fresh shrimp

6 1/2 ounces marinated artichoke hearts, chopped, with juice

1/4 cup silvered almonds

1/2 cup mayonnaise

1/4 cup lemon juice

1 tablespoon curry powder

Melt butter in skillet. Add bulgur and noodles and brown. Pour in chicken broth. Reduce heat, cover and simmer 15 minutes, stirring often. Place in large bowl and cool. Add the celery, green onions, parsley, shrimp, artichoke hearts and almonds. Toss to mix. Combine mayonnaise, lemon juice and curry powder. Add to bulgur mixture and mix. Serve cold.

Serves 4.

CALIFORNIA BROCCOLI SALAD

2 heads broccoli, cut into flowerettes

1 small red onion, thinly sliced

1 cup sunflower seeds

1 cup golden raisins

8 strips bacon, cut into 1/4-inch pieces, cooked and drained

1 cup mayonnaise

1/4 cup sugar

2 tablespoons vinegar

Blanch broccoli until bright green and still crisp, 1 to 2 minutes. Cool. Combine broccoli, onions, sunflower seeds and raisins in a large glass bowl. Blend mayonnaise, sugar and vinegar together until smooth. Toss into salad gently. Sprinkle with bacon. Chill for at least 2 to 4 hours. Serve as a side or luncheon salad.

Serves 6.

MARINATED BROCCOLI AND CAULIFLOWER WITH CHAMPAGNE VINAIGRETTE

1 bunch broccoli

1 head cauliflower

Cut the broccoli and cauliflower into small flowerettes, leaving some of the stem. Blanch in water, cooking the cauliflower first and then the broccoli. Marinate the flowerettes in Champagne Vinaigrette for 1 hour. Arrange 2 pieces of broccoli and 2 pieces of cauliflower alternately on a skewer. Remove the skewer before serving.

Serves 8.

CHAMPAGNE VINAIGRETTE

1 tablespoon Dijon mustard

1 teaspoon minced shallots

$^1/_4$ cup champagne vinegar

Salt and pepper

$^1/_4$ cup white wine

1 cup oil

Combine mustard, vinegar, wine, shallots and salt and pepper. Gradually whisk in the oil until emulsified.

MARINATED MUSHROOM AND RED PEPPER SALAD

2 pounds small mushrooms, stems removed

$^1/_2$ cup chopped red onions

Red bell peppers, cut into strips

$^1/_3$ cup chopped parsley

2 garlic cloves, minced

1 cup olive oil

1 teaspoon sugar

$^3/_4$ cup red wine vinegar

Salt and pepper

Clean mushrooms with damp paper towels. Do not wash them. Blend oil, vinegar, onions, parsley, garlic, sugar, salt and pepper. Pour over mushroom caps. Marinate at least 2 hours. Add pepper strips just before serving.

Serves 6 to 8.

TOASTED WALNUT SPINACH SALAD

1 bunch fresh spinach, cleaned and stems removed

1 avocado, sliced

1/2 cup crumbled feta cheese

1/2 cup coarsely chopped toasted walnuts

Coarsely ground black pepper

Tear spinach into medium-sized pieces. Top with avocado and feta cheese. Chill. When ready to serve, toss lightly with Basil Dressing. Garnish each serving with coarsely ground pepper and toasted walnuts.

Serves 6 to 8.

BASIL DRESSING

1/4 cup red wine vinegar

2 tablespoons chopped fresh basil leaves

1 tablespoon sugar

2 garlic cloves, minced

1/2 cup olive oil

1/2 teaspoon salt

1/2 teaspoon freshly ground pepper

Combine vinegar, basil, sugar and garlic. Slowly whisk in oil until emulsified. Add salt and pepper.

SPINACH SALAD WITH CURRY GINGER VINAIGRETTE

2 bunches spinach leaves, cleaned and stems removed

1 head romaine lettuce

2 cups thinly sliced red onions

2 large red apples, unpeeled and thinly sliced lengthwise

1/2 cup raisins

3/4 cup dry roasted peanuts

Toss spinach, lettuce and red onions in Curry Ginger Vinaigrette and place on individual serving plates. Toss apple slices gently in vinaigrette and arrange in a fan-like design on top of spinach. Sprinkle on raisins and peanuts. Serve immediately.

Serves 6 to 8.

CURRY GINGER VINAIGRETTE

1/4 cup white wine vinegar

1/4 cup ginger jelly

2 tablespoons curry powder

1/4 teaspoon Tabasco sauce

Salt and pepper

3/4 cup oil

Combine vinegar, jelly, curry powder, Tabasco sauce, salt and pepper. Slowly whisk in oil until emulsified. Cover and chill until ready to use.

ROMAINE AND SPINACH SALAD WITH WALNUTS AND CHUTNEY DRESSING

2 heads romaine lettuce, torn into bite-sized pieces

1 bunch spinach, washed, stems removed and torn into bite-sized pieces

2 red apples, peeled, cored and thinly sliced

$^3/_4$ cup coarsely chopped walnuts, toasted

Combine greens with apples and walnuts. Toss with Walnut Chutney Dressing and serve.

Serves 8.

CHUTNEY DRESSING

$^1/_2$ cup oil

2 tablespoons rice wine vinegar

2 tablespoons chutney

$^1/_2$ teaspoon curry powder

1 teaspoon lemon juice

Dash Tabasco sauce

Salt and pepper

Combine all dressing ingredients and mix well.

BABY LETTUCE AND BRIE WITH WALNUT PORT WINE VINAIGRETTE

2 heads baby frisée lettuce

2 heads baby red leaf lettuce

2 heads baby green leaf lettuce

2 heads baby romaine lettuce

1 cup walnut halves and pieces

$^1/_2$ pound Brie cheese, diced and chilled

Carefully wash and dry the lettuces, leaving each whole. Cut each head of lettuce in half without cutting the heels off so that the leaves stay together. Arrange 1 of each type of lettuce on plates, ends to the center. In the center, place the walnuts and Brie. Pour the Port Wine Vinaigrette around and over the lettuce before serving.

Serves 4.

PORT WINE VINAIGRETTE

2 cups port wine

2 teaspoons Dijon mustard

$^1/_4$ cup red wine vinegar

$^1/_2$ cup walnut oil

In a skillet reduce port wine from 2 cups to $^1/_4$ cup. Wine will thicken as it reduces. In a bowl place the mustard, vinegar and wine reduction. Gradually add the walnut oil while stirring with a whisk. Beat until emulsified.

WATERCRESS, EGG AND BACON WITH HERB VINAIGRETTE

8 ounces smoked slab bacon	2 bunches watercress, washed and trimmed
1 teaspoon sugar	2 hard-boiled eggs, chopped

HERB VINAIGRETTE

2 teaspoons Dijon mustard	1 tablespoon chopped fresh thyme
1 teaspoon chopped shallots	1 tablespoon snipped fresh chives
1/4 cup champagne vinegar	1/2 cup oil
1 tablespoon chopped fresh basil	

Cut the bacon into 1/2-inch squares and place in a skillet with the sugar. Add enough water to barely cover the bacon and bring to a boil. Continue cooking until the water evaporates and the sugar begins to caramelize. Drain bacon on paper towels and set aside to cool. Do not refrigerate. Arrange a bed of watercress in the center of each plate. Sprinkle with the bacon and the egg. Pour the Herb Vinaigrette around and over the salad and serve immediately.

Serves 4.

In a bowl place the mustard, shallots, vinegar and herbs. Gradually add the salad oil while stirring with a whisk. Beat until emulsified and set aside.

SHIITAKE MUSHROOMS WITH ASPARAGUS AND GREENS

16 fresh shiitake mushrooms, stems removed	Pinch of salt and pepper
1 cup olive oil	20 fresh asparagus spears, cut to 5-inch lengths
1/2 cup balsamic vinegar	1 cup diced red tomatoes
1 teaspoon minced garlic	Any combination of lettuce or garden greens, enough for 4
1 teaspoon chopped shallots	1 egg yolk
1 tablespoon chopped fresh basil	

Quickly wash and dry the mushrooms with a towel. Mix together the olive oil, vinegar, garlic, shallots, basil, salt and pepper. Place the mushrooms in the oil/vinegar mixture and leave at room temperature for at least 1 hour. The mushrooms will absorb the vinegar before the oil. Refrigeration could cause the oil to solidify, preventing the marinade from working. Blanch the asparagus and chill in an ice bath to stop cooking. On the top half of each serving plate arrange the asparagus in a fan over the diced tomatoes. On the bottom half of the plate arrange the greens. Remove the mushrooms from the marinade and place them in the center of the plate overlapping the asparagus and greens. With a whisk beat the remaining marinade with 1 egg yolk to make the dressing. Add a little more vinegar if necessary. Pour the dressing around and over the salad.

Serves 4.

STUFFED CLAMS

12 medium clams	1 teaspoon dry sherry
1 tablespoon olive oil	Salt
2 tablespoons minced onions	Freshly ground pepper
1 garlic clove, minced	Paprika
1/4 pound chorizo sausage	Minced parsley
1/3 cup bread crumbs	Butter

Place clams in a 400 degree oven just until they open. Remove clams from their shells and chop. Place half the shells in a shallow baking pan. Heat oil and sauté onions and garlic for 2 minutes. Crumble chorizo and sauté until just lightly browned. Drain well. Stir chorizo, bread crumbs and sherry into onion/garlic mixture. Season with salt, pepper, paprika and parsley. Stir in chopped clams. Spoon mixture into clam shells. Dot with butter. Return to oven and bake for 10 minutes until lightly browned.

Serves 4 as a first course.

CRAB CAKES MARYLAND STYLE

2 pounds crabmeat	2 teaspoons Old Bay Seasoning
4 egg yolks	1 teaspoon salt
1/4 cup heavy cream	1/2 teaspoon pepper
1/4 cup chopped parsley	4 tablespoons minced fresh dill
1 cup minced onions	Oil
1/4 cup melted butter	1 cup flour
4 cups bread crumbs	2 eggs
Juice of 1 lemon	1/2 cup milk
2 teaspoons Tabasco sauce	
1 tablespoon dry mustard	

Beat egg yolks, cream and parsley together. Set aside. In a large bowl combine crab and onions. Add butter and 3 cups of the bread crumbs, lemon juice, Tabasco and seasonings. Mix thoroughly and add egg mixture. Chill for 1/2 to 1 hour. Form into 3-inch cakes, 1/2 inch thick. Lightly flour cakes, then dip in egg which has been whisked with milk, then in remaining bread crumbs. Place oil in frying pan to a depth of 1/2 inch and heat to high. Fry cakes for about 5 minutes or until golden brown. More oil may be needed. Drain on paper towels and keep warm in oven while frying remaining cakes. Serve with lemon, cocktail, chili or tartar sauce or flavored mayonnaise.

Serves 6.

QUINTESSENTIAL CRAB CASSEROLE

12 ounces flaked crabmeat

12 ounces cocktail shrimp

1/2 pound mushrooms, sliced

1/4 cup finely minced green onions

6 tablespoons butter

1/3 cup flour

3 cups half and half

2 tablespoons tomato paste

1/2 cup grated Gruyère cheese

1/2 cup grated sharp Cheddar cheese

1 1/2 teaspoons paprika

1/2 teaspoon garlic powder

1/8 teaspoon cayenne pepper

1 tablespoon lemon juice

3 tablespoons minced pimento

2 tablespoons dry sherry

4 cups cooked wild or white rice

Slivered almonds, toasted

A wonderful recipe for any combination of shellfish!

Sauté mushrooms and green onions in butter until soft. Slowly sprinkle with flour and cook 3 minutes. Gradually add half and half, stirring constantly. Stir over low heat until thickened and smooth. Add tomato paste, cheeses, seasonings and lemon juice. Cook and stir to melt cheese. Stir in crab, shrimp, pimento and sherry. Serve the crab and shrimp mixture on top of the rice and sprinkle with toasted almonds, or the crab and shrimp mixture may be combined with rice in a casserole, topped with toasted almonds and baked at 350 degrees until bubbly, 20 to 30 minutes.

Serves 8.

SCALLOPS WITH ASPARAGUS AND WATER CHESTNUTS

1/2 pound scallops

1 pound asparagus, cut diagonally into 2-inch pieces

1/2 to 3/4 cup sliced water chestnuts

1 tablespoon oil

2 garlic cloves, minced

2 slices fresh ginger

1/4 teaspoon white pepper

2 tablespoons oyster sauce

1 tablespoon soy sauce

Salt

Try this with pea pods when asparagus is not available.

Heat oil in skillet and brown garlic and ginger. Add scallops and heat quickly until just barely cooked. Remove to platter. Add asparagus and water chestnuts to pan and stir fry over high heat. Add remaining ingredients. Return scallops to the pan with vegetables and adjust seasonings. Serve immediately.

Serves 4.

POACHED SCALLOPS WITH ORANGE SAUCE

1¼ pounds scallops

1½ cups chicken broth

2 tablespoons julienned orange peel

4 large mushrooms, sliced

½ pound snow peas, stems removed and blanched

1 tablespoon cornstarch combined with 2 tablespoons water

1 tablespoon orange-flavored liqueur

In 10-inch skillet over medium heat, bring broth and orange peel to a boil. Reduce heat to low and add scallops and mushrooms. Cover and simmer about 3 minutes until scallops are tender. Remove scallops and mushrooms with slotted spoon. Arrange on 4 serving plates with snow peas and keep warm. Increase heat to high. Stir cornstarch mixture into boiling broth and cook, stirring constantly until sauce thickens. Add liqueur and blend. Pour sauce over scallops on prepared serving plates.

Serves 4.

SCALLOPS À LA MOUTARDE

1 pound sea scallops

2 tablespoons butter

6 tablespoons chicken broth or white wine

2 tablespoons whole grain mustard

2 teaspoons honey

2 tablespoons heavy cream

2 teaspoons capers

Make a sauce by combining chicken broth or white wine, mustard and honey over medium heat. Add cream and capers. Reduce to desired thickness. Sauté scallops in butter or grill for about 3 minutes, depending on size. Do not overcook. To serve, ladle sauce onto 4 serving plates and set scallops on top of the sauce.

Serves 4 as a first course, 2 as a main course.

SCALLOPS VERONIQUE

1 pound fresh scallops

¼ cup chopped green onions

½ cup sliced fresh mushrooms

3 tablespoons unsalted butter

1 teaspoon cornstarch combined with 2 tablespoons dry sherry

½ cup halved seedless green grapes

½ teaspoon salt

Dash pepper

2 tablespoons fine dry bread crumbs

Sauté onions and mushrooms in butter in a large skillet over medium heat until soft. Add scallops, cover and simmer 5 minutes. Add constarch mixture to scallops. Stir gently until mixture comes to a boil. Cook 1 minute or until slightly thickened. Add grapes, salt and pepper. Spoon scallop mixture into 4 individual shells or cups and sprinkle with bread crumbs. Broil 5 inches from heat for 2 minutes or until lightly browned.

Serves 4.

CIOPPINO

1 large onion, chopped

1 green pepper, chopped

1 cup sliced celery

1 carrot, thinly sliced

3 garlic cloves, minced

3 tablespoons olive oil

56 ounces
chopped tomatoes,
canned or fresh

8 ounces tomato sauce

2 tablespoons
chopped parsley

2 teaspoons
dried basil

1 teaspoon
dried oregano

1 bay leaf

1 teaspoon salt

$1/4$ teaspoon pepper

2 cups white wine

1 pound fresh white
fish, orange roughy,
swordfish or halibut, cut
into bite-sized pieces

$1^1/2$ pounds medium
shrimp, unpeeled

$1/2$ pound large
scallops, halved

$1^1/2$ pounds crab legs
in shell, disjointed

1 can chopped clams

1 dozen clams or
mussels in shells,
washed and bearded

Bibs and hand towels are a must for this feast!

In a large soup pot, sauté onions, green pepper, celery, carrots and garlic in oil until soft. Stir in tomatoes, tomato sauce, parsley, basil, oregano, bay leaf, salt and pepper. Heat to boiling. Reduce heat and let simmer for $1^1/4$ hours. While sauce simmers, prepare fish. Wash shellfish. After removing bay leaf, stir in wine, fish, shrimp, scallops and crab. Bring to a boil, reduce heat and simmer, covered, for 10 minutes. Place clams or mussels over top. Cover and simmer again for 10 minutes. Clams or mussels that do not open should be discarded.

Serves 6 to 8.

PAELLA

²/₃ cup olive oil

1¹/₂ tablespoons
fresh oregano

1¹/₂ tablespoons
fresh basil

3 garlic cloves, minced

2 teaspoons salt

1 teaspoon pepper

2 pounds boneless
chicken breasts, cut
into bite-sized pieces

12 large shrimp,
peeled and deveined

9 ounces
chorizo sausage,
casings removed

2 large yellow
onions, chopped

1 large green bell
pepper, seeded,
and chopped

2 cups raw rice

3 cups hot chicken broth

4 large tomatoes, peeled,
seeded, and chopped

¹/₂ to 1 teaspoon
saffron

1 teaspoon coriander

1 cup fresh peas or
10 ounces frozen
peas, thawed

¹/₂ to ³/₄ pound medium-
sized scallops

12 clams, well scrubbed

2 pimentos, cut
into strips

Combine oil, oregano, basil, garlic, salt and pepper and blend well. Place chicken and shrimp in separate bowls and pour marinade over each. Cover and chill for at least 4 hours. Cook chicken in 3 tablespoons marinade until lightly browned. Remove from pan and set aside. Cut chorizo into pieces and add to pan. Cook over medium heat until well browned. Remove chorizo and set aside. Add onions and green pepper to pan drippings. Raise heat to medium high and cook until vegetables are soft. Stir in rice and brown slightly. Add chicken broth, tomatoes, saffron, coriander, chicken and chorizo. Bring mixture to a boil. Cover, reduce heat and simmer for 25 minutes, stirring occasionally, or until rice is tender. Add peas and scallops and toss gently. Transfer paella to a paella pan or deep, covered dish. Drain shrimp and push into rice mixture along with clams. Bake, covered, at 350 degrees for 15 to 20 minutes or until shrimp are pink and clams open. Garnish with pimento.

Serves 8.

OYSTERS FLORENTINE

2 dozen fresh oysters

2 tablespoons finely
chopped onions

1 garlic clove, minced

3 tablespoons butter

¹/₂ cup finely chopped
cooked spinach

2 tablespoons
heavy cream

1 teaspoon salt

Freshly ground
black pepper

1 egg

1 egg yolk

6 tablespoons
dry bread crumbs

Drain oysters, reserving liquid. Chop 12 of the oysters and set aside. Sauté onions and garlic in 1 tablespoon of the butter for 5 minutes. Add chopped oysters, spinach, cream, salt and pepper. Cook over low heat for 5 minutes, stirring constantly. Remove from heat and add to combined egg and egg yolk, stirring briskly. Add enough water to the oyster liquor to make 1 cup and simmer whole oysters until edges curl. Drain and place 2 oysters each in 6 individual baking dishes or scallop shells. Cover with oyster/spinach mixture, sprinkle with bread crumbs and dot with remaining 2 tablespoons butter. Bake at 450 degrees for 15 minutes.

Serves 6.

GINGER SHRIMP WITH PEA PODS

³/₄ pound medium shrimp, peeled and deveined

2 tablespoons soy sauce

2 tablespoons sherry

2 tablespoons cornstarch

1 teaspoon sesame oil

1 teaspoon sugar

2 tablespoons oil

1 garlic clove, minced

¹/₄ pound snow peas, stems removed

³/₄ cup sliced water chestnuts, drained

¹/₂ cup chicken broth

1 tablespoon grated fresh ginger

Marinate shrimp for 15 minutes in soy sauce, sherry, cornstarch, sesame oil and sugar which have been mixed together. Heat oil in wok or pan until hot but not smoking. Add shrimp and marinade and sauté until shrimp turns pink. Remove shrimp. Scrape bottom of wok to clean. Add a little more oil, add garlic and stir until it is browned. Add snow peas, water chestnuts and broth. Stir for 2 minutes. Return shrimp to wok, add ginger and stir until heated through. Serve immediately over hot rice.

Serves 4.

SHRIMP PROVENÇAL

1 pound medium shrimp, peeled and deveined

Clarified butter

¹/₂ cup white wine

2 tablespoons minced shallots

1 teaspoon minced garlic

2 tomatoes, peeled, seeded and chopped

1 cup heavy cream

¹/₂ tablespoon minced fresh basil

Salt and pepper

¹/₂ tablespoon minced parsley

Heat butter in sauté pan. Add shrimp and cook approximately 2 minutes until shrimp turns pink. Remove shrimp from pan and place in a strainer to drain. Pour off fat. Add wine, shallots and garlic and bring to a boil. Add tomatoes and cook until mixture is reduced by half. Add cream and basil. Salt and pepper. Continue to reduce to sauce consistency. Add shrimp with parsley. Serve immediately with rice.

Serves 4.

SHRIMP KIWI SAUTÉ

1 pound medium shrimp, peeled and deveined

3 kiwis, peeled

2 to 3 tablespoons olive oil

¹/₃ pound prosciutto, julienned

3 shallots, finely chopped

¹/₄ teaspoon chili powder

³/₄ cup dry white wine

Reserve 4 slices of kiwi for garnish and coarsely chop remaining fruit. Set aside. In a heavy skillet heat oil and sauté shrimp for about 1 minute. Add prosciutto, shallots and chili powder. Sauté another 30 seconds. Add the chopped kiwi and sauté 30 seconds. Add wine and reduce by half. Serve immediately with rice.

Serves 4.

KUNG PAO SHRIMP

2 pounds large shrimp, peeled and deveined

1 teaspoon sherry

1 tablespoon cornstarch

1 tablespoon sesame oil

Pinch of salt

Oil

3 dried chile peppers

3 garlic cloves, crushed

1-inch piece fresh ginger, crushed

4 green onions, slivered

$\frac{1}{2}$ cup sliced water chestnuts

1 red bell pepper, sliced

1 yellow bell pepper, sliced

1 pound snow peas, stems removed

$\frac{1}{2}$ cup peanuts

1 tablespoon chicken stock

1 tablespoon soy sauce

2 teaspoons wine vinegar

1 teaspoon hot chile oil

Pinch of sugar

This is hot and spicy at its best!

Marinate shrimp for 30 minutes in sherry, cornstarch, sesame oil and salt. In a wok heat 3 tablespoons oil and blacken the chile peppers. Remove the peppers and save. Stir fry garlic, ginger and green onions in the oil left in the wok. More oil may be needed. Add water chestnuts, peppers and snow peas until slightly cooked. Vegetables should be crisp and snow peas a bright green. Remove and set aside. Add a small amount of oil to the wok. Heat to high and quickly stir fry the marinated shrimp until pink. In small bowl combine stock, soy sauce, vinegar, chile oil and sugar. Add to the wok, cooking only until it thickens. Add peanuts, vegetables and chile peppers and toss gently to combine flavors.

Serves 6 to 8.

PRAWNS WELLINGTON

12 jumbo prawns, peeled and deveined, tail on

3 tablespoons butter

$\frac{1}{2}$ cup finely diced celery

1 onion, chopped

6 to 8 mushrooms, sliced

Lemon juice

2 tablespoons sherry or brandy

1 cup flaked crabmeat

Puff pastry, cut into 12 squares, each 4 x 4 inches, page 234

Dash of white pepper

1 egg white

3 tablespoons water

Sauté together butter, celery, onion, mushrooms and 1 squeeze of lemon until onion is translucent. Add sherry or brandy and simmer for 5 minutes. Add crab the last 2 minutes. Slit bottom side of prawns and put a tablespoon of vegetable/crab mixture inside and also on top of prawn. Wrap in puff pastry in a triangle fashion, leaving tail out. Combine water, egg white and pepper, whisking until frothy. Seal pastry with egg white mixture. Place on an oiled cookie sheet and bake in a preheated oven at 350 degrees for 30 minutes or until pastry is browned. Serve with Lemon Sherry Sauce.

Serves 6.

LEMON SHERRY SAUCE

$\frac{1}{4}$ pound butter

4 egg yolks, slightly whipped

3 tablespoons lemon juice

2 tablespoons sherry

Dash of white pepper

Melt butter. Blend in egg yolks, lemon juice, sherry and pepper. Stir mixture constantly until smooth and warm and serve over the prawns.

SHRIMP ORLEANS

4 pounds raw shrimp, peeled and deveined

1/4 cup peanut oil

2 1/2 cups finely chopped onions

1 3/4 cups finely chopped celery

1 1/2 cups finely chopped green bell peppers

4 tablespoons unsalted butter

2 teaspoons minced garlic

1 bay leaf

2 teaspoons salt

1 1/2 teaspoons white pepper

1/2 teaspoon cayenne pepper

1/2 teaspoon black pepper

1 1/2 teaspoons Tabasco sauce

1 tablespoon dried thyme

1 1/2 teaspoons dried basil

2 1/2 cups chicken broth

3 cups finely chopped, peeled tomatoes

1 1/2 cups tomato sauce

2 teaspoons sugar

5 cups hot cooked rice

Heat the oil over high heat in a 4-quart saucepan. Add 1 cup of the onions and cook for 3 minutes, stirring frequently. Lower the heat to medium and continue cooking until onions are a rich brown color and not burned, about 3 to 5 minutes. Add remaining 1 1/2 cups onions, celery, bell peppers and butter. Cook the peppers and celery about 5 minutes, stirring occasionally. Add garlic, bay leaf, salt and peppers. Add Tabasco, thyme, basil and 1/2 cup of the chicken broth. Cook over medium heat, stirring so the vegetables brown further. Add tomatoes, turn heat to low and simmer for 10 minutes, stirring occasionally and scraping pan bottom. Stir in the tomato sauce and simmer for 5 minutes. Add remaining 2 cups broth and sugar. Continue simmering for 15 minutes. The sauce is best when prepared 24 hours in advance. Store in refrigerator and reheat to near boiling. Add shrimp, cover pot and cook until they are done. Serve over hot rice.

Serves 12.

ORANGE ROUGHY IN WINE SAUCE

4 orange roughy fillets

4 tablespoons butter

1 tablespoon lemon juice

2 tablespoons soy sauce

1 teaspoon Worcestershire sauce

1/4 teaspoon Tabasco sauce

1 tablespoon dry white wine

1/8 teaspoon garlic powder

1/8 teaspoon onion powder

1/8 teaspoon paprika

2 tablespoons chopped green onions

Rinse fillets and place in a single layer in a shallow casserole. Place butter and remaining ingredients in a small saucepan. Heat and stir until butter is melted. Pour over fillets and turn each to coat thoroughly. Pour remaining sauce back into saucepan, heat and set aside. Grill 5 minutes, turn and baste with sauce. Grill 5 minutes longer or until fish tests done.

Serves 4.

SADDLE ROCK OYSTER LOAF

20 ounces small
fresh oysters

4 tablespoons flour

1 egg, beaten

24 salted soda crackers,
finely crushed

1 pound loaf unsliced
firm bread or oblong
sourdough loaf

1/2 cup plus 2
tablespoons butter,
room temperature

1 lemon, halved

1 garlic clove,
finely minced

1/2 teaspoon
Worcestershire sauce

Oil

Parsley sprig

Lemon slices for garnish

Paprika

1 dill pickle, thinly sliced

1 bacon strip,
cooked until crisp

This was called the "Peacemaker Loaf" in historic Sacramento. Husbands who had stayed too long at the saloon could still get a warm welcome from their wives if they brought home this delicious offering.

Drain oysters and pat dry on paper towels. Dredge in flour and dip in egg before rolling in cracker crumbs. Cover and chill at least 2 hours. To form a box for the oysters, cut rectangle from top of the loaf of bread and set aside. Scoop out inside of loaf enough to hold the oysters. Butter the inside and top of the "box" heavily, using 1/2 cup of the softened butter. Squeeze juice of half of the lemon throughout the inside. Wrap the loaf in a tea towel and set aside. Cream together remaining 2 tablespoons butter, garlic, Worcestershire sauce and 1 teaspoon lemon juice. Set aside. Place loaf "box" and lid separately on a baking sheet in a 350 degree oven and watch carefully while the crust crisps and butter melts, about 10 minutes. Meanwhile, fry the oysters in just enough oil to keep them from sticking. When golden brown, dab with seasoned butter mixture. Immediately stuff the oysters into the bread "box" and top with a sprig of parsley. Sprinkle lemon slices with paprika. Add to bread "box" and top with dill pickle slices. Place bacon on pickles and top with "lid." Wrap the loaf in a white linen tea towel and let stand 10 minutes to blend flavors. Serve in slices.

Serves 6 to 8.

GRILLED HALIBUT WITH SAGE, ROSEMARY AND CAPERS

4 halibut steaks,
1 inch thick

4 sage leaves, crumbled

2 sprigs
rosemary, crumbled

4 garlic cloves, minced

1/2 cup olive oil

2 tablespoons
lemon juice

Salt and pepper

1 cup pitted, chopped
kalamata olives

3 teaspoons capers

Mix sage, rosemary, garlic, olive oil and lemon juice plus salt and pepper in a 13 x 9-inch glass baking dish. Add fish and turn to coat. Cover and chill for 6 hours, turning occasionally. Heat and oil grill. Remove fish from marinade and pat dry. Reserve marinade. Grill steaks, turning once, about 9 minutes total. Heat marinade and olives in small saucepan over low heat. Remove from heat and stir in capers. Pour sauce over steaks and serve.

Serves 4.

SALMON MOUSSELINE EN CROÛTE

4 ounces sea scallops	1 cup heavy cream
10 ounces salmon fillet	12 ounces puff pastry, page 234
1 cup egg whites	1 whole egg
4 tablespoons butter, softened	1 tablespoon milk
1 teaspoon salt	6 spinach leaves

A beautiful presentation! Photograph, page 15. Technique, page 236.

In a food processor purée scallops and half of the salmon fillet until smooth. Using the pulse switch, add egg whites. Purée until smooth. Add the butter, a little at a time, and salt, scraping the sides of the bowl with a spatula. With food processor running, gradually add the cream until completely incorporated. Chill for 15 minutes. On a floured surface roll out prepared puff pastry to an 11 x 16-inch rectangle about $1/8$ inch thick. Cut rectangle in half to make 2 11 x 8-inch rectangles. Beat the whole egg with milk to make an egg wash. Place 1 piece of dough on a cookie sheet. Brush dough with egg wash and place 2 spinach leaves on dough, slightly off center, in an oval. This will be the body of the fish shape. Slice remaining salmon into long thin strips. Place half of the salmon strips on the spinach, then a mound of the mousseline following the oval shape. Some mousseline will be left over. Place the remaining salmon over the mousseline. Cover with remaining spinach. Place the other piece of pastry over the first and form a seal around the mound. Cut the pastry into fish shape, add fins and make scales with a large pastry tube on the top of the pastry . Brush with egg wash. Bake in a preheated 400–degrees oven for 25 minutes.

Serves 2.

SALMON IN PARCHMENT

4 individual serving size fish fillets such as salmon, red snapper or halibut	1 tablespoon chopped fresh tarragon or dill
3 shallots, minced	Dry white wine
8 small cherry tomatoes	Butter, melted
8 large mushrooms, quartered	Salt and pepper
2 zucchini or summer squash, sliced	Beurre blanc sauce, page 247
$3/4$ cup baby carrots, blanched	

Fold 4 12-inch squares of parchment or aluminum foil in half diagonally, and butter the bottom half. Divide the shallots among the 4 parchment pieces and place 1 fillet of fish on top of the shallots. Surround each fillet with the vegetables. Sprinkle each portion with wine and fresh herbs. Fold the upper triangle of parchment over the fish and vegetables and seal the 2 open edges with a double foldover, being careful to seal completely. Place the 4 triangular packets in a baking dish and bake at 450 degrees for 10 to 15 minutes. Serve immediately with beurre blanc sauce.

Serves 6.

STUFFED SALMON POACHED IN CHAMPAGNE

5 to 6-pound whole salmon, boned	1 to 1½ cups California champagne
3 lemons, thinly sliced	Parsley
3 strips bacon	Rice stuffing
¼ pound mushrooms, sliced	Sour Cream Sauce

Wash and dry salmon. Stuff with Rice Stuffing and secure with toothpicks. Place large piece of heavy foil in bottom of large baking dish and place salmon on it. Lay some of the lemon slices over salmon and place bacon over them. Scatter mushrooms over all and drizzle with champagne. Loosely cover fish with more heavy foil. Seal edges by folding them together. Bake at 400 degrees for 25 to 35 minutes or until fish is flaky. Serve with Sour Cream Sauce and garnish with parsley.

Serves 8 to 10.

RICE STUFFING

½ cup butter	2 bunches green onions, chopped
2 cups long grain rice	1 cup minced parsley
4 cups chicken stock	Salt and pepper
¾ cup pine nuts	

Melt ¼ cup of the butter in heavy saucepan over medium heat. Add rice and stir for 3 minutes. Add stock. Cover and bring to a boil. Reduce heat and simmer for 20 to 25 minutes. Melt remaining ¼ cup butter in medium skillet. Add pine nuts and stir until golden brown. Add green onions and parsley until heated through. Mix into rice. Season with salt and pepper.

SOUR CREAM SAUCE

2 large onions, chopped	1 cup sour cream, room temperature
¼ pound plus 2 tablespoons butter	1 tablespoon lemon juice
1 cup dry sherry	2 tablespoons juice from baked salmon
5 tablespoons flour	Salt and pepper
3 cups half and half	

Sauté onions in 2 tablespoons of the butter until softened. Add sherry and cook until liquid is absorbed. Add remaining butter and stir until melted. Sprinkle with flour and cook on medium heat, stirring constantly for 2 to 3 minutes. Slowly add half and half, stirring until thickened. Blend in sour cream and lemon juice. Just before serving add 2 tablespoons juice from baked salmon, salt and pepper.

GRILLED MARINATED SWORDFISH

2 pounds swordfish steaks, ½ inch thick, cut into 4 serving pieces	¼ cup red wine vinegar
3 garlic cloves, finely chopped	¼ cup water
½ cup fresh oregano leaves	½ cup extra virgin olive oil
2 tablespoons chopped Italian parsley	Juice of 1 large lemon
	Salt and freshly ground pepper

This recipe comes from sunny Capri and is perfect fare for a warm summer evening.

In a small bowl combine garlic, oregano, parsley, vinegar, water, oil and lemon juice. Season with salt and pepper and set aside. Brush fish steaks lightly with oil. Place on a hot grill or under broiler 2 to 3 minutes on each side or until fish is lightly golden. Place fish in a large, shallow dish and pour marinade over steaks. Marinate about 30 minutes. Serve at room temperature.

Serves 4.

SALMON IN PHYLLO WITH RED PEPPER SAUCE

8 salmon fillets, 4 to 5 ounces each, boned	Salt and white pepper
8 sheets phyllo dough	Pesto
Butter	Red Pepper Sauce

Brush butter on a half sheet of phyllo. Place another half sheet on top of the first and brush again with butter. Place each salmon fillet in the center of 1 long edge of the phyllo sheet. Spread 1 tablespoon Pesto on the salmon. Season with salt and white pepper. Roll the phyllo in a cylinder and crimp the ends to look like a party favor. Brush tops with butter. Repeat to make 8 rolls. Bake on a cookie sheet in a preheated 400 degree oven until nicely browned, about 10 minutes. Spread the Red Pepper Sauce on individual serving plates and place the phyllo rolls on the sauce.

Serves 8.

PESTO

2 cups fresh basil leaves	2 garlic cloves
2 tablespoons pine nuts	1 teaspoon salt
$^1/_2$ cup grated Parmesan cheese	$^1/_2$ cup olive oil
3 tablespoons butter, softened	

Place basil, pine nuts, Parmesan cheese, butter, garlic, and salt in food processor. Pulse until evenly blended. Drizzle olive oil into mixture while the machine is still running.

RED PEPPER SAUCE

3 large red bell peppers	$^1/_2$ cup sour cream
$^3/_4$ cup dry white wine	

Roast peppers over flame or broil until black. Place in a paper bag until cool. Peel and seed. Purée the peppers with the wine in a blender or food processor. Simmer the purée in a saucepan for 5 minutes. Add the sour cream and simmer over low heat another 5 minutes or until smooth.

CEVICHE

$^3/_4$ pound medium shrimp, peeled and deveined	$^1/_3$ cup chopped parsley or cilantro
$^3/_4$ pound raw scallops, thinly sliced	2 tablespoons minced red pepper
$^3/_4$ cup lime juice	$^1/_2$ teaspoon dried oregano
3 tablespoons olive oil	Tabasco sauce
2 tablespoons rice wine vinegar	Salt and pepper
$^1/_2$ cup finely chopped red onions	2 avocados, peeled and sliced

Ceviche is a great accompaniment to pasta when served as a main course.

Cook shrimp in boiling water for 2 to 3 minutes or just until they turn pink. Drain and cool. Cut prawns lengthwise and marinate prawns and scallops in lime juice in a bowl, covered, at room temperature for 2 to 3 hours or in refrigerator overnight. This "cooks" the fish. Drain and discard lime juice. Combine oil, vinegar, onion, parsley, red pepper, oregano, Tabasco sauce to taste, salt and pepper. Mix with prawns and scallops and chill overnight. To serve, arrange avocados on a plate or shell and top with chilled prawn/scallop mixture.

Serves 4 as a main course or 6 as an appetizer.

SWORDFISH WITH FRESH PINEAPPLE COULIS

4 swordfish steaks,
1 inch thick

1 large pineapple,
peeled, cored
and quartered

1 red bell
pepper, diced

1 green bell
pepper, diced

1 red onion, diced

1/4 cup olive oil

3 tablespoons finely
chopped cilantro

2 tablespoons
lime juice

2 tablespoons
chopped chives

2 tablespoons
chopped parsley

1 serrano chile pepper,
minced with seeds

Olive oil

Freshly ground pepper

For pineapple coulis, place pineapple on baking sheet and broil until just beginning to brown, about 5 minutes per side. Remove and chop finely. Mix with bell peppers, onions, olive oil, cilantro, lime juice, chives, parsley and chile pepper. Cover and chill 2 hours. Brush swordfish with oil, season with pepper and grill about 5 minutes per side or until tender. Transfer to plates and garnish with pineapple coulis. Serve immediately.

Serves 4.

TUNA STEAKS NIÇOISE

6 tuna steaks,
1 inch thick

1/4 cup lemon juice

1/4 cup vermouth

1 tablespoon minced
fresh ginger

1/4 teaspoon sugar

5 tablespoons olive oil

1 large onion,
finely chopped

6 garlic cloves, minced

1 cup tomato sauce

2 tomatoes, peeled,
seeded and
coarsely chopped

1/4 cup chopped
green olives

3 tablespoons brandy

1 tablespoon chopped
fresh basil

Pinch dried red
pepper flakes

Freshly ground pepper

6 green olives, sliced into
thin strips, for garnish

Combine lemon juice, vermouth, ginger and sugar. Add 3 tablespoons of the olive oil and freshly ground pepper. Mix and pour over tuna. Cover and marinate at least 2 hours in the refrigerator, turning occasionally. In a skillet, heat 1 tablespoon of the olive oil. Add onions and garlic. Cover and cook over low heat until softened, stirring occasionally. Add tomato sauce, fresh tomatoes, chopped green olives, brandy, basil, red pepper flakes and pepper. Cook over very low heat, stirring occasionally, until the sauce thickens, about 20 minutes. Remove from heat. Preheat oven to 400 degrees. Remove the tuna steaks, reserving marinade. Pour marinade into a saucepan and cook over high heat until slightly thickened, about 5 minutes. In a large skillet, preferably cast iron, heat 1 tablespoon olive oil. Add tuna steaks and sear about 1 minute per side. Transfer tuna to a baking dish and brush with marinade. Reduce oven temperature to 350 degrees and bake 8 to 9 minutes or until done. Reheat the tomato sauce. Spoon the sauce onto 6 plates. Arrange tuna steaks on top and garnish with sliced olives.

Serves 6.

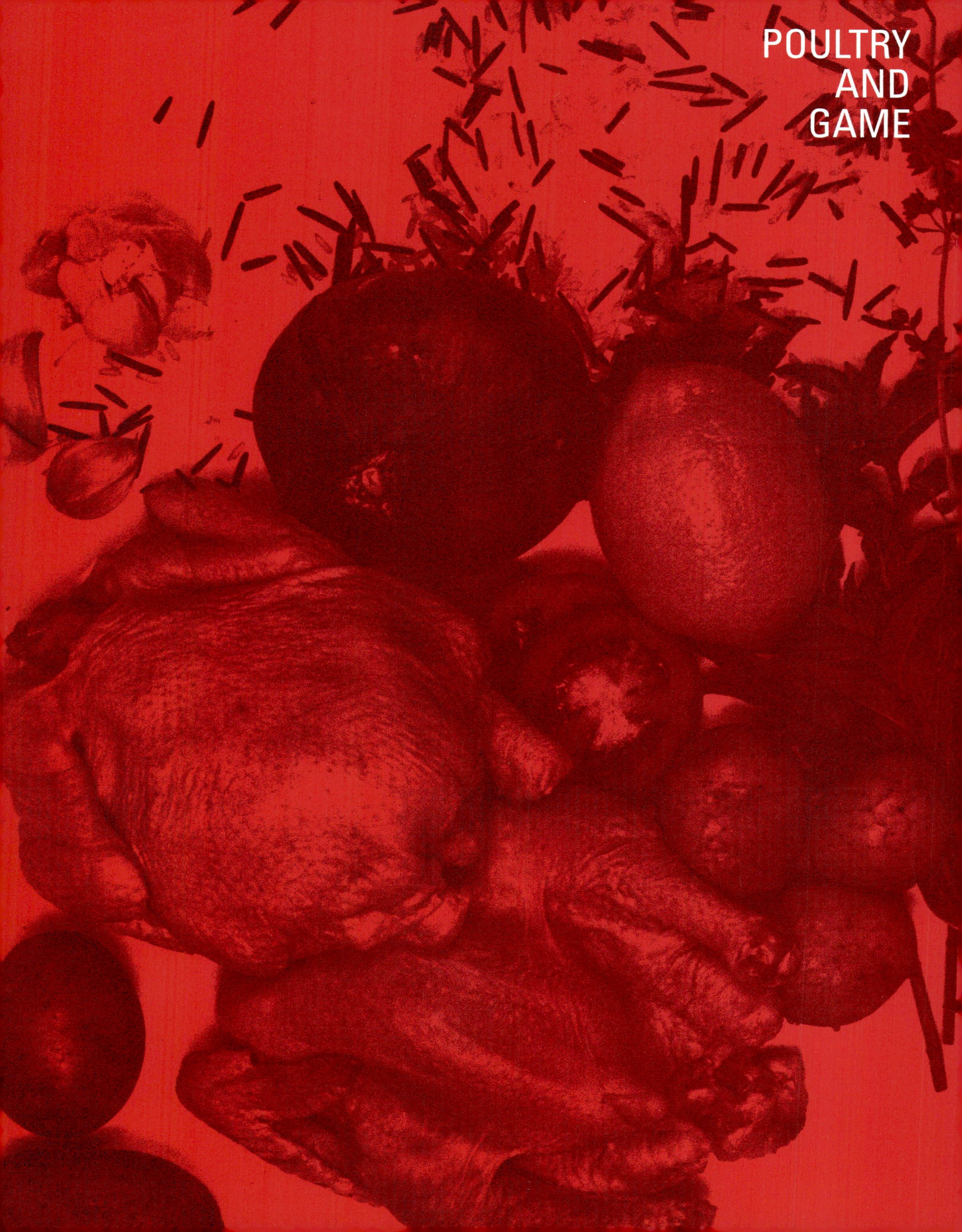
POULTRY
AND
GAME

THREE MUSHROOM CHICKEN

2 whole chicken breasts, skinned, boned and sliced into thin strips

1½ tablespoons oil

¼ cup sliced bamboo shoots

¼ cup sliced water chestnuts

½ cup fresh white mushrooms

½ cup fresh shiitake mushrooms*

½ cup fresh oyster mushrooms*

1 cup chicken broth

½ teaspoon salt

⅛ teaspoon white pepper

1 tablespoon oyster sauce

1 tablespoon cornstarch mixed with 2 tablespoons water

2 green onions, slivered, for garnish

*Use dried mushrooms if not available. If dried, soak in warm water overnight.

Heat a wok and swirl in oil. Sauté chicken until browned. Add bamboo shoots, water chestnuts and all mushrooms and continue to brown. When mushrooms are aromatic, add chicken broth and cover with lid. Simmer, covered, for 1 minute. Open lid and season with salt, pepper and oyster sauce. Bring to a boil. Add cornstarch/water mixture to thicken. Garnish with green onions. Serve over pan-fried noodles.

Serves 4.

CHICKEN JERUSALEM

6 whole chicken breasts, split

Oregano

Basil

Salt and pepper

Flour

1½ tablespoons olive oil

2 tablespoons butter

1 large garlic clove, minced

¾ pound fresh mushrooms, sliced

1½ cups white wine

½ to ¾ cup sliced large black olives

6 ounces artichoke hearts, halved

2 cups grated mozzarella, Port Salut, Gouda or Edam cheese or combination of all

Season chicken with oregano, basil, salt and pepper. Lightly flour chicken and sauté in olive oil, butter and garlic until browned . Place in a 9 x 13-inch glass dish, overlapping slightly. Add mushrooms to the pan in which the chicken was browned and sauté with wine, olives and artichokes. Pour over chicken and cover with foil. Bake at 350 degrees for 25 minutes. Remove foil and sprinkle with cheese. Return to the oven and bake, uncovered, at 400 degrees for 5 more minutes.

Serves 8 to 10.

ARTICHOKE CHICKEN TURNOVERS

2 cups diced, cooked chicken

1 cup diced Monterey Jack cheese

16 ounces marinated artichokes, drained

1/2 cup sour cream

4 ounces diced green chiles

1/2 teaspoon garlic salt

2 green onions, chopped

1 tablespoon lemon juice

1 pound puff pastry, page 234

1 egg yolk

1 tablespoon milk

Combine chicken and cheese. Add artichokes, sour cream, green chiles, garlic salt, green onions and lemon juice. Roll puff pastry on a lightly floured board and cut into an 8-inch circle. Off center, fill with 1/2 cup of the chicken mixture. Lightly moisten 2 opposite edges of circle, bring to top, overlap and pinch to seal. Repeat to make 6 turnovers. Place pastries on ungreased, rimmed baking sheet, seam sides down. Mix egg yolk and milk and brush the tops of the turnovers lightly. Bake at 400 degrees for 30 minutes until puffed and lightly browned. Serve warm or hot.

Serves 6.

SAVORY CHICKEN BUNDLES

3 whole chicken breasts, halved, skinned and boned

3/4 cup chopped green onions

3/4 cup mayonnaise

3 tablespoons lemon juice

3 garlic cloves, minced

3/4 teaspoon dry tarragon

1 pound phyllo dough

2/3 cup melted butter with 1 additional garlic clove, crushed

Salt and pepper

Grated Parmesan cheese

Mix together green onions, mayonnaise, lemon juice, garlic and tarragon and set aside. For each bundle, place 1 sheet of phyllo dough on board and brush with garlic butter. Arrange a second sheet on top and brush again with garlic butter. Lightly sprinkle chicken breasts with salt and pepper. Spread 1 side with mayonnaise mixture and turn over onto phyllo. Top with more mayonnaise mixture. Wrap breasts in phyllo, folding like a flag. Repeat to make 6 bundles. Place the bundles slightly apart on an ungreased cookie sheet. Brush with remaining garlic butter and sprinkle with Parmesan cheese. Bake at 375 for 20 to 25 minutes or until golden brown. Serve hot. These can be frozen in single layers in air-tight containers. They must be thawed completely before baking. Cover with foil while thawing.

Serves 6.

ENCHILADAS VERDES

3 cups cooked, shredded chicken

1 medium green pepper, chopped

1/4 cup chopped onions

2 to 3 large romaine lettuce leaves, washed and dried

1/2 cup diced green chiles

3/4 cup chicken broth

3 tablespoons oil

3/4 cup salsa

1/4 teaspoon salt

1 cup sour cream

10 6-inch flour tortillas

2 cups grated Monterey Jack cheese

Fresh cilantro leaves, chopped, for garnish

In a food processor or blender mix the green pepper, onions, lettuce, green chiles and broth together until smooth. Heat the oil in a medium saucepan over medium-high heat. Add the green pepper mixture, salsa and salt. Turn heat to medium and cook for 5 minutes. Remove from heat and whisk in 3/4 cup of the sour cream. Mix 1 cup of the sauce with the shredded chicken. Roll the mixture into the flour tortillas. Place into greased 9 x 13-inch pan. Pour remaining sauce over rolled tortillas. Cover with cheese. Bake until hot and bubbly. Dot with remaining sour cream and cilantro.

Serves 4 to 6.

GENERAL'S CHICKEN

1 pound chicken thighs, skinned and boned

1 egg

$^1/_4$ cup cornstarch

2 tablespoons oil

1 tablespoon finely minced fresh ginger

1 teaspoon minced garlic

2 green onions, chopped, for garnish

SAUCE

1 cup chicken broth

3 tablespoons white wine

3 tablespoons sugar

2 tablespoons vinegar

1 tablespoon sesame oil

$^1/_4$ cup soy sauce

1 teaspoon chile paste or 1 teaspoon hot chile oil

1 tablespoon cornstarch mixed with 2 tablespoons water

Cut chicken into 1-inch cubes. Mix egg and $^1/_4$ cup cornstarch together, forming a thin paste. Cover chicken with paste. Place oil in a frying pan and heat until very hot. Add ginger and garlic, stirring constantly. Add chicken and sauté for 5 minutes. Remove chicken to a platter. To the pan, add all sauce ingredients, except the cornstarch and water and bring to a boil. Add cornstarch and water mixture and add to sauce while stirring constantly. Return chicken to the sauce and garnish with green onions. Serve immediately with rice.

Serves 4.

PHOENIX AND DRAGON

2 tablespoons oil

$^1/_2$ cup mirepoix, equal parts julienned carrot, celery and onions

1 teaspoon minced garlic

1 pound chicken, skinned, boned and cut into bite sized pieces

8 large mushrooms, sliced

6 to 7 ounces clams with juice

1 cup heavy cream

1 teaspoon dried thyme

$^1/_2$ pound large shrimp, peeled and deveined with tails left on

$^1/_2$ teaspoon salt

2 teaspoons oyster sauce

$^1/_8$ teaspoon white pepper

1 tablespoon lemon juice

1 tablespoon cornstarch mixed with 2 tablespoons water

1 avocado, cubed

1 tablespoon pine nuts, toasted, for garnish

Sprig of thyme for garnish

Heat a frying pan or wok until very hot. Add the oil, mirepoix, garlic and sauté briefly. Add chicken and mushrooms. Sauté until aromatic and lightly browned. Add the clams with juice all at once and deglaze. Add the cream and thyme. Cover and simmer about 3 minutes. Add prawns and continue to simmer, uncovered. Season with salt, oyster sauce, white pepper and lemon juice. Make sure sauce is bubbling before adding cornstarch mixture. Boil until thickened. Add the avocado and transfer mixture from the pan or wok to the center of a plate. Garnish with pine nuts and sprig of thyme. You may serve this on a bed of pasta or steamed rice.

Serves 6.

CHICKEN EN CROÛTE

5 whole chicken breasts	Cream Cheese Pastry
6 peppercorns	Duxelle Sauce
1 carrot, halved	Lemon Butter Sauce
1 celery stalk, halved	1½ cups grated Jarlsberg or Swiss cheese
1 bay leaf	
3 cups cooked wild rice	1 egg, separated

In a saucepan with water bring peppercorns, carrot, celery and bay leaf to a boil. Add chicken breasts and simmer for 15 to 20 minutes. Remove chicken and cut into small cubes. Spoon wild rice into a buttered casserole to cover the bottom. Distribute chicken evenly over the rice. Pour Duxelle Sauce over chicken. Spoon Lemon Butter Sauce over all and sprinkle with cheese to cover the sauces. Roll Cream Cheese Pastry to ¼ inch thick. Cut ½ to ¾-inch strips and crisscross to form a lattice pattern for the top. Brush with egg white. Decorate top of the casserole with different pastry shapes made from the leftover dough. Brush shapes with egg yolk. Bake casserole for 30 minutes at 375 degrees or until pastry is golden.

Serves 8.

CREAM CHEESE PASTRY

½ cup butter, softened	1½ cups flour
3 ounces cream cheese, softened	½ teaspoon salt
2 tablespoons heavy cream	

Cream butter and cream cheese together. Add cream and blend well. Gradually stir in flour and salt until combined. Wrap in wax paper and chill for 2 hours. This can be made a day in advance.

DUXELLE SAUCE

¼ cup butter	½ cup lemon juice
¼ cup olive oil	2 cups heavy cream
1 cup minced onions	Salt and pepper
2½ pounds mushrooms, minced	½ cup chopped parsley

Heat butter and oil in a saucepan. Add onions and sauté over medium heat until translucent. Lower flame and add mushrooms and lemon juice. Cook until moisture evaporates. Add cream and reduce by half. Season with salt and pepper. Blend in parsley.

LEMON BUTTER SAUCE

½ cup plus 1 tablespoon butter	¾ cup lemon juice
	Salt
3 tablespoons flour	
1½ cups milk	

Melt butter in a small saucepan and gradually add flour stirring to make a roux. Cook 3 minutes. Add milk slowly to roux, whisking to avoid lumps. Bring to a boil and add lemon juice. Season with salt.

SAUTÉED CHICKEN BREAST WITH GREEN PEPPERCORNS AND COGNAC

2 whole chicken breasts

Salt and pepper

4 tablespoons flour

3 tablespoons oil

1/4 cup plus 2 tablespoons butter

2 tablespoons green peppercorns

1/4 cup cognac

1/2 cup chicken stock

Remove any excess fat or undesired skin from the chicken breasts. Season with salt and pepper and dust with flour. In a skillet place the oil and 1/4 cup of butter over medium heat. When the butter turns golden brown gently sauté the breasts, skin side first. Once browned turn over and continue to cook for 5 minutes. Pour out any excess oil or fat and add the peppercorns. Add cognac and chicken stock. Bring to a boil and then remove from the heat. Arrange the chicken breasts on plates. Return the skillet to the burner and bring to a boil once again. Whisk in the 2 tablespoons of butter. If the liquid has evaporated, add a little more chicken stock until an emulsion is achieved. Pour the sauce over the chicken and serve.

Serves 4.

CHICKEN WITH FOIE GRAS AND PORT WINE

2 whole chicken breasts, halved, skinned and boned

Salt and pepper

4 tablespoons flour

3 tablespoons oil

3 tablespoons butter

2 cups port wine

1/3 cup fresh berries, raspberry, blueberry, blackberry or combination

6 ounces pâté de foie gras

Crème fraîche, page 249

Photograph, page 242.

Season chicken with salt and pepper and dust with flour. Heat oil and 2 tablespoons of the butter in a skillet on medium heat. When the butter turns golden brown, gently sauté the breasts, skin side first for 5 minutes. Turn and continue to cook 4 minutes. Transfer to 350-degree oven, and roast 5 minutes. Remove chicken from pan, set aside and keep warm. While pan is still hot, pour off excess fat, deglaze with the port and simmer. When wine is reduced by half, about 10 minutes, add remaining 1 tablespoon of the butter and stir until melted. Add berries and stir gently, adding a little more port if necessary. To serve, slice chicken in 1/2-inch slices and arrange on individual plates. Place small triangles of pâté on top. Spoon port/berry sauce either around the chicken or over top. Garnish with designs made with Crème fraîche.

Serves 4.

LEMON VELVET CHICKEN

2 whole chicken breasts, boned and skinned

1/2 cup butter, melted and clarified

Flour

Salt and pepper

1 tablespoon lemon juice

2 tablespoons chopped parsley

Cover the bottom of a large skillet with butter, reserving any remaining butter for later. Pound the chicken breasts flat. Lightly flour and sprinkle with salt and pepper. Place in a hot skillet and sear for 3 minutes. Turn and sauté for an additional 3 to 4 minutes. Remove to a hot platter. Add remainder of butter to skillet and heat. Add lemon juice and parsley. Pour over chicken and serve immediately.

Serves 2 to 4.

CHICKEN STANLEY SAUTÉ

3-pound chicken,
cut into 8 pieces

6 tablespoons butter

3 medium onions, sliced

1/2 pound
mushrooms, sliced

3/4 cup white wine

1 tablespoon
curry powder

1 teaspoon lemon juice

1/2 teaspoon salt

1 truffle, thinly sliced,
for garnish

Melt 4 tablespoons of the butter in large skillet and brown chicken on all sides. Add onions and mushrooms and cook for 15 minutes, covered. Combine wine, curry powder, lemon juice and salt. Pour over chicken. Simmer 15 to 20 minutes more. Whisk in the remaining 2 tablespoons butter. Garnish with truffle slices.

Serves 4.

RASPBERRY CHICKEN

6 to 8 chicken pieces,
skinned and boned

3 tablespoons butter

1 tablespoon oil

3/4 cup
raspberry vinegar

1 1/4 cups chicken stock

1/2 teaspoon salt

1/4 teaspoon pepper

1 1/4 cups heavy cream

Raspberries for garnish

Sauté chicken in butter and oil for 3 to 5 minutes until golden brown. Remove chicken, drain fat, and add vinegar, stock and salt. Return chicken to the pan and simmer, uncovered, until done, about 20 minutes. Add pepper, remove chicken and keep warm. Add cream and another splash of vinegar to the broth. Boil vigorously, stirring until thickened. Pour over chicken and serve.

Serves 6 to 8.

GAME HENS WITH GARLIC AND LIME

4 Cornish game hens,
1 1/2 pounds each,
backbone removed

1/2 cup lime juice

1/3 cup tequila

1 cup olive oil

2 tablespoons triple sec

1 cup chopped fresh
cilantro leaves

4 to 5 garlic
cloves, minced

2 teaspoons red
pepper flakes

1/2 teaspoon salt

1 teaspoon freshly
ground pepper

Flatten game hens, using the palm of your hand. Combine lime juice, tequila, olive oil, triple sec, cilantro, garlic, red pepper flakes, salt and pepper. Pour over game hens and marinate overnight in refrigerator. Remove game hens from marinade. Grill on the barbeque or bake on the upper rack of the oven at 400 degrees, basting occasionally with the drippings, until the skin is golden and the juices are clear, 25 to 30 minutes.

Serves 4.

CHICKEN BOUILLABAISSE

1 large whole roasting chicken

2 yellow onions, diced

1 whole garlic bulb, minced

2 pounds tomatoes, peeled, seeded and coarsely chopped

1 large can plum tomatoes, drained

1 1/2 cups dry white wine

2 cups chicken stock

1/2 teaspoon dried thyme

1/2 teaspoon dried oregano

1 teaspoon dried basil

2-inch piece orange rind

Pinch of cayenne pepper

1 pound small new potatoes, unpeeled

1/2 cup capers, rinsed

1 cup pitted small green olives

Freshly ground pepper

3 medium zucchini, sliced

Lemon juice

Chopped parsley for garnish

Roast chicken for 1 hour at 350 degrees. Cool the chicken, discard skin, remove meat from carcass and cut into bite-sized pieces. Simmer the onions, garlic, tomatoes, wine, stock, herbs, orange rind and cayenne pepper in a covered stock pot for 45 minutes. Add potatoes, capers and olives to tomato mixture, continuing to cook 45 minutes longer. Remove the orange rind and add additional cayenne pepper to taste. Add freshly ground pepper, zucchini, lemon juice and chicken. Cover and cook 15 minutes. Garnish with chopped parsley and serve in wide, shallow soup bowls.

Serves 6.

CHICKEN STUFFED WITH SPINACH AND RICOTTA

3-pound chicken

1 cup ricotta cheese

4 tablespoons butter, softened

1/2 cup grated Parmesan cheese

1/2 dried teaspoon each marjoram, thyme, savory and oregano

1/4 teaspoon white pepper

3 packages frozen chopped spinach

1 medium onions, minced

3 garlic cloves, minced

1 tablespoon butter

1 tablespoon oil

1 egg, beaten

Salt

1/4 cup white wine

1/4 cup olive oil

1 teaspoon minced garlic

Pinch each of thyme, savory and oregano

Mix ricotta and butter. Add Parmesan cheese and spices. Cook the spinach and drain well, pressing out all water. Sauté onions and 3 minced garlic cloves in butter and oil until soft and add to cheese mixture. Add spinach and egg. Season with salt. Chill. Cut chicken down back and cut backbone out. Cut tail off and cut wings off at the first joint. Turn over on back and flatten with hand until the breast bone cracks. Starting at neck, loosen skin from meat but not to edge. Marinate flattened chicken in white wine, olive oil, 1 teaspoon minced garlic and additional herbs. Stuff chicken between the meat and skin with spinach mixture. Bake at 400 degrees for 15 minutes. Reduce heat to 375 and continue baking for 30 to 40 minutes. Remove and cut into fourths. Serve immediately. Instead of a whole chicken, chicken breast halves can be used. Stuff mixture between meat and skin. Bake at 375 degrees for 30 minutes. This can be sliced and served at room temperature.

Serves 4.

CHUTNEY CHICKEN IN PHYLLO

3 whole chicken
breasts, halved

Pepper

2 garlic cloves, minced

1 cup melted butter

$^{1}/_{2}$ cup dry vermouth
or sherry

$^{1}/_{2}$ cup brandy

6 sheets phyllo dough

$^{1}/_{4}$ pound mozzarella
cheese, shredded

$^{1}/_{4}$ pound Monterey Jack
cheese, shredded

1 cup peach chutney

6 cooked or canned
artichoke hearts

$^{3}/_{4}$ cup pine nuts

Marjoram

Season chicken with pepper and garlic. Place in shallow roasting pan and pour $^{1}/_{4}$ cup of the melted butter over the top. Add vermouth and brandy and cook for 15 minutes. Cool chicken and remove from bone. Brush 1 sheet of phyllo with melted butter. Lightly sprinkle with cheeses. Place 1 breast at end of phyllo leaving about 3-inch margin. Brush top of chicken with chutney and top with an artichoke heart. Sprinkle with more cheese and pine nuts. Season with marjoram. Wrap chicken with phyllo by folding phyllo over chicken, brushing with melted butter and sprinkling with cheeses between folds. Tuck in end pieces and continue to wrap. Place on shallow buttered baking pan, seam side down. Brush with butter. Repeat procedure for each chicken breast. Bake at 375 degrees for 20 minutes or until golden brown.

Serves 6.

CHICKEN IN PARCHMENT WITH WILD RICE AND RASPBERRY PAPAYA SALSA

1 whole chicken
breast, halved,
skinned and boned

Flour

2 tablespoons butter

2 tablespoons oil

$^{1}/_{2}$ small white
onions, chopped

$^{1}/_{2}$ cup wild rice,
uncooked

1 cup water

Salt and pepper

2 tablespoons
butter, softened

1 egg white,
beaten slightly

RASPBERRY
PAPAYA SALSA

1 jalapeño pepper,
roasted, seeded
and chopped

$^{1}/_{4}$ cup chopped cilantro

2 tablespoons
chopped mint

1 cup diced papaya

1 pint fresh raspberries

Juice of 1 lime

Juice of $^{1}/_{2}$ orange

Juice of 1 lemon

2 tablespoons sugar

Salt

Perfect for two and easy to multiply!

Season and flour the chicken breasts. In a skillet sear the chicken in 1 tablespoon of the butter and 1 tablespoon of the oil and set aside. In a sauce pan sauté the onions in remaining 1 tablespoon each of butter and oil until translucent. Add the rice and water, season with salt and pepper and simmer for 45 minutes. Cut 2 10 x 10-inch pieces of parchment paper and brush with softened butter. Off to 1 side of the paper, place half the rice and 1 seared chicken breast half. Brush some egg white on the edges of the paper. Fold the paper over the chicken and twist the edges together. Repeat. Place in a pan and bake in a preheated 350-degree oven for 10 minutes. Remove from oven and let cool. To ready to serve, open the paper and sprinkle the Raspberry Papaya Salsa over the chicken or serve it on the side.

Serves 2.

In a bowl place the peppers, cilantro, mint, papaya and raspberries. Add lime, orange and lemon juices and sugar. Gently toss. Season with salt.

"MOTHER LODED" CHICKEN

2 whole chicken
breasts, halved,
skinned and boned

4 slices jalapeño jack
cheese, 1/4 inch thick

1/2 teaspoon
dried oregano

2 eggs

1 tablespoon grated
Parmesan cheese

1/4 teaspoon salt

1/4 teaspoon pepper

1 tablespoon minced
parsley

Flour

2 tablespoons oil

2 tablespoons butter

1 lemon, cut into wedges

Cut a pocket in each half chicken breast about 2 x 3 inches but do not cut through. Roll cheese in oregano and insert in pockets. Chill 15 minutes. In a medium bowl beat eggs, Parmesan cheese, salt, pepper and parsley. Dip breasts in flour and then in egg mixture. Heat oil and butter and sauté breasts until crisp and golden brown. Arrange in baking dish and bake at 375 degrees for 8 to 10 minutes. Serve immediately with fresh lemon.

Serves 4.

SAMOAN CHICKEN WITH LIME CREAM SAUCE

2 whole chicken
breasts, halved,
skinned and boned

4 slices prosciutto
ham, thinly sliced

1/4 papaya, diced

5 tablespoons coconut

1/2 teaspoon
dried thyme

1 teaspoon curry powder

2 tablespoons butter

3 tablespoons oil

Juice of 1 lime

1 cup heavy cream

1 tablespoon lime zest

1 tablespoon butter

Flatten chicken breasts with a mallet. Layer proscuitto and papaya on each breast. Roll and secure ends with a toothpick. Coat the rolled breasts with a mixture of coconut, thyme and curry. Sear chicken breasts in butter and oil, seam side down. Transfer to oven and bake at 375 degrees for 15 minutes. Remove from oven and strain fat from pan, retaining the browned coconut for the sauce. On high heat, add lime juice to the pan, deglazing briefly. Add cream and bring to a boil over high heat. Reduce heat and simmer for 10 minutes or until reduced and thickened. Stir in lime zest and butter. Stir for 1 to 2 minutes. Remove from heat and pour over chicken.

Serves 4.

ROLLED CHICKEN BREAST WITH POTATO PÂTÉ

2 whole chicken breasts, halved and boned	1 cup grated mozzarella cheese
Salt and pepper	2 tablespoons butter
1 bunch spinach, washed and stemmed	1 tablespoon oil

Pound chicken breasts flat. Season with salt and pepper. Blanch the spinach, and lay evenly over chicken and sprinkle with grated cheese. Roll up chicken fillets, sear in butter and oil and then roast 15 minutes at 350 degrees. Cool. To serve, slice chicken crosswise and serve on the Potato Pâté. Top with Port Wine Vinaigrette.

Serves 4.

POTATO PÂTÉ

2 potatoes, peeled and thinly sliced	1 teaspoon minced garlic
1 cup heavy cream	1/4 cup grated Parmesan cheese
1 teaspoon minced shallots	Salt and pepper

In an ovenproof skillet, place the potatoes, cream, shallots, garlic and cheese. Slowly bring to a boil over medium heat. Remove from heat, cover with foil and bake at 350 degrees for 30 minutes. Remove from oven and place in a mold. Chill overnight. Remove from mold and cut into any shape.

PORT WINE VINAIGRETTE

1 cup port wine	1 cup walnut oil
1/4 cup Dijon mustard	
1/4 cup champagne vinegar	

Place port wine in saucepan and reduce to 1/4 cup. Cool. Stir in mustard and vinegar. Add the walnut oil slowly while stirring with a whisk until smooth.

GRILLED LIME CHICKEN WITH FRESH PAPAYA SALSA

3 to 4 whole chicken breasts, halved, skinned and boned	Juice of 6 to 8 limes

Pour lime juice over chicken and let stand at least 30 minutes. Grill chicken 3 to 4 minutes per side. Serve with Papaya Salsa.

Serves 6 to 8.

PAPAYA SALSA

1 papaya, skinned, seeded and finely chopped	3 tablespoons lime juice
1/4 medium red onions, chopped	1/4 cup chopped cilantro
4 1/2 ounces diced green chiles	6 tablespoons rice wine vinegar
	1 red bell pepper, finely chopped

Combine all ingredients and let stand for 1 hour.

GRILLED BLUEBERRY CHICKEN

4 whole chicken breasts, halved, skinned and boned

3/4 cup unsweetened pineapple juice

1/4 cup soy sauce

2 tablespoons lime juice

1 garlic clove, minced

1 medium star fruit, sliced, for garnish

2 medium kiwis, peeled and sliced, for garnish

8 medium strawberries, for garnish

Pound chicken with mallet. Place chicken in a 9 x 13-inch baking dish. Combine pineapple juice, soy sauce, lime juice and garlic, stirring well. Pour over chicken, reserving 1/4 cup for basting, and marinate in refrigerator 8 hours or overnight, turning occasionally. Drain and grill chicken over medium hot coals, 5 minutes on each side or until chicken is done and tender, basting once with reserved marinade. Remove chicken from grill and chill thoroughly. Spoon 2 tablespoons Blueberry Sauce onto 8 individual serving plates. Place a chicken breast in the sauce. Top each serving with 1 slice of star fruit, 2 slices of kiwi and 1 strawberry.

Serves 8.

BLUEBERRY SAUCE

1 cup fresh blueberries

2 tablespoons water

2 tablespoons crème de cassis

1 teaspoon lemon juice

Combine blueberries, water and creme de cassis in a small saucepan. Bring to a boil. Reduce heat and simmer 1 to 2 minutes. Remove from heat and cool. Transfer mixture to a food processor and process until smooth. Stir in lemon juice. Cover and chill.

SHASTA CHICKEN WITH GRILLED VEGETABLES

1 whole chicken, cut up

3 zucchini, sliced lengthwise to desired thickness

2 Japanese eggplants, sliced lengthwise to desired thickness

1 cup soy sauce

1/2 cup sugar

1/4 cup olive oil

2 teaspoons ginger

1 garlic clove

1/2 cup sherry

Mix all ingredients except chicken and vegetables in a blender at low speed for 30 seconds. Pour three-fourths of the marinade over chicken, reserving one-fourth for basting later. Marinate chicken, turning to coat occasionally, for at least 6 hours, preferably overnight. Grill chicken using reserved marinade for basting. During the last 5 minutes, grill vegetables, turning once.

Serves 4.

TURKEY SHISH KABOBS

3 pounds turkey breast, skinned, boned and cut into 1½-inch cubes

4 large leeks, washed thoroughly and cut crosswise into 6 pieces

2 large zucchini, cut crosswise into 6 pieces

4 red bell peppers, cut into squares

Parsley for garnish

MARINADE

3 tablespoons sherry

3 tablespoons dark brown sugar

½ cup oil

⅔ cup soy sauce

1 tablespoon minced fresh ginger

1 garlic clove, minced

1 teaspoon grated lemon rind

2 teaspoons red pepper flakes

4 green onions, minced

1 tablespoon minced parsley

Marinate the turkey in a covered bowl at least 4 hours, preferably overnight. Thread skewers, alternating vegetables and turkey. Brush with reserved marinade. Barbecue or broil about 4 minutes per side, turning once. Sprinkle with parsley and serve immediately.

Serves 8 to 10.

Combine marinade ingredients in a bowl. Reserve ¼ cup for basting.

TURKEY PICCATA

1 pound turkey breast, sliced into ¼-inch steaks

⅓ cup flour

2 tablespoons oil

2 tablespoons butter

2 tablespoons chopped shallots

¼ pound mushrooms, sliced

½ cup chicken broth

½ cup dry white wine

1½ tablespoons lemon juice

1 tablespoon capers

½ lemon, thinly sliced

Chopped parsley

A method for either veal or chicken.

Pound turkey steaks, dredged in flour, between sheets of plastic wrap to ⅛ inch thickness. Brown turkey quickly in oil and butter. Set aside and keep warm. Add shallots and mushrooms to skillet. Sauté until browned. Add broth, wine, lemon juice and capers, mixing well. Return turkey to skillet, spooning sauce over top. Lay lemon slices on turkey. Cover and simmer just until turkey is hot. Serve with sauce and parsley.

Serves 4.

MARINATED TURKEY LEGS WITH FRESH HERBS

8 turkey legs

1 cup white wine

1/4 cup olive oil

2 tablespoons butter

1 medium onion, minced

1 garlic clove, minced

1 teaspoon salt

1/4 teaspoon paprika

2 teaspoons fresh rosemary

2 teaspoons fresh thyme

3 tablespoons minced parsley

1 teaspoon freshly ground pepper

Use this delicious marinade for any poultry.

Combine all of the ingredients, except the turkey legs, in a 3-quart saucepan and simmer for 15 minutes. Pour over turkey legs in a roasting pan. Bake at 350 degrees for 45 minutes, basting every 20 minutes until done, or turkey can be grilled on the barbeque. The basting sauce can be made ahead of time, chilled and reheated when ready to use.

Serves 8.

TURKEY BREAST MARSALA

8 thick slices cooked turkey breast

4 to 6 tablespoons butter

Pepper

8 slices prosciutto

8 slices Monterey Jack cheese

1/2 cup Marsala wine

Chopped parsley for garnish

Sauté the turkey in butter until golden brown on both sides. Sprinkle with pepper. Place 1 slice each of prosciutto and cheese on each. Pour the Marsala over all and cover. Cook until heated through and cheese is melted. Sprinkle with parsley.

Serves 8.

FLAMING GINGER DUCK

2 whole duck breasts, halved, skinned, boned and cut into strips

2 tablespoons butter

3 oranges, cut into segments

1 tablespoon minced fresh ginger

2 shallots, minced

Salt and pepper

Cayenne pepper

1/4 cup Grand Marnier

Sauté duck in butter. Add orange segments, ginger, shallots, salt, pepper and cayenne pepper. Add Grand Marnier slowly, ignite and flambé. Serve immediately.

Serves 4.

ROASTED DUCK WITH FRESH PEACHES

3 to 4-pound duck

8 chestnuts, peeled

2 peaches, peeled and quartered

1/2 lemon, quartered and thinly sliced

2 tablespoons butter

2 tablespoons finely diced onions

1 tablespoon minced garlic

2 tablespoons balsamic vinegar

1 cup duck or chicken stock and 1 tablespoon glace de viande, page 245

Salt and pepper

Paperdelli noodles

Stuff duck with chestnuts, peaches and lemons. Roast at 400 degrees for 45 minutes and cool. Remove duck and pour off fat, reserving the drippings. Take the stuffing from the cavity and reserve. Take the legs, thighs and breasts off the carcass, leaving the leg and thigh intact. Put half the butter and the reserved drippings in a saucepan. Add onions, garlic and stuffing. Cook for 4 minutes. Deglaze with balsamic vinegar and reduce by half. Add stock and the remaining 1 tablespoon butter. Reheat duck in oven. At the same time cook the paperdelli in boiling, salted water. Place duck pieces on noodles and spoon sauce over the top. Serve immediately.

Serves 2.

ROAST DUCK WITH PORT-SOAKED APRICOTS

2 5-pound ducks, trimmed of excess fat

6 garlic cloves, minced

1/2 teaspoon cinnamon

1 tablespoon plus 1 teaspoon lemon juice

3/4 teaspoon freshly ground pepper

16 dried apricots, approximately 8 ounces

1 1/2 cups port wine

2 cups small pearl onions

2 tablespoons butter

1 teaspoon sugar

1 cup chicken stock

1/4 cup orange juice

1 teaspoon orange zest, finely grated

1 cup small green olives, pitted, drained and rinsed

In a small bowl, combine the garlic, cinnamon and lemon juice. Crush with the back of a spoon into a rough paste. Rub the insides of the ducks with the paste and lightly season outsides with 1/4 teaspoon of the pepper. Place on a rack in a large roasting pan and roast 1 hour at 500 degrees, until browned and the juices run clear when the thigh is pierced with a knife. Meanwhile, combine the apricots with 1 cup of the port. Bring to a simmer over moderately high heat. Remove from the heat, cover and set aside for at least 30 minutes and up to 2 hours. Make a cross in the root end of each pearl onion. Boil in salted water 5 to 7 minutes. Drain, peel and cool. In a small sauté pan, melt the butter over high heat. Add the cooked onions and sprinkle with sugar. Cook, shaking the pan constantly, until the onions have caramelized to a rich brown, about 3 minutes. Set aside. Place the remaining 1/2 cup port and chicken stock in a saucepan. Bring to a boil over high heat and reduce to 1 cup, approximately 10 minutes. Add the orange juice, orange zest, apricots and their liquid, olives and onions to the sauce. Season with remaining pepper. Cook to warm through, about 3 minutes. Cut the breasts from the ducks and slice each in half. Remove the legs and separate the drumsticks and thighs. Arrange the duck pieces on a large, warmed serving platter. Spoon the apricots, onions, olives and sauce on top. Serve hot.

Serves 6.

PHEASANT BREASTS VERONIQUE

4 whole pheasant breasts, about 4 pounds, halved, skinned and boned

Salt

4 tablespoons butter

2 tablespoons orange marmalade

½ teaspoon dreid tarragon

1 cup dry white wine

16 medium-sized mushrooms, quartered, for garnish

1 cup heavy cream

1 teaspoon cornstarch mixed with 1 tablespoon water

1½ cups seedless grapes

Parsley sprigs for garnish

In a pan over medium heat, melt 2 tablespoons of the butter. Add mushrooms and cook, stirring, until liquid has evaporated. Set aside. Sprinkle pheasant breasts lightly with salt. In a large skillet melt remaining 2 tablespoons of the butter over medium heat. Add pheasant breasts and cook, turning, until golden on each side. Stir in marmalade, tarragon and wine. Cover, reduce heat and simmer until meat in thickest portion is no longer pink when slashed, about 15 to 20 minutes or longer, if necessary. Transfer pheasant to a warm serving dish, reserving juices. Add cream to pan juices. Quickly bring to a full rolling boil over medium-high heat. Add cornstarch mixture. While stirring, return sauce to a boil. Add grapes, return sauce to a boil again and pour over pheasant. Garnish with mushrooms and parsley.

Serves 6.

PHEASANT WITH ARTICHOKES

4 whole pheasant breasts, about 4 pounds, halved, skinned and boned

Flour

½ cup butter

1 teaspoon salt

⅛ teaspoon white pepper

¼ teaspoon nutmeg

1 cup sliced mushrooms

10 ounces artichoke hearts or bottoms, diced

1 cup dry sherry

1 cup heavy cream

¼ cup chopped chives

Dredge pheasant in flour and sauté in butter until golden brown. Sprinkle with salt, pepper and nutmeg. Add mushrooms, artichokes and sherry and simmer, covered, for 15 to 20 minutes or longer, if necessary. Transfer pheasant to a warm platter, reserving juices. Stir cream into juices and bring to a boil. Stir in chives. Mix thoroughly and pour over pheasant. Serve with rice or noodles.

Serves 6.

VEAL MARCI

1½ pounds
veal scallops

½ cup flour

3 tablespoons shortening

1 medium onion,
thinly sliced

1 green bell pepper,
cut into strips

2 cups chicken broth

½ pound mushrooms,
browned in butter

¾ cup pimento-stuffed
green olives

MARINADE

2 teaspoons salt

2 teaspoons paprika

1 cup oil

½ cup lemon juice

2 garlic cloves, minced

2 teaspoons
prepared mustard

½ teaspoon nutmeg

1 teaspoon sugar

Combine marinade ingredients and mix well. Pour over veal and marinate overnight in refrigerator. Remove veal from marinade and reserve the marinade. Dredge veal in flour and brown in shortening in a large Dutch oven. Add onions, bell peppers, broth, reserved marinade, mushrooms and olives. Cover and simmer slowly until veal is tender, about 2 hours. Add water, if necessary. Serve over rice.

Serves 4 to 6.

VEAL STUFFED CABBAGE ROLLS

1 head white
cabbage, cored

1½ pounds ground veal

1 onion, chopped

2 tablespoons
chopped parsley

1 garlic clove, minced

1 egg, slightly beaten

½ cup bread crumbs

3 slices cooked
ham, diced

Salt and pepper

Butter

Grated
Parmesan cheese

Place whole cabbage head in a large pot of salted, simmering water for 10 minutes, or until the outer leaves are easy to remove. Loosen as many leaves as possible and set aside to cool. Return the rest of the cabbage to the water and repeat this procedure until all the leaves are loosened. Use the smaller leaves as a liner for the larger leaves. Mix the veal with onions, parsley, garlic, egg, bread crumbs, ham, salt and pepper. Place 1½ tablespoons of meat mixture in center of each cabbage leaf. Folding outer edges in first, roll cabbage around mixture. Place rolls in a buttered casserole dish, seam side down. Dot with butter and Parmesan cheese. Bake at 400 degrees for 45 minutes or until slightly browned. Serve with your favorite tomato sauce.

Serves 6 to 8.

VEAL PACIFIC

2½-pound veal fillet, cut into 6 medallions

½ avocado, cut into 12 wedges

2 eggs, slightly beaten

6 slices Monterey Jack cheese

¼ cup flour

Olive oil

Pound veal medallions between 2 pieces of waxed paper. Dip in beaten eggs and dredge in flour. Sauté in olive oil until golden brown. Arrange veal in a baking dish. Top each medallion with two wedges of avocado, a dollop of Crab Sauce and a slice of Monterey Jack cheese. Bake at 500 degrees until cheese has browned slightly. Watch carefully. Remove from oven. Heat the Avocado Sauce and spoon over each serving.

Serves 6.

CREAM SAUCE

2 tablespoons butter

¼ cup heavy cream

¼ cup flour

2 tablespoons grated Parmesan cheese

¾ cup chicken stock

Salt, pepper and nutmeg

¼ cup white wine

To be used in both Crab and Avocado Sauces.

In a saucepan, melt butter and add flour. Stir until it forms a roux. Cook 2 to 3 minutes. Add chicken stock and wine slowly, stirring constantly, while heating. After sauce thickens slightly, add cream and bring to a slow boil. Reduce heat and simmer for a few minutes, watching carefully. Remove from heat and stir in cheese and spices. Set aside.

CRAB SAUCE

¾ cup chopped green onions

1 tablespoon chopped dill

1 cup sliced mushrooms

1 tablespoon brandy

1 garlic clove, minced

⅓ cup Cream Sauce

2 tablespoons butter

1 cup cooked and flaked Alaskan king crab meat

2 tablespoons minced parsley

Sauté green onions, mushrooms and garlic in butter. Add parsley, dill, brandy and Cream Sauce. Heat thoroughly, then gently fold in the crabmeat.

AVOCADO SAUCE

1 avocado

1 tablespoon lemon juice

2 tablespoons sour cream

½ tablespoon chopped fresh dill

½ cup Cream Sauce

Salt and white pepper

¼ cup heavy cream

Purée avocado with cream and sour cream in a blender or food processor. Add Cream Sauce, lemon juice and dill. Blend thoroughly and season with salt and pepper. Set aside.

COLD HERBED VEAL ROAST WITH SAUCE VERTE

4½-pound veal shoulder, boned and butterflied

¼ cup Worcestershire sauce

1 tablespoon fresh thyme

1 teaspoon crushed red pepper

½ teaspoon coarsely cracked black pepper

2 large yellow bell peppers

2 large red bell peppers

1 cup fresh bread crumbs

2 tablespoons olive oil

In a baking dish, lay veal flat and brush with 2 tablespoons Worcestershire sauce. Sprinkle with half of the thyme, red pepper and cracked pepper. Turn the meat over and repeat procedure with Worcestershire and seasonings. Cover with plastic wrap and marinate in refrigerator for 2 to 3 hours or overnight. Roast yellow and red bell peppers under a broiler or over a flame until charred. Place peppers in a sealed brown bag and let steam for 10 minutes. Peel, discarding the cores, seeds and ribs. Cut into 1½ inch thick strips. Remove veal from the baking dish and place on a work surface, skin side down. Evenly distribute ½ cup of the bread crumbs over the meat. Arrange alternating strips of bell peppers in a single layer over the bread crumbs. Sprinkle with remaining bread crumbs. Carefully roll up the veal to form a neat package. Tie securely with kitchen string. In a large, heavy, cast iron skillet, heat olive oil until it just begins to smoke. Sear the veal, then place in a 450 degree oven. Roast meat, turning every 10 minutes, for 40 minutes until evenly browned all over. Reduce oven temperature to 350 degrees and continue to cook another 40 to 50 minutes. Internal temperature should read 150 degrees. Remove from the oven and place on a rack to cool completely. The meat can be prepared ahead to this point and refrigerated overnight. Just before serving remove the strings and thinly slice the meat. Carving is easier when the roast is cold. Serve cold or at room temperature with Sauce Verte.

Serves 12.

SAUCE VERTE

½ bunch watercress

½ bunch spinach

½ bunch tarragon

1 cup mayonnaise

Salt and pepper

Blanch watercress, spinach and tarragon in hot water for 5 minutes. Drain thoroughly and cool. Place mayonnaise in food processor and add greens. Purée until well blended. Season with salt and pepper.

OSSO BUCCO

5 to 6 veal shanks

½ cup flour

1 garlic clove, minced

3 tablespoons olive oil

3 tablespoons butter

½ cup finely chopped carrots

½ cup finely chopped celery

¼ cup finely chopped parsley

1 cup prepared brown sauce or demi-glace, page 245

3 tablespoons tomato paste

¼ cup vermouth

Tie veal shanks with butcher's string to hold them together. Lightly flour. Sauté garlic in oil and butter until lightly browned. Add carrots, celery and parsley and sauté for 5 minutes. Add brown sauce, tomato paste and vermouth. If the sauce seems too thick, add water to achieve desired consistency. Arrange shanks in a casserole with sauce. Bake at 350 degrees for 1 to 1½ hours.

Serves 4 to 6.

VEAL CHOPS WITH LEMON COGNAC SAUCE

4 veal chops, 1 inch thick	2 teaspoons cognac
Flour	1/4 pound shallots, thinly sliced
5 tablespoons butter	1 teaspoon minced fresh rosemary
3 tablespoons olive oil	1/2 cup dry white wine
12 mushroom caps	Pepper
1/2 teaspoon lemon juice	Minced parsley
	Lemon zest

Lightly flour the veal chops and shake off excess. In a skillet melt 1 tablespoon of the butter with 1 1/2 tablespoons of the oil over medium-high heat. Sear chops on both sides. Transfer to a 350-degree oven and bake for about 12 minutes for medium rare. In another skillet, heat remaining oil and butter until lightly browned. Add mushrooms, cap side down and sauté, shaking pan, until mushrooms are browned, 2 to 3 minutes. Stir in lemon juice and cognac and remove from heat. Cover with foil to keep warm. Add shallots and rosemary to first skillet and sauté over medium-high heat. Stir, scraping bottom, until shallots are softened, about 5 minutes. Add wine and simmer, stirring constantly, until sauce is slightly reduced, about 3 minutes. Season with pepper. Combine parsley and lemon zest. Place chops on warmed plates. Spoon shallot sauce over each chop and top with 3 mushroom caps. Sprinkle with parsley/lemon mixture. Serve immediately.

Serves 4.

VEAL CUTLETS WITH SHIITAKE MUSHROOMS

4 veal cutlets, 3 to 4 ounces each, flattened	4 wedges of peeled ripe tomato
Cornflake or bread crumbs	Salt and pepper
2 tablespoons butter	4 ounces grated Monterey Jack cheese
1 tablespoon oil	

Evenly coat veal cutlets with crumbs and sauté in 1 tablespoon of the butter and oil until done. Top each with a wedge of tomato. Brush tomato with 1 tablespoon melted butter. Season with salt and pepper. Place veal and tomato on top of Shiitake Mushroom Sauce. Sprinkle tomato with cheese and heat in oven until cheese is melted.

Serves 4.

SHIITAKE MUSHROOM SAUCE

2 shallots, minced	1/4 cup Madeira wine
2 garlic cloves, minced	1 cup chicken stock
6 tablespoons butter	2 cups heavy cream
1/2 pound shiitake mushrooms, thinly sliced	

Sauté shallots and garlic in 4 tablespoons of the butter until soft. Add mushrooms and sauté for 5 minutes. Add wine and cook for a few more minutes. Add stock, bring to a boil and reduce by half. Add cream and reduce until thick and sauce coats the back of a spoon. Whisk in the remaining 2 tablespoons butter.

STUFFED BREAST OF VEAL

6-pound breast of veal, boned and trimmed

½ cup plus 2 tablespoons butter

1½ cups minced onions

2 garlic cloves, minced

2 cups cooked, drained spinach

⅓ cup heavy cream

1 cup fresh bread crumbs

¼ cup grated Parmesan cheese

2 eggs, slightly beaten

1 tablespoon lemon juice

1 tablespoon grated lemon rind

1 teaspoon dried thyme

¼ teaspoon grated nutmeg

Salt and pepper

¼ pound ham, shredded

¼ pound Gruyère cheese, grated

3 tablespoons olive oil

½ cup diced celery

½ cup diced carrot

1 cup dry white wine

2 cups chicken stock

5 tablespoons flour

This is worth the effort!

Pound veal with a mallet to as even a thickness as possible. In a large skillet melt 4 tablespoons of the butter over medium heat and sauté 1 cup of the onions and garlic. Stir for 3 minutes until softened. Add spinach and cream, and cook another 3 minutes. Place spinach mixture in a food processor and purée. Add bread crumbs, Parmesan cheese, eggs, lemon juice and rind, thyme and nutmeg. Season stuffing mixture with salt and pepper. Set aside to cool. Sprinkle the surface of the veal with salt and pepper and spread cooled stuffing mixture on top, leaving a ½-inch border. Cover stuffing with ham and Gruyère cheese. Roll veal, jelly-roll style, starting with the shorter side, tightening as it rolls. Tuck the ends into the roll and tie with kitchen string. In a large Dutch oven brown veal in oil and 3 tablespoons of the butter. Remove veal roll from the pan. Add to the pan remaining ½ cup onions, celery and carrots. Sauté mixture over medium heat for 5 minutes or until mixture is golden. Add white wine to deglaze pan. Add stock. Bring liquid to a boil, stirring constantly. Place veal in liquid, cover and braise 2 hours at 350 degrees, basting often. Remove from oven and cool veal in the pan juices for 30 minutes. Transfer to a plate and cover to keep warm. Strain the cooking liquid, skim off the fat and reduce to 3 cups. In another saucepan make a roux of 3 tablespoons of the butter and 5 tablespoons flour. Stir for 3 minutes, remove from heat and whisk in hot pan juices until thick and smooth. Return pan to heat and simmer for 10 minutes. Season with salt and pepper. Remove string from veal and slice into ½-inch slices. Arrange on individual plates or a large platter and serve sauce on the side.

Serves 10 to 12.

ROAST PORK WITH SAUCE ROBERT

2½ to 3-pound pork roast

1 cup brown or beef stock, page 245

1 tablespoon butter

⅓ cup finely minced onions

1 tablespoon flour

½ cup dry white wine

1 tablespoon Dijon mustard

Salt and pepper

Roast pork at 325 degrees until done. Remove from roasting pan and keep warm. Pour all the fat from the pan and deglaze with brown stock. Pour off the stock and reserve. Sauté onions in butter until brown. Sprinkle with flour and cook a little bit longer. Stir in the stock and wine. Simmer until sauce is reduced to ¾ of the original amount. At the last minute stir in the mustard, salt and pepper. Serve sauce over roasted pork.

Serves 6 to 8.

CITRON CHOPS

4 center cut pork chops, 1 inch thick

Salt and pepper

Vegetable oil

2 to 4 tablespoons water

5 tablespoons sugar

1½ teaspoons cornstarch

¼ teaspoon salt

¼ teaspoon cinnamon

10 whole cloves

½ cup orange juice

Grated orange rind

Season chops with salt and pepper. Heat oil in a skillet and brown chops. Reduce heat, add water and simmer for 45 minutes, turning once. Add more water if necessary. In a saucepan stir together sugar, cornstarch, salt, cinnamon, cloves, orange juice and orange rind. Cook until thick and clear. Serve sauce over chops.

Serves 4.

FRUIT STUFFED PORK LOIN WRAPPED IN RED CABBAGE LEAVES

3 pounds trimmed pork loin

Salt

Freshly ground pepper

Several bay leaves, crumbled

1 tablespoon dried thyme

½ cup diced dried apricots

½ cup diced dried prunes

1 cup red wine

⅓ cup chopped pecans

⅓ cup chopped hazelnuts

1 large head red cabbage

1 cup chicken stock or ½ cup each white wine and water

1 cup heavy cream

Watercress for garnish

Rub pork all over with salt, pepper, bay leaves and half of the thyme. Chill overnight, loosely covered. Place fruits in bowl with wine and soak at least 1 hour. Drain. Combine nuts with fruits. Chill. Sear meat on all sides. Bring a large pot of water to a boil and dip cabbage in it briefly to soften leaves. Keep dipping cabbage head as necessary while removing leaves. With the handle of a wooden spoon, make a hole through the center of the loin along its length. Push fruit/nut stuffing into hole using the handle of the wooden spoon to force the stuffing all the way into the middle. Make a bed of the blanched cabbage leaves. Place meat on it. Sprinkle with salt, pepper and remaining thyme. Bring edges of leaves up so meat is fully encased in cabbage. Tie securely with kitchen string. This may be completed a day ahead. Place meat in a pan, add stock and bake, covered, at 375 degrees for 45 minutes. Remove from oven and let stand 10 minutes. Pour liquid from roasting pan into saucepan and bring to a boil. Add cream, continue to boil and reduce by half or until it becomes a light sauce. Cut the meat into thin slices and garnish with watercress. Serve sauce in a separae bowl.

Serves 8.

PORK TENDERLOIN ITALIANO

1-pound pork tenderloin, sliced

3 tablespoons grated Parmesan cheese

Italian bread crumbs

2 eggs, slightly beaten with 2 tablespoons of milk

1$\frac{1}{2}$ cups thinly sliced onions

1 tablespoon butter

$\frac{1}{3}$ pound fresh mushrooms, sliced

$\frac{1}{2}$ pound bacon, diced and fried until crisp

1 cup chicken stock

Add cheese to bread crumbs and dredge meat in crumbs, egg mixture and again in crumbs. Let stand on wax paper for approximately 20 minutes. Sauté onions in butter and set aside. Sauté meat in the same pan until lightly browned. Place meat in baking dish with pieces overlapping slightly. Spread onions over the top of the pork followed by the mushroom slices and top with bacon. Pour stock over all, cover and bake at 325 to 350 degrees for 40 minutes.

Serves 4.

MOONGATE PORK

1$\frac{1}{2}$-pound boneless pork loin roast

$\frac{1}{2}$ cup sugar

$\frac{1}{4}$ cup plum jam

$\frac{1}{4}$ cup soy sauce

$\frac{1}{4}$ cup apple butter

1 teaspoon chili powder

1 teaspoon salt

$\frac{1}{4}$ teaspoon fresh ginger, thinly sliced

Toasted sesame seeds for garnish

Combine all ingredients, except sesame seeds, pour over pork roast and marinate for at least 6 hours or overnight, turning several times. Remove pork from marinade and roast at 325 degrees for 1 hour, uncovered. Slice thinly. Bring marinade to a boil and pour over slices. Sprinkle with toasted sesame seeds.

Serves 4.

APRICOT GLAZED RIBS

6 pounds pork ribs

1$\frac{1}{2}$ cups water

1 cup dried apricots, coarsely chopped

1 cup apricot jam

$\frac{1}{2}$ cup packed brown sugar

1 teaspoon vinegar

1 tablespoon lemon juice

1 tablespoon minced fresh ginger

$\frac{1}{2}$ teaspoon kosher salt

Combine all ingredients, except ribs, in a saucepan and bring to a boil. Cook for 5 minutes. Remove from heat and cool slightly. Purée in food processor. Brush glaze on ribs and grill over hot coals until crisp, approximately 45 minutes. Continue to brush with glaze while grilling.

Serves 6.

PORK TENDERLOIN WITH TWO MARINADES

4 whole pork tenderloins

Two choices for grilling pork–either one is exceptional!

HONEY GINGER MARINADE

1 piece fresh ginger, peeled and minced	⅔ cup honey
	6 tablespoons soy sauce
¼ teaspoon crushed red pepper flakes	6 tablespoons sesame oil

CANTONESE MARINADE

1 cup hoisin sauce	3 tablespoons sugar
3 to 4 garlic cloves, chopped	3 tablespoons dry sherry
1 teaspoon five spice seasoning	

Marinate pork tenderloins in either marinade for at least 1 hour or overnight in refrigerator. Remove meat from marinade and discard marinade. Broil 6 to 8 minutes per side, or barbecue over medium hot coals approximately 5 minutes per side. Thinly slice pork on the diagonal and serve.

Serves 6 to 8.

MINTED MEDALLIONS OF PORK

1-pound pork loin, boned, trimmed and cut into 8 medallions	2 tablespoons butter
	Mint leaves for garnish
½ cup flour seasoned with salt and pepper	Orange segments, peeled and seeded, for garnish
1 tablespoon oil	

Dredge medallions in seasoned flour, shaking off excess. Sauté in oil and butter for 3 to 4 minutes on each side. Arrange on serving plate and spoon Mint Sauce over the pork. Garnish with mint leaves and orange segments.

Serves 4.

MINT SAUCE

1½ cups dry white wine	2 tablespoons light brown sugar
1 cup orange juice	
1 tablespoon grated orange rind	¼ cup beef stock or glace de viande, page 245
1 teaspoon grated lemon rind	2 tablespoons hoisin sauce
½ cup minced onions	1 tablespoon cornstarch mixed with 2 tablespoons water
1 teaspoon minced fresh ginger	
2 tablespoons butter	3 tablespoons minced mint leaves

Combine white wine, orange juice and citrus rinds. Bring to a boil. Reduce to approximately 2 cups. Sauté onions and ginger in 2 tablespoons butter until onions are translucent. Add brown sugar, stock and hoisin sauce. Reduce heat and simmer for 5 minutes. Return sauce back to a boil and stir in cornstarch mixture until sauce thickens. Add mint leaves and keep warm.

CURRIED LAMB IN CRÊPES

CRÊPES

1 cup cold water	2 cups flour
1 cup cold milk	5 tablespoons melted butter
4 eggs	
1/2 teaspoon salt	

Place water, milk, eggs and salt in a mixing bowl. While mixer is running, add flour and mix until smooth. Add butter. Let batter sit for 4 or more hours. To cook crêpes, heat a buttered non-stick pan or crepe pan. Place approximately 1/4 cup batter in pan, tilting in a circular motion to distribute batter evenly. Cook approximately 1 minute, flip and cook other side for 30 seconds. Place crêpes between sheets of waxed paper. These may be frozen.

Makes 16 crêpes.

CURRY SAUCE

3 medium onions, sliced	1 teaspoon dried thyme
1 medium-sized tart apple, sliced	1 small bay leaf
1 1/2 tablespoons oil	1 sprig parsley
2 1/2 tablespoons curry powder	1 teaspoon salt
3 1/2 tablespoons flour	1/2 teaspoon black pepper
2 garlic cloves, coarsely chopped	Pinch of cayenne pepper
	5 cups beef stock

Sauté onions and apples in oil until onions are translucent. Add curry powder and flour and sauté for a few more minutes. Add remaining ingredients and simmer for 3 hours. Strain and purée.

FILLING

2 medium onions, chopped	2 garlic cloves, minced
1 tablespoon oil	1 cup Major Grey chutney for garnish
2 1/2 pounds ground lamb	1 cup applesauce for garnish
2 teaspoons salt	
1/2 teaspoon black pepper	

Sauté onions in oil, add ground lamb and continue to sauté. Add salt, pepper and garlic and cook until meat is thoroughly cooked but not browned. Pour off fat. Place approximately 1 tablespoon Curry Sauce in individual casseroles. Add enough Curry Sauce to lamb mixture to moisten it. Roll approximately 2 tablespoons of lamb mixture in each crêpe. Place 2 crêpes in each dish and cover with more sauce. Chill until serving time. When ready to serve, heat crêpes at 450 degrees for 15 minutes or until very hot. Combine chutney and applesauce and garnish each serving with 2 tablespoons of this mixture.

Serves 8.

BUTTERFLIED LEG OF LAMB WITH DIJON AND PARMESAN

6 to 7-pound leg of lamb, boned and butterflied

1/4 cup olive oil

3 garlic cloves, minced

1 teaspoon dried tarragon

1/4 cup Dijon mustard

1/2 cup grated Parmesan cheese

3 tablespoons chopped parsley

2 tablespoons bread crumbs

1 teaspoon salt

1 teaspoon pepper

Technique, page 230.

Blend oil, garlic and tarragon in a small bowl. Brush over lamb. Let stand at room temperature for 2 hours. Place meat fat side down on hot grill. Brush top with half of the mustard. Grill on first side 5 minutes. Turn meat, brush with remaining mustard and grill 5 minutes. Reduce heat. Blend cheese, parsley, bread crumbs, salt and pepper in a small bowl. Sprinkle over meat, patting gently so crumbs adhere. Continue to grill until meat is done, approximately 30 minutes for rare. Let stand 10 minutes before carving.

Serves 6 to 8.

GRILLED LAMB ROSEMARIE

6 to 7-pound leg of lamb, boned and butterflied

MARINADE

1/2 cup olive oil

1 cup dry red wine

2 to 3 sprigs rosemary, chopped

2 to 3 sprigs thyme, chopped

2 to 3 sprigs marjoram, chopped

2 tablespoons snipped parsley

2 tablespoons chopped chives

1/2 teaspoon black pepper

1/2 teaspoon Worcestershire sauce

2 garlic cloves, minced

1 teaspoon salt

Technique, page 230.

Mix marinade ingredients until well blended and pour over lamb. Marinate 24 hours or more, turning occasionally. Remove lamb from marinade and reserve marinade. Grill lamb for 45 minutes to 1 hour. Spoon warmed marinade over slices of lamb before serving.

Serves 8.

CROWN OF LAMB WITH WHOLE GRAIN MUSTARD, SPINACH AND COUSCOUS

2 racks of lamb, trimmed and chime bone removed

3 bunches spinach, chopped

1 egg

2 tablespoons heavy cream

1 cup Dijon mustard

1 teaspoon salt

2 cups couscous

6 cups water or stock

1 tablespoon minced shallots

2 tablespoons olive oil

Salt and pepper

Fresh rosemary for garnish

Pink peppercorns for garnish

Photograph, page 20. Technique, page 231.

Sear racks in a skillet. After lamb has cooled enough to handle bring both ends together to form the crown. Tie the two end bones together with kitchen string to hold in place. Repeat this procedure with the other rack. Using a little lamb stock or water, wilt the spinach by tossing in a skillet over high heat. Place in a large bowl. Beat the egg with the cream and add to the spinach. Add the mustard and salt and blend well. Place the spinach mixture in the center of each crown of lamb. Cover the tops of the bones with aluminum foil and roast at 350 degrees for 40 minutes. In a 2-quart saucepan place the water or stock, shallots and oil and bring to a boil. Add the couscous and stir. Reduce heat, cover and simmer 5 to 10 minutes or until done. Stir and season with salt and pepper. To serve, spread the couscous on a serving platter. Remove string from the end bones. Place on the platter end to end so that the tied ends are not exposed. Garnish the tops of the bones with paper booties. Place fresh rosemary and pink peppercorns around lamb.

Serves 8.

FIRE PAN BURRITOS

1 pound chicken breasts, skinned, boned and cut into thin strips

1-pound sirloin steak or top round, cut into thin strips

2 teaspoons cumin

2 teaspoons chili powder

1 teaspoon garlic salt

$1/2$ pound chorizo sausage

1 onion, thinly sliced

1 green bell pepper, thinly sliced

1 red bell pepper, thinly sliced

1 golden bell pepper, thinly sliced

2 garlic cloves, minced

1 Anaheim chile, thinly sliced in rings

2 tablespoons chile oil

Flour tortillas

Monterey Jack cheese

Guacamole

Salsa

The chile pepper gives a wonderful zing!

Season chicken and steak strips with a mixture of cumin, chili powder and garlic salt. Set aside for 15 minutes. In a pan, cover chorizo with water and simmer, covered, for 15 minutes. Drain and set aside. Over high heat sauté onions, peppers, garlic and chile in oil for 3 to 5 minutes. Add more oil if necessary and sauté chicken and steak with onions and peppers until cooked. Slice chorizo on the diagonal and add to pan until hot. Serve meat mixture with warmed flour tortillas, cheese, guacamole and salsa.

Serves 6.

CHINESE T-BONE STEAK

2 t-bone steaks, 1 inch thick, seasoned with salt and white pepper

Oil

1 yellow onion, sliced

1/2 cup chicken stock

1 tablespoon oyster sauce

1 teaspoon hoisin sauce

1/4 teaspoon salt

1/8 teaspoon white pepper

1 tablespoon cornstarch, dissolved in 2 tablespoons water

4 to 8 tablespoons unsalted butter

Cook steaks in a medium hot heavy skillet. Remove and place on large plates. Keep warm. Add a small amount of oil to the skillet and brown onion. Add chicken stock and season with oyster sauce, hoisin sauce, salt and pepper. Thicken with cornstarch mixture. Turn off the heat. Whisk in the butter. Pour sauce over steaks and serve immediately.

Serves 2.

GRILLED TEQUILA LIME BEEF

1 pound flank steak, sliced diagonally into strips 1/8 inch thick and 2 inches long

1 tablespoon brandy

1 tablespoon minced garlic

1 tablespoon minced fresh ginger

1 1/2 tablespoons soy sauce

2 tablespoons sugar

2 tablespoons tequila

2 tablespoons lime juice

Oil

1/2 cup julienned red bell pepper

1/2 cup julienned green bell pepper

1/2 cup julienned yellow bell pepper

Flour tortillas or mu shu pork wrappers, found in Chinese grocery stores

Marinate flank steak in brandy, garlic, ginger, soy sauce and sugar for at least 2 hours. Add tequila and lime juice and continue to marinate for another 2 to 4 hours. Grill meat and vegetables quickly on a hot grill or in a skillet using very little oil. Roll in warmed flour tortillas or mu shu pork wrappers. Serve with Lime Ginger Sauce.

Serves 6.

LIME GINGER SAUCE

3/4 cup sugar

1/4 cup white vinegar

1/4 cup white wine

1/4 cup water

2 teaspoons sesame oil

1 teaspoon ground black pepper

1 tablespoon minced fresh ginger

1/2 teaspoon minced garlic

1/4 teaspoon red pepper flakes

1 tablespoon lime juice

1 tablespoon minced green onion

Combine sugar, vinegar, wine, water and simmer until clear. Add remaining ingredients. Reserve for dipping.

MEDALLIONS OF BEEF WITH WILD MUSHROOM CABERNET SAUCE

4 thick filet mignon medallions, 4 to 5 ounces each

2 tablespoons olive oil

2 cups chopped wild mushrooms, morels, shiitake and chanterelles

2 shallots, minced

2 teaspoons minced garlic

2 teaspoons chopped dried thyme

4 to 5 tablespoons butter

2 cups cabernet sauvignon

1 cup beef stock or glace de viande, page 245

Salt and pepper

Lightly season medallions with salt and pepper. Heat olive oil in a heavy skillet. When oil begins to smoke, add medallions and cook to the desired degree of doneness, about 3 to 4 minutes per side for rare. Remove medallions from skillet to a warm oven. Reduce heat to medium high. In the same skillet sauté mushrooms, shallots, garlic and thyme in 2 tablespoons of the butter until lightly browned. Pour cabernet into skillet and bring to a boil. Reduce by half. Add beef stock and return to a boil. Reduce to 1 cup. Remove skillet from heat and whisk in remaining 2 to 3 tablespoons butter. Finish with salt and pepper. Pour sauce over medallions.

Serves 4.

STEAK AU POIVRE WITH PORCINI SAUCE

6 center-cut filet mignon steaks, 1 1/2 inches thick

1 1/2 teaspoons coarsely ground pepper

1/2 cup Madeira wine

1 1/2 ounces dried porcini mushrooms

1 cup boiling water

1 tablespoon olive oil

2 tablespoons butter

1/2 cup minced shallots

3 garlic cloves, minced

3/4 cup heavy cream

Rub 1/8 teaspoon pepper on each side of steaks. Place in shallow dish and sprinkle with 1/4 cup of the Madeira. Cover with plastic wrap and set aside at room temperature for 1 to 2 hours, turning occasionally. Cover the mushrooms with boiling water and soak for 20 minutes. Strain mushrooms, reserving liquid. Rinse well, drain and chop. Strain the mushroom liquid through cheesecloth, reserving 1/2 cup. In a large skillet heat oil and butter over high heat. Add steaks and cook until browned, 2 minutes per side. Remove from heat and add the remaining 1/4 cup Madeira to the pan. Flame sauce with a long match, shaking the pan until the flame dies down. Transfer steaks to an ovenproof dish and cook at 350 degrees for 15 minutes for medium. Meanwhile, add shallots and garlic to the skillet and cook, covered, until softened, 6 to 8 minutes. Increase heat, add reserved mushroom liquid and cook, stirring constantly, until syrupy. Stir in the cream and cook until slightly reduced. Stir in reserved mushrooms, reduce heat and cook 2 minutes longer. Transfer steaks to 6 warmed plates. Stir any juices from the steaks into the sauce and spoon over the steaks.

Serves 6.

THREE PEPPER STEAK WITH BOURBON CREAM

2 New York or filet mignon steaks, thick cut and trimmed

Salt

2 garlic cloves, minced

1 tablespoon three-colored whole peppercorns, green, white and pink

1 tablespoon olive oil

1 green onion with top, julienned

1/2 teaspoon crumbled dried thyme

1/2 cup bourbon whiskey

1 teaspoon Worcestershire sauce

1 tablespoon lemon juice

1/4 cup heavy cream

Fresh thyme sprig for garnish

Colored peppercorns for garnish

Season steaks with salt and garlic. On a cutting board, crush peppercorns with a pressing, rolling motion of a rolling pin. Press steaks into the crushed peppercorns, forming a light crust of peppercorns on both sides, about 1 1/2 teaspoons per steak. Add olive oil to hot heavy skillet and add steaks. Cook steaks 2 to 3 minutes per side for medium rare. Transfer to a dish and hold in a warm oven. Reduce heat to medium high. Add onions and thyme and sauté until softened, about 1 minute. Add bourbon, ignite and flame, stirring to deglaze pan. Add Worcestershire sauce and lemon juice. Bring to a boil and reduce liquid by half. Whisk in cream and continue to cook for another minute until sauce is well heated. Pour sauce over steaks. Garnish with whole fresh thyme sprig and a trio of colored peppercorns.

Serves 2.

FILLET OF BEEF IN PUFF PASTRY

6 to 7-pound whole fillet of beef, butterflied

1/2 pound fresh mushrooms, minced

3 shallots, minced

6 to 7 ounces liver pâté

2 tablespoons Dijon mustard

3/4 cup finely chopped pecans

2 red apples, cored and chopped

10 ounces spinach, thawed and drained

3/4 cup ricotta cheese

Salt and pepper

1/2 cup unsalted butter

2 pounds puff pastry, page 234

2 egg whites, slightly beaten

Combine mushrooms, shallots, pâté and Dijon. Set aside. In a separate bowl, mix pecans, apples, spinach and ricotta. Set aside. Roll out fillet. Spread mushroom mixture evenly over it, leaving a 1-inch border. Spread nut mixture on top of mushroom mixture, being careful not to mix. Roll up fillet firmly and tie. Rub with salt and pepper. Melt butter in a heavy skillet and sear all sides of the roast. Remove and let cool. Roll out puff pastry and cut to fit around fillet. Brush with some of the egg white. Cut ties and place fillet on top of pastry. Wrap fillet with pastry and seal edges with more egg white. Brush entire surface of pastry with remaining egg white. Bake at 400 degrees for 25 minutes, until medium rare. Cool 15 minutes before slicing. Spoon Madeira Sauce over slices and serve.

Serves 12.

MADEIRA SAUCE

6 tablespoons butter

3 tablespoons flour

1 1/2 cups beef stock

1/2 cup Madeira wine

In a saucepan melt butter and stir in flour. Cook for 5 minutes, stirring constantly. Slowly add beef stock and Madeira. Cook, while stirring, for an additional 5 minutes or until thick.

SUPER BOWL SHORT RIBS

4 pounds boneless
beef short ribs

16 ounces tomato sauce

1 cup dark brown sugar

1/2 cup soy sauce

2 to 3 medium red
onions, sliced or
coarsely chopped

3 tablespoons cinnamon

After the aroma of these ribs has permeated the house for two hours, the fans are more anxious to eat than watch the half-time show.

Remove all visible fat from the short ribs and slice into 2-inch strips, about 1/2 inch thick. Place in an ovenproof casserole and add the other ingredients which have been mixed together thoroughly. Bake at 325 degrees for 2 hours, occasionally stirring to turn exposed pieces into sauce. Serve over seasoned rice.

Serves 8.

TENDERLOIN OF BEEF AND LOBSTER

4 pounds beef
tenderloin, trimmed

3 lobster tails

2 tablespoons grated
fresh ginger

2 garlic cloves, minced

1 onion, sliced

1/2 cup soy sauce

3/4 cup sherry

1 tablespoon
chopped parsley

3 tablespoons
melted butter

Rub beef with ginger and garlic on both sides. Place the onions on the bottom of pan and place tenderloin on top. Combine soy sauce and sherry to make a basting liquid. Pour half of the baste over the beef, reserving the other half for basting while baking lobster. Bake at 450 degrees for 25 to 35 minutes, or until a desired doneness. Remove meat from oven and make a slice vertically down the middle, halfway through. Split the shells of the 3 lobster tails and rub the lobster meat with soy/sherry baste. Bake at 350 degrees for 10 minutes. Remove lobster from shell. Stuff lobster tail into tenderloin. Place under broiler only to heat, again basting with soy/sherry baste. Sprinkle with chopped parsley and melted butter. Slice and serve.

Serves 6 to 8.

CALF LIVER DIJON

1 pound calf liver, sliced
1/4 to 1/8 inch thick

1/2 cup flour, seasoned
with 1/2 teaspoon
each salt and pepper

2 tablespoons butter

Dredge the liver in seasoned flour. Shake off the excess. Heat the butter in a sauté pan. Sauté the liver in a single layer over high heat for 30 to 45 seconds a side. Serve immediately and top with Dijon Sauce.

Serves 4.

DIJON SAUCE

2 cups dry white wine

3 tablespoons
minced shallots

2 tablespoons
Dijon mustard

3/4 cup butter, cut into
1/2-inch pieces

1/4 teaspoon pepper

1 tablespoon
minced parsley

In a saucepan, reduce the wine and shallots to approximately 2 tablespoons. Keep pan moving as liquid reduces. Whisk in mustard. Remove from heat and whisk in the butter pieces. Stir in the pepper and parsley. Set the pan in a warm, not hot, place. Sauce will separate if overheated.

VEGETABLES
AND RICE

CREAMED SPINACH WITH FRESH PARMESAN

1 pound spinach, stems removed

1 onion

8 ounces cream cheese, cut into pieces

3 eggs

½ teaspoon dried basil

2 tablespoons brandy

Salt and pepper

3 tablespoons grated Parmesan cheese

Wash spinach well and cook until limp in the water that clings to the leaves. Using the steel blade of a food processor, chop onion, add remaining ingredients, except Parmesan cheese, and process until smooth. Pour the mixture into a buttered au gratin dish. Sprinkle with grated Parmesan cheese. Bake at 350 degrees for 20 minutes.

Serves 6.

BAKED ASPARAGUS WITH PARMESAN AND ALMONDS

½ cup whole almonds, blanched, coarsely chopped and toasted

½ cup grated Parmesan cheese

½ teaspoon salt

1½ pounds asparagus, trimmed

8 tablespoons butter

Lemon wedges for garnish

Mix chopped almonds with Parmesan cheese and salt and set aside. Plunge asparagus into boiling, salted water and cook until barely tender. Asparagus should be crisp and bright green. Drain and refresh in cold water. Butter a shallow baking dish with 1 tablespoon of the butter. Arrange asparagus in a dish and top with the almond mixture. Dot with remaining butter and bake at 450 degrees for 20 minutes. Serve with lemon wedges.

Serves 4.

ASPARAGUS CAESAR

2 pounds asparagus, peeled and blanched

1 can anchovy fillets

6 tablespoons grated Parmesan cheese

3 tablespoons capers

2 tablespoons olive oil

While asparagus is still warm, arrange on a serving platter. Drizzle oil from the anchovy fillets over the top. Sprinkle with Parmesan cheese and capers. Drizzle with the olive oil, and garnish with anchovy fillets, as desired.

Serves 4 to 6.

FROSTED CAULIFLOWER

1 whole cauliflower, cored

½ cup mayonnaise

1 teaspoon dry mustard

1 cup grated Cheddar cheese

Paprika

Place cauliflower in covered dish and microwave 6 minutes per pound on high. Place on serving platter. Combine mayonnaise and mustard. Frost top of cauliflower. Sprinkle with Cheddar cheese. Microwave uncovered for 45 seconds. Sprinkle with paprika before serving.

Serves 4 to 6.

CHINESE LONG BEANS WITH TOASTED PECANS

2 bunches of Chinese long beans, about 2 pounds

2 tablespoons balsamic or red wine vinegar

1 teaspoon salt

1 tablespoon Dijon mustard

1/4 cup olive oil

1/4 cup oil

2 tablespoons maple syrup

2 teaspoons dried tarragon

2 eggs, hard-boiled and chopped

1/2 cup chopped pecans, toasted

Cook beans in boiling salted water until barely tender, about 8 minutes. Run under cold water, drain and pat dry. Cut ends from beans and trim each to 4-inch lengths. Arrange on a platter and chill, covered, for at least 2 hours. Mix vinegar, salt and mustard. Whisk in oils vigorously. Add maple syrup and tarragon. Chill, covered, for at least 2 hours. Just before serving, spoon vinegar mixture over beans and sprinkle the top with eggs and pecans. You may serve this at room temperature. As a variation, asparagus may be used in place of beans.

Serves 8.

DRUNKEN SWEET POTATOES

4 6-inch sweet potatoes, rubbed with oil and pricked with a fork

1/2 cup melted butter

1/4 teaspoon salt

4 tablespoons brown sugar

1 cup crushed pineapple, drained

3/4 cup chopped walnuts

1/4 teaspoon nutmeg

1/8 teaspoon cinnamon

1/2 cup bourbon or whiskey

Bread crumbs

Bake potatoes at 350 degees for 1 hour. Halve and scoop out the pulp, reserving shells. Combine pulp with all other ingredients except bread crumbs. Stuff shells with the mixture and top with bread crumbs. Bake at 350 degrees for 30 minutes.

Serves 8.

APPLE AND YAM CASSEROLE

1 1/2 pounds yams, baked and sliced

7 Pippin apples, peeled and quartered

4 tablespoons cornstarch

1/2 cup butter

2 cups sugar

2 cups water

1/2 teaspoon salt

Juice of 1/2 lemon

1 teaspoon vinegar

Zest of 1/2 orange

Zest of 1/2 lemon

Place all ingredients except yams and apples in a saucepan. Cook and stir until thick. Arrange yams and apples in casserole dish. Pour sauce over all. Bake at 300 degrees for 1 hour.

Serves 6 to 8.

COGNAC CARROTS

12 carrots, peeled
and sliced

4 tablespoons butter

2 teaspoons sugar

$^{1}/_{4}$ to $^{1}/_{2}$ teaspoon salt

$^{1}/_{4}$ cup cognac

$^{1}/_{4}$ cup chopped parsley
for garnish

Steam carrots until barely tender, 10 to 15 minutes. In a saucepan melt butter, add carrots and sauté briefly. Add sugar, salt and cognac. Sauté for 5 minutes. Just before serving, sprinkle with parsley.

Serves 4.

CREAMY CARROT CASSEROLE

3 cups peeled and
sliced carrots

12 soda
crackers, crushed

2 teaspoons
minced onions

2 tablespoons
melted butter

1 cup grated sharp
Cheddar cheese

$^{2}/_{3}$ cup carrot liquid

$^{1}/_{2}$ teaspoon salt

$^{1}/_{2}$ teaspoon
white pepper

Boil carrots in salted water until soft. Reserve $^{2}/_{3}$ cup of the cooking liquid. Mash or process carrots and stir in remaining ingredients. Bake at 400 degrees for 15 minutes.

Serves 10 to 12.

CALIFORNIA ORANGE CARROTS

1 pound carrots, peeled
and sliced $^{1}/_{2}$ inch thick

$^{1}/_{2}$ teaspoon salt

$^{3}/_{4}$ cup water

$^{1}/_{2}$ teaspoon freshly
grated orange peel

1 orange, peeled and cut
into bite-sized pieces

2 tablespoons butter,
softened

1 tablespoon chopped
green onions

In a covered saucepan cook carrots in salted water for 10 to 15 minutes or until tender. Drain. Add remaining ingredients and heat, stirring occasionally. Serve immediately.

Serves 4.

EGGPLANT CANNELONI

2 medium-sized eggplants, peeled and sliced 1/4 inch thick

1 teaspoon finely chopped garlic

1/4 cup olive oil

Salt and pepper

16 ounces ricotta cheese

12 ounces grated Provolone cheese

3/4 cup grated Parmesan cheese

2 tablespoons chopped parsley

Pinch of nutmeg

2 cups tomato sauce

Parsley or watercress for garnish

In a frying pan gently heat the garlic in the olive oil without allowing the garlic to brown. Brush the warm garlic olive oil onto both sides of the eggplant slices. Lightly season with salt and pepper. Place on baking sheets and bake at 350 degrees for 15 minutes or until softened. Combine the ricotta, Provolone and 1/2 cup of the Parmesan cheese in a small bowl. Season with parsley, salt, pepper and nutmeg. Thinly spread the cheese filling on 1 side of each of the eggplant slices. Roll up the slices, beginning at the narrowest end, and place seam side down in a large casserole or au gratin dish. Pour tomato sauce over eggplant and sprinkle with remaining Parmesan cheese. Return to the oven and bake at 350 degrees for 15 minutes or until heated through. Before serving, place under the broiler briefly to melt and lightly brown the cheese on top. Garnish each serving with more chopped parsley or a sprig of watercress.

Serves 8.

EGGPLANT TIAN

1/4 cup plus 1 tablespoon olive oil

1 small eggplant, about 1 pound, unpeeled and cut into 1/2-inch cubes

1 large onion, thinly sliced

1 medium-sized green bell pepper, thinly sliced

2 teaspoons minced garlic

1 teaspoon dried thyme

Salt and pepper

2 small zucchini

3 medium-sized tomatoes, thinly sliced

1/4 cup grated Parmesan cheese

In a large skillet, heat 1/4 cup of the oil over moderately low heat. When hot, add eggplant, onion, green pepper, garlic, thyme, 1 teaspoon salt and 1/4 teaspoon pepper. Cook 20 to 25 minutes, stirring often, until vegetables are soft but not browned. Regulate heat to maintain even cooking. Meanwhile, peel zucchini lengthwise with a vegetable peeler, alternating peeled and unpeeled strips and creating striped zucchini. Slice thinly. Spread eggplant mixture in the bottom of a shallow 2-quart baking dish. Arrange alternate rows of overlapping tomato and zucchini slices on top. Sprinkle with salt and pepper and drizzle with 1 tablespoon oil. Bake 20 minutes. Sprinkle with cheese and bake 15 to 20 minutes longer or until vegetables on top are tender. If desired, broil a few minutes to brown the top. Serve hot, warm or at room temperature with additional cheese on the side.

Serves 6.

HUNAN EGGPLANT IN GARLIC SAUCE

1 large eggplant, peeled and cut into 1-inch cubes

Oil

3 ounces pork, finely chopped

2 tablespoons chopped water chestnuts

1 tablespoon minced garlic

1 teaspoon red pepper flakes

3/4 cup chicken broth

1/3 cup soy sauce

3 tablespoons sugar

1/2 teaspoon salt

3 tablespoons white vinegar

1/4 cup white wine

2 tablespoons sesame oil

1 tablespoon cornstarch mixed with 2 teaspoons water

2 tablespoons chopped green onions

Sauté eggplant in oil until golden brown. In a wok or frying pan heat 2 tablespoons oil. Add pork, water chestnuts, garlic and pepper flakes. Stir together. Add broth, soy sauce, sugar, salt, vinegar, wine and sesame oil. Bring to a boil. While stirring, slowly add cornstarch mixture to thicken. Place browned eggplant and green onions on a serving platter. Pour sauce over and serve.

Serves 4.

CRISPY EGGPLANT

1/2 cup mayonnaise

1 tablespoon minced onions

1/4 teaspoon salt

1/3 cup fine dry bread crumbs

1/3 cup grated Parmesan cheese

1/2 teaspoon dried Italian seasoning

1 eggplant, 1 pound, cut into 1/2-inch slices

Stir together the mayonnaise, onions and salt. In a shallow dish or on sheet of waxed paper, combine bread crumbs, cheese and Italian seasoning. Brush both sides of eggplant with mayonnaise mixture and coat with crumb mixture. Place in a shallow roasting pan or on a baking sheet. Bake at 425 degrees for 15 to 17 minutes or until browned.

Serves 4 to 6.

EGGPLANT AND MUSHROOMS

1 eggplant, cut into 1/4-inch slices

1/3 cup butter

1/2 cup canned sliced mushrooms, drained, broth reserved

1 tablespoon chopped pimento

1 tablespoon chopped parsley

Salt and pepper

2/3 cup heavy cream

2 tablespoons grated Parmesan cheese

Brown eggplant slices on both sides in butter. Arrange eggplant, mushrooms, pimento and parsley in layers in a shallow 1 1/2-quart baking dish. Sprinkle each layer with salt and pepper. Combine mushroom broth and cream and pour over the eggplant. Sprinkle with cheese. Bake at 300 degrees until the sauce is thick, approximately 1 hour. Baste with the sauce while cooking. Before serving, garnish with more grated cheese and chopped parsley.

Serves 4.

FRITTATA DI CIPOLLE

4 to 5 medium onions, chopped	2 slices bread soaked in $1/2$ cup milk and broken
3 tablespoons oil	6 eggs, beaten
2 garlic cloves, minced	$1/2$ cup grated Parmesan cheese
Salt and pepper	

Fry onions in oil until soft. Add garlic and sauté a few minutes more. Add remaining ingredients. Stir, cover and cook for 5 minutes. Turn over and cook the other side for 5 minutes. If perferred, this may be baked in a flat pan at 350 degrees for 30 minutes. Serve hot or slice into squares and serve cold as an appetizer.

Serves 6.

CHEESE ONION TART

1 cup crumbled soda crackers	1 tablespoon flour
$1/4$ cup butter, softened	1 teaspoon salt
2 onions, thinly sliced	3 eggs, beaten
$1/2$ cup butter	1 cup milk, scalded
$1/2$ pound grated Swiss cheese	

Combine crumbs with $1/4$ cup softened butter. Press into a 9-inch tart pan. Sauté onions in $1/2$ cup butter until tender but not brown. Place in the tart pan. Combine cheese, flour and salt and mix well. Add eggs and milk and pour over onions. Bake at 325 degrees for 40 minutes.

Serves 6.

SWISS CHARD TORTE

$1 1/2$ pounds Swiss chard	$3/4$ teaspoon salt
3 eggs, beaten	$1/4$ teaspoon dried marjoram
2 cups ricotta cheese	$1/8$ teaspoon nutmeg
$1/2$ cup bread crumbs	$1/8$ teaspoon pepper
$3/4$ cup grated Parmesan cheese	1 pound puff pastry, page 234
1 cup grated Monterey Jack cheese	6 hard-boiled eggs
$1/2$ cup chopped onions	1 egg white, beaten
$1/2$ cup chopped parsley	

In a food processor or blender, finely chop the chard. Add 3 beaten eggs. Stir in ricotta cheese, bread crumbs, Parmesan and Monterey Jack cheeses, onions, parsley, salt, majoram, nutmeg and pepper. On a floured board, roll the puff pastry into a 15-inch circle. Fit the pastry into an 8-inch springform pan. Spoon in half of the chard mixture. Evenly space the hard-boiled eggs on top and cover with the remaining chard. Roll out another circle of puff pastry, 8 inches in diameter. Place over filling and pinch edges to seal. Slash the top in several places. Brush with egg white. Place pan on a rimmed baking sheet. Bake at 450 degrees for 35 to 40 minutes or until crust is golden brown and toothpick inserted in center comes out clean. Cool on a wire rack for 15 minutes. Remove sides of pan and cool completely. Serve at room temperature.

Serves 10 to 12.

ZUCCHINI GENOA

6 small zucchini,
halved lengthwise

3 onions, halved

2 cups cubed day-old
French bread, soaked in
water and squeezed dry

1 garlic clove, minced

¹/₂ cup grated
Parmesan cheese

¹/₂ teaspoon dried thyme

¹/₂ teaspoon dried
marjoram

¹/₂ teaspoon dried
oregano

3 eggs, beaten

1 tablespoon oil

¹/₂ teaspoon salt

¹/₄ teaspoon pepper

Parboil squash and onions in 4 quarts of salted water. Drain and cool with cold water. Scoop the pulp from the zucchini and onions, reserving outer shells. Squeeze moisture from the pulp. Combine pulp and bread and chop. Add remaining ingredients. Stuff zucchini shells and onion halves. Put on a lightly oiled cooking sheet. Bake at 400 degrees for 45 minutes to 1 hour or until golden brown.

Serves 6.

PUMPKIN AU GRATIN

16 ounces pumpkin,
canned or fresh, puréed

¹/₂ teaspoon salt

Freshly ground
black pepper

Dash of nutmeg

¹/₄ teaspoon
ground cloves

2 tablespoons
melted butter

1 egg

¹/₂ cup heavy cream

3 tablespoons grated
Parmesan cheese

Combine pumpkin, salt, pepper, nutmeg, cloves and butter. Place in a small, lightly buttered casserole. Beat the egg lightly and mix in the cream and Parmesan cheese. Pour over the pumpkin. Bake at 400 degrees for 30 minutes or until top is puffed and lightly browned.

Serves 6.

ITALIAN SPAGHETTI SQUASH

1 small spaghetti
squash, 2 pounds

1 red bell
pepper, chopped

1 green bell
pepper, chopped

2 garlic cloves, minced

Salt and pepper

8 tomatoes, chopped

¹/₂ red onion, chopped

1 tablespoon mixed
Italian seasonings

¹/₄ cup toasted pine nuts

³/₄ cup grated
Parmesan cheese

Split squash in half lengthwise and scoop out seeds. Bake at 400 degrees for 1 hour. Combine remaining ingredients except Parmesan cheese. Remove spaghetti squash from the oven and fill cavity with the mixture. Sprinkle top with cheese and bake for approximately 30 minutes or until squash is tender and can be pulled into spaghetti-like strands.

Serves 6.

POTATA BAGA

1 tablespoon butter

1/2 cup chopped onions

1/2 teaspoon minced garlic

2 cups heavy cream

1 teaspoon salt

1/2 teaspoon pepper

1/8 teaspoon nutmeg

1 pound potatoes, peeled and sliced 1/8 inch thick

2 cups grated Gruyère cheese

1 pound rutabagas, peeled and sliced 1/8 inch thick

Heat butter in a small sauté pan, add onions and garlic and sauté until onions have softened. Remove from heat and combine with cream, salt, pepper and nutmeg. Spread half of the potatoes in a 7 x 11-inch baking pan. Sprinkle with 1/2 cup of the cheese. Spread half of the rutabagas on top, then 1/2 cup cheese. Repeat, using a layer of potatoes, 1/2 cup cheese and ending with a layer of rutabagas. Pour the cream mixture over all. Bake at 350 degrees for 35 minutes. Remove from the oven and sprinkle with the remaining 1/2 cup of cheese. Return to oven and bake for 10 to 15 minutes, or until vegetables are tender and most of the cream has been absorbed.

Serves 6.

POTATO PUFF SOUFFLÉ

2 teaspoons minced onions

1/4 cup butter

1/4 cup flour

1 teaspoon salt

Pepper

1 cup sour cream

2 cups mashed potatoes

4 egg yolks, well beaten

4 egg whites, stiffly beaten

Sauté onions in butter until tender. Blend in flour, salt and pepper. Heat until bubbly. Remove from heat. Stir in sour cream and potatoes. Beat until smooth. Add small amounts of hot mixture to egg yolks, stirring constantly. Add to remaining hot mixture and mix well. Fold in egg whites. Pour into 1 1/2-quart soufflé dish. Bake at 350 degrees for 30 to 35 minutes or until knife inserted in center comes out clean. Serve immediately.

Serves 6 to 8.

FRENCH SCALLOPED POTATOES

1 pound red potatoes, peeled and sliced

1/4 cup butter

Salt and white pepper

1 1/2 to 2 cups heavy cream

Rinse potatoes in cold water to remove starch. Pat dry and layer in a casserole with butter, salt and white pepper, reserving about 2 tablespoons of butter. Pour the cream over potatoes. Cover with foil and bake at 350 degrees for 30 to 35 minutes. Remove foil, dot with remaining butter and bake another 10 to 15 minutes.

Serves 4 to 6.

OVEN ROASTED RED POTATOES WITH ROSEMARY

2 pounds red
potatoes, quartered

2 tablespoons
melted butter

2 tablespoons olive oil

1 teaspoon minced garlic

1 teaspoon
minced shallots

1½ teaspoons salt

1 teaspoon pepper

¼ cup chopped fresh
rosemary

Place potatoes in a pot of boiling water. Return to a boil, remove from heat and drain. In a large mixing bowl, mix all other ingredients. Add potatoes and mix gently until well coated. Place on a cookie sheet and bake at 400 degrees for 10 minutes.

Serves 8.

TOMATOES STUFFED WITH SPINACH, RICE AND PINE NUTS

1 cup water

⅛ teaspoon saffron

½ cup rice

½ teaspoon salt

2 teaspoons olive oil

2 teaspoons
minced shallots

5 ounces spinach,
stemmed, blanched,
drained and chopped

¼ teaspoon pepper

¼ cup pine nuts, toasted

6 to 8 small tomatoes

Sour cream or crème
fraîche, page 249,
for garnish

Bring the water to a boil in a 1-quart saucepan. Stir in the saffron, rice and ¼ teaspoon of the salt. Cover and cook over medium-low heat until water is absorbed and rice is tender. Remove to a bowl and cool. Heat the oil in a small skillet. Add the shallots and spinach and sauté briefly. Add the remaining ¼ teaspoon salt, pepper and pine nuts and sauté for 1 minute. Add the rice and heat thoroughly. There should be about 2 cups of filling. Cut the tops from the tomatoes. Hollow them out and sprinkle the insides lightly with salt and pepper. Stuff the tomatoes with the warm rice mixture and set in a baking pan. Cover with foil and bake at 350 degrees for 5 to 10 minutes or until heated through. Serve, if desired, with a spoonful of sour cream or crème fraîche. As a variation, add cooked shellfish or sausage to the filling. Stuff 4 large tomatoes instead of 6 to 8 small ones to serve as a light entrée. Dust with grated Parmesan cheese before baking.

Serves 6 to 8.

MARINATED SUMMER TOMATOES

¼ cup white wine
vinegar

3 to 4 tablespoons sugar

3 slices fresh
ginger, slivered

⅓ cup water

1 tablespoon sesame oil

3 large tomatoes,
cored and cut into
½-inch slices

Watercress for garnish

Toasted sesame seeds
for garnish

Heat the vinegar, sugar, ginger and water until the sugar completely dissolves. Stir in sesame oil. Remove from heat and cool. Place tomatoes slices in a plastic container and pour cooled sauce over them. Marinate in the refrigerator for at least 4 hours, preferably longer. To serve, garnish with watercress and toasted sesame seeds.

Serves 4.

CALIFORNIA RANCH RICE

1 cup chopped onions	1 bay leaf, crushed
2 garlic cloves, minced	Salt and pepper
4 tablespoons butter	14 ounces whole green chiles, rinsed, seeded and cut into strips
4 cups cooked rice	
2 cups sour cream	2$^{1}/_{2}$ cups grated Cheddar cheese
1 cup small curd cottage cheese	

In a large frying pan sauté onions and garlic in butter until limp. Add rice, sour cream, cottage cheese, bay leaf, salt and pepper and mix. In a greased casserole put a layer of rice mixture, layer of chiles and layer of cheese, reserving $^{1}/_{2}$ cup cheese. Repeat, ending with a layer of rice. Bake at 375 degrees for 25 minutes. Sprinkle reserved cheese over the top and return to oven to bake 20 minutes longer.

Serves 8 to 10.

AROMATIC YELLOW RICE

2 cups long grain or basmati rice, rinsed and drained	3 to 4 cloves
2$^{2}/_{3}$ cups of water	1-inch stick of cinnamon
1$^{1}/_{4}$ teaspoons salt	1 bay leaf
$^{3}/_{4}$ teaspoon turmeric	3 tablespoons unsalted butter, cut into pieces

After initial rinsing, soak rice in 5 cups of water for 30 minutes. Drain. Combine the rice, water, salt, turmeric, cloves, cinnamon and bay leaf in a heavy pot. Bring to a boil, cover and cook over low heat for 25 minutes. Turn off heat and let the pot stand for 10 minutes, covered and undisturbed. Add the butter and mix in gently with a fork. Remove the whole spices before serving.

Serves 6.

WINE RICE

1 cup rice	1 teaspoon salt
1 cup fresh tomatoes, chopped and seeded	$^{1}/_{4}$ teaspoon pepper
$^{1}/_{2}$ cup chopped onions	1 cup tiny peas or petit pois
1 pound mushrooms, sliced	2 tablespoons butter
1$^{1}/_{2}$ cups chicken broth	$^{1}/_{4}$ to $^{1}/_{2}$ cup grated Parmesan cheese
$^{1}/_{2}$ cup red wine	

Place rice, tomatoes, onions, and mushrooms in a large skillet. Add chicken broth, wine, salt and pepper and mix well. Cover and simmer for 30 to 40 minutes or until liquid is absorbed and rice is tender. Gently stir in peas and butter. Sprinkle with cheese and serve immediately.

Serves 8.

HERBED LENTILS AND RICE

2²/₃ cups chicken broth

³/₄ cup lentils

³/₄ cup chopped onions

¹/₂ cup brown rice

¹/₄ cup dry white wine

¹/₃ cup water

¹/₂ teaspoon dried basil

¹/₂ teaspoon salt

¹/₄ teaspoon dried oregano

¹/₄ teaspoon dried thyme

¹/₈ teaspoon garlic powder

¹/₈ teaspoon pepper

¹/₂ cup grated Swiss cheese

2 ounces Swiss cheese, sliced into strips

Combine chicken broth with all other ingredients, except the cheeses, in a bowl. Stir in the grated Swiss cheese. Place mixture in an ungreased 1¹/₂ quart casserole dish and bake at 350 degrees for 1¹/₂ hours, or until lentils and rice are tender. Arrange the strips of Swiss cheese on top. Return to oven and bake an additional 2 to 3 minutes, until topping melts.

Serves 4.

SOUTHWESTERN BLACK BEANS AND RICE

1 cup dry black beans

³/₄ cup sliced carrots

³/₄ cup sliced celery

¹/₂ cup chopped onions

1 garlic clove, minced

1 jalapeño pepper, minced

¹/₈ teaspoon ground red pepper

Black pepper

1 cup diced cooked ham or turkey

¹/₂ cup red bell pepper strips

¹/₂ cup green bell pepper strips

2 teaspoons oil

3 cups cooked rice

Bring 1 quart water to a boil in a Dutch oven or large saucepan. Stir in beans and add carrots, celery, onions, garlic, jalapeño, red and black peppers. Cover and simmer 2¹/₂ hours, stirring occasionally. Add ham or turkey and simmer 15 minutes. Sauté red and green peppers in oil until tender crisp. Stir into rice. Salt to taste. Serve beans with rice.

Serves 4.

WILD RICE WITH SNOW PEAS

1 cup rice

1/2 cup wild rice, rinsed 3 times

2 1/2 cups chicken broth

1 tablespoon butter

1 teaspoon salt

1/3 cup olive oil

1/3 cup oil

1/3 cup lemon juice

1 garlic clove, minced

1/2 teaspoon garlic salt

1/4 teaspoon celery seed

1/8 teaspoon cayenne or black pepper

1/4 teaspoon dried oregano

2 green onions, sliced

6 ounces snow peas

3 ounces water chestnuts, drained and sliced

4 ounces mushrooms, sliced

6 cherry tomatoes, halved

In a large, covered saucepan bring the chicken broth to a boil and add white rice, wild rice, butter and salt. Cover and simmer over low heat 35 minutes or until rice is tender and liquid is absorbed. If necessary, add more broth as rice cooks. Combine oils, lemon juice, garlic, garlic salt, celery seed, pepper and oregano and mix well. Pour over hot rice. Sauté green onions, snow peas, water chestnuts and mushrooms lightly. Add vegetables to the rice just before serving. Add cherry tomatoes. May be served warm or cold.

Serves 6.

MONTEREY CASSEROLE

3 to 4 cups cooked rice

Butter

7 ounces green chiles, diced

1 pound Monterey Jack cheese

3 zucchini, sliced into 1/4-inch slices and parboiled

1 tomato, sliced

2 cups sour cream

1 teaspoon dried oregano

1 teaspoon salt

2 tablespoons chopped green bell peppers

2 tablespoons chopped green onions

1 tablespoon chopped parsley

Place rice in a buttered casserole. Cover with chiles and three-fourths of the cheese, cut into strips, zucchini and tomato. Mix sour cream with the seasonings and spread over all. Sprinkle remaining cheese, which has been grated, over the top. Bake at 350 degrees for 30 minutes.

Serves 12 to 16.

SPICY BLACK-EYED PEAS

2 cups chopped onions

2 cups chopped green
bell pepper

2 cups chopped celery

$^1/_4$ cup oil

2 pounds fresh or frozen
black-eyed peas

5 tomatoes, peeled,
seeded and chopped

1 cup diced green chiles

1 teaspoon chili powder

1 teaspoon cumin

Salt and pepper

1 jalapeño pepper,
finely chopped

White vinegar

Sauté the onions, green peppers and celery in the oil. Pour peas into a soup pot. Add the sautéed vegetables, tomatoes, green chiles, chili powder, cumin, salt, pepper and jalapeño pepper. Cook over medium low heat for 1 hour. Before serving, add vinegar. For best results, prepare 1 day in advance.

Serves 8.

COUSCOUS WITH SAFFRON AND RED BELL PEPPER

1 cup couscous

2 cups chicken broth

1 tablespoon butter

$^1/_2$ teaspoon salt

$^1/_4$ teaspoon saffron

$^1/_2$ cup diced red
bell pepper

In a saucepan combine all ingredients and bring to a boil. Boil for 2 minutes. Remove from heat and let stand covered for 10 minutes. Stir before serving.

Serves 4 to 6.

WHEAT AND BARLEY BOWL

3 tablespoons butter

$^3/_4$ cup barley

3 cups water

2 teaspoons bouillon
concentrate, any kind

$^1/_2$ teaspoon salt

$^1/_4$ teaspoon pepper

$^1/_4$ cup bulgur

2 cups shredded fresh
spinach leaves

$^1/_2$ cup sliced
green onions

$^1/_4$ cup snipped parsley

1 tablespoon lemon juice

1 large tomato,
cut into wedges

$^1/_4$ cup unsalted
sunflower seeds
for garnish

Melt butter over high heat in a large skillet. Add barley. Reduce heat and cook, stirring constantly, 5 to 10 minutes or until browned. Stir in water, bouillon, salt and pepper. Bring to a boil, reduce heat and cover tightly. Simmer 40 minutes. Stir in bulgur and simmer, covered, for 15 minutes. Add spinach, green onions, parsley and lemon juice. Cook and stir until liquid is absorbed, approximately 10 minutes. Add tomatoes. Serve hot, garnished with sunflower seeds.

Serves 6 to 8.

PASTA DOUGH

2 cups
unbleached flour

Pinch of salt

2 large eggs,
room temperature

1 to 2 teaspoons water

Pasta dough can be seasoned with fresh herbs and spices, such as basil, rosemary, sage, saffron or red pepper.

Mound flour and salt on a pastry board or in a large mixing bowl. Make a well in the middle of the flour. Crack eggs into the well and add water. Using a fork, gently beat the eggs and begin to incorporate the flour, using a circular motion. When all the flour has been moistened, gather dough into a ball. Turn the dough out onto a work surface and begin to knead. Work dough until it is smooth and elastic, 10 to 15 minutes. Wrap dough in plastic and let rest for about 45 minutes. Form pasta into desired shape using a pasta machine or other device. In salted, boiling water cook pasta al dente, about 3 to 5 minutes. Serve with your favorite pasta sauce.

Makes 1 pound.

BLACK PASTA DOUGH

1 package squid
or cuttlefish ink,
available frozen in
Asian or Italian markets

2 teaspoons
warm water

2 cups
unbleached flour

Pinch of salt

2 large eggs,
room temperature

Steep squid ink package with the 2 teaspoons warm water until ink is liquified. Following directions for Pasta Dough, prepare black pasta, substituting black squid liquid for the 1 to 2 teaspoons water.

Makes 1 pound.

BUCATINI WITH MUSHROOMS, TOMATOES AND TUNA

12 ounces fresh tuna

1 cup olive oil

5 garlic cloves,
minced

1 tablespoon
fresh oregano

1 tablespoon fresh basil

4 tablespoons
chopped parsley

4 cups imported
Italian tomatoes

$^1/_2$ pound small
mushrooms, cleaned
and thinly sliced

2 tablespoons capers

Salt

Freshly ground pepper

1 pound bucatini,
spaghetti or penne

Grill tuna until done and marinate for 1 hour in $^1/_2$ cup of the olive oil, 2 cloves of the minced garlic, oregano, basil and parsley. Place tomatoes and their juices in the food processor and purée. Remove and press through a sieve to remove seeds. Set aside. Heat remaining oil in a large skillet. Add mushrooms and sauté over high heat until lightly colored. Add remaining garlic and sauté briefly. Add tomatoes. Cook, uncovered, over medium heat, 6 to 8 minutes. Cut tuna into small pieces, add capers and combine with tomatoes. Season with salt and coarsely ground black pepper. Cook 2 to 3 minutes longer. Bring a large pot of water to a boil. Add 1 tablespoon of salt and pasta. Cook pasta, uncovered, until tender. Drain pasta and place in skillet with sauce. Toss well until pasta and sauce are thoroughly blended. Serve immediately.

Serves 4.

ANGEL HAIR PASTA WITH TOMATO AND BASIL

1 cup peeled, seeded and chopped tomatoes

1/4 cup chopped fresh basil

1/2 cup olive oil

2 large shallots, chopped

Salt

Freshly ground pepper

1 pound angel hair pasta

Combine tomatoes, basil, olive oil, shallots, salt and pepper. Toss with freshly cooked pasta and serve immediately. You may substitute garlic for shallots.

Serves 4.

ANGEL HAIR PASTA WITH EGGPLANT

5 tablespoons olive oil

1 cup chopped onions

2 garlic cloves, minced

12 ounces tomatoes, chopped

1 teaspoon sugar

1 tablespoon fresh basil

1 tablespoon fresh oregano

Salt and pepper

12 to 16 slices eggplant, 1/4 inch thick

8 ounces angel hair pasta

Fresh basil for garnish

Freshly grated Parmesan cheese

Heat 2 tablespoons of the olive oil in frying pan. Add onions and garlic and sauté for 5 minutes. Add tomatoes to onion mixture. Add sugar, basil, oregano, salt and pepper. Bring to a boil. Reduce heat and simmer, covered, for 15 to 30 minutes until it reaches a sauce consistency. Lightly salt eggplant and allow to sit for 10 minutes to draw out the moisture. Brush with the remaining olive oil and grill about 5 minutes per side. Meanwhile, cook and drain pasta. Divide pasta among 4 serving plates and top with sauce. Cut eggplant circles in half. Fan across top of pasta and top with more sauce. Garnish with a fresh basil sprig and a sprinkle of Parmesan.

Serves 4.

PASTA BONINO

4 to 5 garlic cloves, minced

1 pound mushrooms, sliced

1 medium yellow onion, sliced

28 ounces whole tomatoes, drained and cut into pieces

3/4 pound spinach, stems removed and reserved

3 tablespoons olive oil

1/4 cup chicken broth

1 pound tagliarini

1/2 cup grated Parmesan cheese

Simmer garlic, mushrooms, onions, tomatoes and spinach stems in olive oil 5 to 10 minutes. Coarsely chop remaining spinach and add to mixture with chicken broth. Bring to a boil and simmer for 3 minutes. Cook and drain pasta and add to sauce. Top with Parmesan cheese.

Serves 4 to 6.

LINGUINE WITH PESTO

1 pound linguine

1/2 teaspoon salt

Grated Parmesan cheese

Pesto may be made ahead and refrigerated for up to two weeks in a sealed glass container.

Cook pasta al dente, about 3 to 5 minutes. Drain. Place Pesto in a large skillet and simmer for 5 minutes. Add linguine and toss. Serve with grated Parmesan cheese.

Serves 4.

PESTO

1 cup fresh basil

4 sprigs parsley

4 ounces pine nuts

2 garlic cloves

1/3 cup grated Parmesan cheese

1/2 cup grated Romano cheese

1/4 cup olive oil

Combine basil, parsley, pine nuts, garlic, Parmesan and Romano cheeses in a food processor or blender. While processor is running, slowly pour olive oil into basil mixture until smooth. Set aside.

TAGLIARINI WITH PORCINI MUSHROOM SAUCE

2 ounces porcini mushrooms

1 to 2 cups cold water

1 medium onion, minced

1 garlic clove, minced

1 bunch parsley, chopped

2 tablespoons olive oil

2 pounds tomatoes, finely chopped

6 ounces tomato paste

2 teaspoons sugar

2 teaspoons salt

2 teaspoons mixed dried Italian herbs

2 pounds tagliarini, preferably fresh

Soak mushrooms in cold water for 20 minutes. In a frying pan, sauté onions, garlic and parsley in olive oil until onions are translucent. Remove mushrooms, reserving liquid, and chop finely. Pour onion mixture, mushrooms and mushroom liquid into a large stockpot. Add tomatoes, tomato paste, sugar, salt and herbs. Simmer for 5 to 6 hours or all day, if possible. The longer it simmers the better the taste. When ready to serve, cook and drain pasta. Spoon sauce over tagliarini and serve.

Serves 8 to 10.

HAIGHT-ASHBURY PASTA

3 garlic cloves, crushed

1/2 cup olive oil

12 fresh basil
leaves, slivered

1 cup kalamata olives,
pitted and sliced

3/4 cup sun-dried
tomato halves

8 ounces feta
cheese, crumbled

Salt and pepper

1 pound angel
hair pasta, cooked

1/2 cup walnuts, toasted

Sauté garlic in olive oil. Add basil, olives and sun-dried tomatoes. Cook until well heated. Add cheese to the tomato mixture along with salt and pepper. Cook and drain pasta. Immediately toss pasta in the sauce. Sprinkle with walnuts and serve immediately.

Serves 4 to 6.

TAGLIOLINI WITH ASPARAGUS, LEEKS AND GARLIC

2 leeks

4 tablespoons olive oil

4 tablespoons
unsalted butter

1 pound asparagus,
trimmed and
thinly sliced on bias

3 to 4 garlic
cloves, minced

1/2 cup coarsely chopped
fresh basil

1 to 2 tablespoons
chopped parsley

Salt and freshly
ground pepper

1 pound fresh tagliolini

Use saffron in the pasta dough for a tantalizing change in flavor.

Cut off root ends and trim outer leaves from leeks. Cut in half lengthwise and wash out any sand between the layers. Slice the leeks very thin. Heat olive oil and butter in a large sauté pan over medium heat. Sauté asparagus and leeks until asparagus is tender but still crisp and leeks are soft, 4 to 5 minutes. Add garlic and sauté 2 to 3 minutes. Add herbs and season with salt and pepper. Cook and drain pasta. Toss with asparagus/leek mixture.

Serves 4.

PASTA WITH HOT WALNUT SAUCE

1/3 cup olive oil

1/2 cup
chopped walnuts

1 small onion, minced

4 tablespoons
red wine vinegar

2 teaspoons sugar

1/2 teaspoon salt

3/4 pound
corkscrew macaroni

4 ounces
smoked turkey or
prosciutto, cut
into thin strips

Heat oil and cook walnuts until lightly browned. Remove from pan and drain on a paper towel. Cook onions in remaining oil until tender. Remove from heat. Stir in vinegar, sugar and salt. Cook and drain pasta. Toss with walnuts and onion/vinegar mixture. Add smoked turkey and serve.

Serves 4.

PASTA WITH FOUR CHEESES

5 ounces Gruyère
cheese, cubed

5 ounces fontina
cheese, cubed

1³/₄ cups grated
Parmesan cheese

1¹/₂ tablespoons flour

¹/₄ cup butter

1 cup milk

1 cup half and half

1 pound fresh fettuccine

5 ounces mozzarella
cheese, grated

Combine Gruyère and fontina cheeses with Parmesan and flour. Keep the mozzarella separate. Heat the butter, milk and half and half in a large saucepan until the butter is melted. Stir in the cubed cheese mixture a little at a time. Continue stirring with a wooden spoon until mixture is smooth. Keep warm over very low heat, stirring occasionally. Cook the pasta. Drain and put into a warm bowl. Pour the cheese sauce over the pasta and stir quickly. Add mozzarella cheese and stir. Serve immediately on heated plates.

Serves 4.

PASTA PUTTANESCA

6 plum tomatoes, peeled,
seeded and chopped

4 to 5 garlic
cloves, minced

8 oil-packed sun-dried
tomatoes, drained and
cut in slivers

¹/₂ cup oil-cured
black olives, pitted
and chopped

¹/₄ cup finely
chopped parsley

¹/₄ cup finely
chopped fresh basil

1 tablespoon chopped
anchovy fillets

¹/₃ cup olive oil

1 pound spaghetti
or fettuccine

Salt and pepper

¹/₂ cup grated
Parmesan cheese

In a bowl place the tomatoes, garlic, sun-dried tomatoes, olives, parsley, basil, anchovy and olive oil. Toss thoroughly, cover with plastic wrap and place in the refrigerator to marinate for at least 2 hours. Bring the sauce to room temperature before serving. Cook the pasta in boiling water until just tender. Drain and place in a serving bowl. Immediately pour the sauce over the hot pasta, toss and season with salt and pepper. Add the Parmesan, toss again and serve. This pasta is meant to be served warm, not hot.

Serves 4.

LINGUINE BOWMANO

1 pound fresh
mushrooms, sliced

8 tablespoons butter

3 tablespoons olive oil

¹/₂ cup minced parsley

6 garlic cloves, minced

1 tablespoon
chopped chives

1 tablespoon chopped
fresh basil

1 teaspoon chopped
fresh oregano

3 tablespoons
lemon juice

¹/₂ cup white wine

1 pound linguine

Grated Parmesan cheese

Minced parsley
for garnish

Sauté mushrooms in 4 tablespoons of the butter and pour off liquid. Melt remaining 4 tablespoons of the butter. Add olive oil and all other ingredients except pasta and cheese. Simmer for 20 minutes, adding more wine if necessary. Cook and drain pasta. Toss mixture gently with pasta. Top with Parmesan cheese and additional parsley.

Serves 4.

PASTA WITH SCALLOPS AND TOMATOES

4 green onions, thinly sliced

3 garlic cloves, minced

1 tablespoon olive oil

2 cups diced tomatoes

³/₄ pound large scallops, rinsed and patted dry

1 cup chicken or seafood stock

Pinch of crushed red pepper

2 teaspoons capers

12 ounces angel hair pasta

Sauté onions and garlic in olive oil. Add tomatoes and cook until just heated through. Add scallops and broth. Simmer 3 minutes. Add red pepper and capers. Heat to boiling, reduce heat and simmer for as long as it takes to cook the scallops. Cook pasta in boiling salted water and drain. Combine with tomato mixture and serve immediately.

Serves 4.

CLAM STUFFED PASTA

20 large pasta shells

6¹/₂ ounces minced clams with juice

¹/₄ cup grated Parmesan cheese

¹/₄ cup seasoned bread crumbs

3 tablespoons butter

¹/₄ teaspoon dried Italian seasoning

Great as a first course!

Cook shells according to directions. Mix clams, clam juice, Parmesan cheese and bread crumbs. Stuff cooked pasta with clam mixture. Melt butter and mix in Italian seasoning. Pour butter mixture over pasta and bake at 350 degrees for 15 minutes.

Makes 20 shells.

FETTUCCINE WITH SMOKED SALMON

4 tablespoons unsalted butter

1 bunch green onions, thinly sliced

¹/₄ cup Scotch whiskey

3 cups heavy cream

1 teaspoon ground white pepper

¹/₂ teaspoon crushed hot red pepper

1 pound smoked salmon, thinly sliced, cut into strips

1¹/₂ pounds fettuccine

³/₄ cup minced Italian parsley

Melt butter over moderate heat. Add onions and cook 3 minutes. Stir in whiskey and cook 4 more minutes or until reduced to 1 tablespoon. Add cream, white and red peppers. Increase heat to moderately high and cook until cream is slightly thickened, about 8 minutes, stirring frequently. Remove from heat and stir in salmon. Cover to keep warm. Cook fettuccine, drain and rinse. Add pasta and parsley to sauce. Cook, tossing for 1 to 2 minutes to blend. Add extra cream if sauce seems too thick. Serve at once.

Serves 4 to 6.

BLACK FETTUCCINE WITH SCALLOPS

1 pound bay or
sea scallops,
rinsed and dried

Salt and pepper

Flour

2 leeks

2 tablespoons olive oil

2 tablespoons
unsalted butter

1 red bell pepper,
cut into thin strips

1 yellow bell pepper,
cut into thin strips

2 garlic cloves, minced

1 cup fish or chicken
stock

Juice of 1 lemon

2 to 3 tablespoons
chopped parsley

1 pound
black fettuccine,
black pasta dough,
page 178

Season scallops with salt and pepper and dust lightly with flour. Cut off root end and trim outer leaves from leeks. Cut in half lengthwise and wash out any sand between the layers. Cut leeks into very fine julienne strips. Sauté scallops quickly over high heat in olive oil until lightly browned. Scallops should not be fully cooked. Set aside. In a large sauté pan, melt butter over medium heat. Add peppers and leeks and cook until softened slightly. Add garlic and cook briefly. Add stock and bring to a boil. Reduce heat, add scallops and season with salt, pepper and lemon juice. Cook fettuccine al dente. Drain and toss with sauce. Toss in the parsley and serve.

Serves 6.

ROSEMARY FETTUCCINE

1 whole chicken breast,
halved, skinned
and boned

2 ounces pancetta,
thinly sliced and
cut into strips

1 leek

2 tablespoons olive oil

Salt

3 to 4 garlic
cloves, minced

$1/4$ teaspoon red
pepper flakes

1 cup chicken stock

1 tablespoon
unsalted butter

1 pound fresh
rosemary fettuccine,
pasta dough, page 178

Grated Parmesan
cheese

Cut chicken breast into $1/2$-inch strips. Cook pancetta over medium heat until brown and crispy. Transfer to a paper towel to drain. Remove fat from pan. Cut off root ends and trim outer leaves from leek. Cut in half lengthwise and wash out any sand between the layers. Slice into very thin julienne strips, 2 to 3 inches long. Heat olive oil in a large sauté pan over high heat. When oil is hot but not smoking, add chicken and season with salt. Sear chicken for 2 to 3 minutes and add pancetta, leeks, garlic and red pepper flakes. Sauté for another 1 to 2 minutes. Do not let garlic brown. Add chicken stock. Heat 1 minute. Do not overcook the chicken. Just before serving, add the butter, while swirling or shaking the pan. Cook fettuccine al dente, drain and toss with sauce. Serve with freshly grated Parmesan cheese.

Serves 4.

PASTA WITH LOBSTER, WHITE CORN, GOLDEN PEPPERS AND BASIL

2 live lobsters, about
1¹/₄ pounds each

3 tablespoons olive oil

1 carrot, diced

1 onion, diced

1 stalk celery, diced

2 tomatoes,
coarsely chopped

2 golden bell peppers or
other sweet
peppers, julienned

¹/₂ red bell
pepper, diced

2 garlic cloves,
thinly sliced

1 sprig parsley

1 sprig thyme

1 bay leaf

2 ears white corn

2 tablespoons
unsalted butter

1 cup heavy cream

1 pound linguine

Fresh basil leaves,
cut into thin ribbons,
for garnish

Cook the lobsters in plenty of salted, boiling water for 7 minutes. Remove and cool. Shell lobster tails and claws, reserving shells. Sauté lobster shells in olive oil over high heat for 2 minutes. Add carrots, onions, celery, tomatoes, peppers and garlic along with parsley, thyme and bay leaf. Sauté briefly and add enough water to cover vegetables and shells. Simmer for 30 to 45 minutes. Strain liquid and reduce to about 2 cups. Reserve for sauce. Chop the claw meat and slice the lobster tails into medallions. Strip the kernels from the ears of corn using a sharp knife. Melt butter in a large sauté pan over medium heat. Add corn and sauté for 2 minutes. Add cream, 1 cup of the lobster stock and reduce slightly. Add lobster meat. Cook pasta, drain and toss with sauce. Garnish with basil ribbons.

Serve 4 to 6.

SPINACH FETTUCCINE WITH PROSCIUTTO

3 tablespoons olive oil

3 tablespoons butter

1 pound mushrooms,
thinly sliced

8 ounces
prosciutto, diced

2 large tomatoes, peeled,
seeded and chopped

1 teaspoon nutmeg

1 fresh sage leaf

1 cup heavy cream

1 pound
spinach fettuccine

1 cup grated
Parmesan cheese

¹/₂ cup
pine nuts, toasted

¹/₂ cup chopped
Italian parsley

Heat olive oil and butter in a large frying pan and sauté mushrooms approximately 10 minutes. Add prosciutto, tomatoes, nutmeg, sage and cream. Cook over high heat for 4 to 5 minutes until sauce is somewhat thickened. Remove from heat and set aside. Cook the fettuccine al dente, 3 to 5 minutes, and drain. Mix fettuccine with the mushroom sauce and half of the Parmesan cheese. Transfer to serving bowl or onto individual plates. Sprinkle with pine nuts, remaining cheese and parsley.

Serves 4 to 6.

GNOCCHI WITH VEAL SAUCE

3 cups mashed
potatoes, approximately
3 large russets

1¹/₂ cups flour

1¹/₂ teaspoons salt

1 tablespoon olive oil

2 eggs, slightly beaten

Flour

3 quarts salted
boiling water

2 to 3 tablespoons
melted butter

1¹/₂ cups grated
Parmesan cheese

Combine mashed potatoes, flour, salt and olive oil. Blend with fork. Add eggs and blend thoroughly into mixture. Turn dough onto a floured board. Knead gently about 15 times. Shape into a flat loaf and set on floured area to prevent sticking. Cut off 1 piece at a time–about ¹/₂ cup. Roll on a lightly floured board into a long cord ³/₈ inch thick. Cut into 1-inch lengths. Press each lightly in center to give bow shape or lightly roll with tines of a fork. Set gnocchi aside on lightly floured baking sheets. The pieces should not touch. Gnocchi can be frozen in a single layer. When frozen, you can place them altogether in an airtight container until ready to use. Cook the gnocchi, one-third at a time, by dropping them in boiling water. Cook for 5 minutes after they return to the surface. Keep water at a slow boil. Remove with slotted spoon, draining well. Place in shallow, rimmed pan and mix gently with melted butter. Cover tightly with foil and keep in warm place. Gnocchi can be held in a 150-degree oven, covered, for a couple of hours. To serve, top with Veal Sauce and serve with Parmesan cheese.

Serves 6.

VEAL SAUCE

¹/₄ cup chopped bacon

3 tablespoons olive oil

1 pound boneless veal,
finely chopped

1 medium
onion, chopped

1 carrot, finely diced

2 stalks celery,
finely chopped

¹/₂ cup
chopped mushrooms

8 ounces tomato sauce

16 ounces whole
tomatoes, with liquid

1 cup dry red wine

1¹/₂ teaspoons salt

¹/₄ teaspoon
allspice

Dash of pepper

Place bacon in a Dutch oven or large frying pan with olive oil. Add veal, onions, carrots and celery. Cook over medium heat, stirring, until vegetables are soft. Add mushrooms, tomato sauce, whole tomatoes, wine, salt, allspice and pepper. Simmer 2 hours or until sauce is reduced to 4 cups. This sauce can be made ahead and stored, covered, in the refrigerator.

SPANISH SPAGHETTI

8 strips bacon

4 large Spanish onions, chopped

1 large green bell pepper, seeded and chopped

1 pound extra lean ground round

1 pound tomatoes, puréed

1 cup tomato soup

1 cup tomato sauce

3 teaspoons chili powder

Salt

Cayenne pepper

1/2 pound mushrooms, thinly sliced

1 pound Cheddar cheese, grated

1 pound spaghetti

Cut bacon into small pieces and brown in a large pan. Remove and set aside. Brown onions and peppers in 1 tablespoon bacon drippings. Add meat and cook until brown. Drain off fat and add puréed tomatoes, tomato soup, tomato sauce and chili powder. Season with salt and cayenne pepper. Bring to a boil and simmer for 35 to 40 minutes, stirring occasionally to prevent sticking. Stir in mushrooms, bacon and cheese, saving enough cheese to make a layer on the top. Cook spaghetti, drain and place in a 2 or 3-quart casserole. Spoon sauce over spaghetti and top with reserved cheese. Bake at 350 degrees for 30 minutes. This may be made ahead and refrigerated. Bring to room temperature before baking.

Serves 8.

LAYERED POLENTA PIE WITH FONTINA CHEESE

4 cups semolina

8 cups chicken stock

3 tablespoons butter

4 ounces fontina cheese, grated

2 tablespoons finely chopped fresh sage

1 cup pesto

Bring chicken stock and butter to a boil. Turn down heat until barely simmering and slowly add semolina while stirring constantly. Continue to stir until mixture begins to come away from the sides of pan, about 20 minutes. Remove from heat, fold in cheese and sage. In a large, buttered ovenproof bowl, place a layer of polenta, a layer of pesto, another layer of polenta, a layer of Sun-Dried Tomato Sauce and ending with a layer of polenta. Bake at 350 degrees for 25 minutes. Turn upside down and unmold. Cut into pie sections and serve.

Serves 10.

SUN-DRIED TOMATO SAUCE

1 tablespoon minced onions

1 tablespoon minced garlic

1 green bell pepper, seeded and minced

5 button mushrooms, minced

1 cup oil-packed sun-dried tomatoes, drained

1 teaspoon minced fresh thyme

1 teaspoon minced fresh oregano

2 tablespoons butter

Sauté onions, garlic, peppers and mushrooms until onions are translucent. Add tomatoes and herbs. Simmer for 5 minutes. Purée and set aside.

CAPELLINI WITH CHICKEN AND CUCUMBERS

2 whole chicken breasts, halved, skinned, boned and diced

1 tablespoon butter

$^1/_2$ English cucumber, diced into $^1/_4$-inch pieces

Juice and zest of 1 lime

1$^1/_2$ cups heavy cream

1 tablespoon fresh tarragon leaves

Salt and freshly ground pepper

$^1/_2$ pound dried capellini

Salt and pepper chicken and sauté in butter for 3 to 4 minutes or until most of it has turned opaque. Add the cucumber, lime juice and zest, cream and tarragon. Bring to a boil and reduce slightly. Sauce should not be thick and heavy. Cook and drain pasta and add to sauce. Garnish with freshly ground black pepper.

Serves 4.

SQUASH RAVIOLI WITH BROWN BUTTER, SAGE AND HAZELNUTS

2 small bulbs garlic

Olive oil

1 medium butternut squash

Salt and pepper

$^1/_3$ cup grated Parmesan cheese

$^1/_2$ cup bread crumbs, toasted

Freshly grated nutmeg

1 pound pasta dough, page 178

Semolina

4 tablespoons unsalted butter, softened

$^1/_4$ cup chopped fresh sage for garnish

3 tablespoons chopped toasted hazelnuts for garnish

To make garlic oil, cut bulbs of garlic in half horizontally. Keeping the heads intact, place the garlic in a baking dish and pour olive oil over them so that there is about $^1/_4$ inch of oil in the bottom of the dish. Cover and bake at 300 degrees for 1$^1/_2$ hours. Garlic should be very soft and sweet. Cut the squash in half, scoop out the seeds and score the flesh in a crisscross pattern. Brush lightly with garlic oil, season with salt and pepper and bake cut side down on a cookie sheet for 45 minutes to 1 hour at 375 degrees. The squash should be quite soft. Scoop the cooked squash out of its skin and cool. Chop squash and garlic in small pieces and mash with a fork. Add Parmesan and bread crumbs. If mixture is too soft or runny, add a bit more Parmesan to absorb any moisture. The filling should have enough body to retain its shape when dropped from a spoon. Season with salt, pepper and nutmeg.

To assemble ravioli, roll out a sheet of pasta dough to a width of 4 inches. Trim edges. Fold the dough lengthwise to make a crease down the center. Then lay out flat again. Place a teaspoon of filling down 1 side of vertical length of dough at 2-inch intervals. Using a spray bottle of water, finely mist the entire sheet. Fold lengthwise to seal, using a little more water, if necessary, to ensure a tight seal. Using a knife or scalloped pastry wheel, cut between the filling in a straight line. With your fingers, ease out the trapped air within each ravioli, beginning at the creased end and working around to the opened end. Place finished ravioli on a cookie sheet generously sprinkled with semolina and cover.

Cook ravioli in boiling, salted water 4 to 5 minutes. Drain. In a small saucepan, heat butter over high heat. Stir constantly until butter is dark brown and has a nutty smell. Pour over the cooked ravioli and garnish with sage, hazelnuts and additional Parmesan.

Serves 4 to 6.

SAFFRON LOBSTER RAVIOLI WITH LEMON BUTTER SAUCE

1½ pounds lobster tails

1 small red bell pepper, seeded and cut into 1-inch slivers

1 pound saffron pasta, pasta dough, page 178

Semolina

Boil lobster tails in a large kettle of boiling salted water for about 7 minutes. Remove and cool. Remove shells and cut meat into small pieces. Steam peppers until tender. Toss lobster and pepper slivers with 2 tablespoons of the Lemon Butter Sauce. Chill until ready to use. Prepare and assemble ravioli as directed in Squash Ravioli. Cook ravioli in boiling, salted water 4 to 5 minutes. Drain. Pour Lemon Butter Sauce over all and serve .

Serves 4 to 6.

LEMON BUTTER SAUCE

1 small garlic clove, crushed

½ cup butter

2 teaspoons lemon juice

2 teaspoons white wine

½ teaspoon sugar

Pinch white pepper

Pinch paprika

Sauté garlic in butter. Add remaining ingredients and gently heat for an additional 2 minutes. Set aside.

CHICKEN AND CHÈVRE RAVIOLI

1 whole chicken breast, halved, skinned and boned

2 leeks

1 teaspoon chopped fresh thyme

2 tablespoons unsalted butter

1 pound pasta dough, page 178

6 ounces chèvre

Salt and pepper

Freshly grated nutmeg

Grill chicken breast over medium heat until done. Finely chop and set aside. Trim leeks of root end and dark green leaves. Cut in half lengthwise and rinse under cold water to remove any sand. Chop into thin ribbons. Stew the leeks and thyme in butter over medium low heat until very soft. Cool and combine with chicken and chèvre. Season with salt, pepper and nutmeg. Prepare and assemble ravioli as directed in Squash Ravioli. Cook ravioli in boiling salted water for 4 to 5 minutes. Drain. Pour Walnut Sauce over all and serve.

Serves 4 to 6.

WALNUT SAUCE

1 tablespoon unsalted butter

2 teaspoons chopped shallots

¼ cup walnuts, chopped

1 cup heavy cream

Salt and pepper

Heat butter in medium sauté pan. Add shallots and soften but do not brown. Add cream, walnuts, salt and pepper. Simmer until completely heated.

PIZZA DOUGH

1 package active
dry yeast

³/₄ cup lukewarm water

2 cups flour

1 tablespoon milk

¹/₂ teaspoon salt

2 tablespoons olive oil

Mix together yeast, ¹/₄ cup of the water and ¹/₄ cup of the flour. Let rise for 20 minutes. Add remaining water and flour. Stir in milk, salt and olive oil and mix with a wooden spoon. Knead for 10 to 15 minutes on a floured board, adding no more flour than necessary to make dough slightly tacky but not sticky. Place dough in bowl rubbed with a little olive oil. Cover the bowl with a towel and place in a warm place. Let dough rise until doubled in volume, about 1 hour. Punch down and let rise another 45 minutes. Roll out on a lightly floured board to desired size of pizza. This basic recipe can be used with a variety of favorite pizza toppings.

Makes dough for 1 12-inch pizza.

ARTICHOKE BRIE PIZZA

1 cup marinara
or pizza sauce

6¹/₂ ounces marinated
artichoke hearts,
drained and sliced

8 ounces Brie
cheese, cubed

¹/₂ cup chopped onions

¹/₄ to ¹/₂ cup
sun-dried tomatoes

12-inch round of
pizza dough or
commercially prepared
Italian bread shell

Spread pizza dough with marinara sauce. Top with artichoke hearts, cheese, onions and tomatoes. Bake on a cookie sheet at 500 degrees for 10 to 12 minutes.

Makes 1 12-inch pizza.

SAUSAGE, PEPPER AND BASIL PIZZA

1 pound Italian
sausage, crumbled

1 tablespoon olive oil

¹/₂ red onion,
thinly sliced

¹/₂ each red and yellow
bell pepper, stemmed,
seeded and sliced
into ¹/₄-inch strips

1 garlic clove, minced

¹/₂ pound mozzarella
cheese, grated

1 tablespoon finely
chopped fresh basil or
cilantro for garnish

1 tablespoon finely
chopped parsley for
garnish

12-inch round
of pizza dough

Sauté sausage on medium high heat until it begins to brown. Drain on paper towels and set aside. Discard fat. Heat olive oil and add onions and peppers. Cook 5 minutes until softened. Mix garlic with mozzarella and spread mixture over pizza dough, leaving a ¹/₂-inch border. Add sausage and top with onion/pepper mixture. Bake on a cookie sheet at 500 degrees for 10 to 12 minutes. Garnish with basil or cilantro and parsley. Cut and serve.

Makes 1 12-inch pizza.

TOMATO, MOZZARELLA AND BASIL PIZZA

3 to 4 garlic cloves

4 tablespoons olive oil

1 cup grated
mozzarella cheese

1 red tomato,
thinly sliced

1 yellow tomato,
thinly sliced

12-inch round
of pizza dough

Fresh basil leaves
for garnish

Crush garlic cloves by smashing them on a cutting board with the flat side of a knife. Place garlic in a small saucepan and cover with olive oil. Warm briefly over a low flame and cool. Brush the surface of the pizza dough with a small amount of the garlic oil. Spread mozzarella evenly over oiled dough. Top with the sliced tomatoes, alternating red and yellow. Drizzle a little more garlic oil over the top. Sprinkle with chopped basil. Bake on a cookie sheet at 500 degrees for 10 to 12 minutes.

Makes 1 12-inch pizza.

EGGPLANT, ROASTED GARLIC AND SUN-DRIED TOMATO PIZZA

6 slices eggplant,
unpeeled and sliced
1/4 inch thick

Olive oil

8 to 10 garlic
cloves, peeled

Salt and pepper

1/2 cup grated
mozzarella cheese

4 oil-packed sun-dried
tomatoes, julienned

12-inch round
of pizza dough

4 to 5 fresh basil leaves,
chopped, for garnish

Brush eggplant slices with olive oil, season with salt and pepper and bake on a cookie sheet at 425 degrees for 12 to 15 minutes, or until golden brown. Place garlic in a small shallow saucepan. Add enough olive oil to cover. Heat on low so that the oil barely bubbles. Cook for 15 minutes, stirring occasionally, or until garlic is golden and soft when pierced with a fork. Remove garlic and reserve oil. Brush dough lightly with the garlic oil and spread mozzarella over the top, leaving a 1/2-inch border around the edges. Lay the eggplant slices over the cheese. Scatter the whole garlic cloves and sun-dried tomatoes over the eggplant. Bake on a cookie sheet at 500 degrees for 8 to 10 minutes. Garnish with basil.

Makes 1 12-inch pizza.

CHINESE BARBECUED PORK PIZZA

1 small red
bell pepper

1 small golden
bell pepper

1 small green
bell pepper

1 tablespoon olive oil

Salt and pepper

2 tablespoons
hoisin sauce

1/2 cup grated
mozzarella cheese

1/4 pound barbecued
pork, thinly sliced, found
in Oriental markets

2 green onions,
thinly sliced

2 teaspoons
chopped cilantro

12-inch round
of pizza dough

Remove stems and seeds from peppers and cut into 1/4-inch strips. In a large sauté pan over medium high heat, sauté the peppers in olive oil briefly until colors intensify. Season with salt and pepper. Remove from heat and set aside. Spread hoisin sauce on pizza dough, leaving a 1/2-inch border around the edges. Scatter with the cheese, then the peppers. Top with slices of barbecued pork. Sprinkle with green onions. Bake on a cookie sheet at 500 degrees for 8 to 10 minutes. Garnish with cilantro.

Makes 1 12-inch pizza.

APPLE, BRIE AND WALNUT BREAKFAST PIZZA

2 tablespoons butter

2 Granny Smith apples, cored, peeled and sliced into 1/4-inch pieces

Cinnamon

8 ounces Brie cheese

1/2 cup chopped walnuts

1 teaspoon fresh rosemary leaves

12-inch round of pizza dough

Melt the butter in a medium sauté pan over medium heat. When butter is hot, add the apples and cook until well browned. Season apples with the cinnamon, and cool. Brush the pizza dough surface with a small amount of additional melted butter or light oil. Dot the surface with broken pieces of Brie. Arrange the cooked apples over the top and sprinkle with walnuts and rosemary. Bake on a cookie sheet at 500 degrees for 10 to 12 minutes.

Makes 1 12-inch pizza.

CALZONE WITH PROSCIUTTO AND GOAT CHEESE

1 pizza dough recipe, page 190

2 ounces goat cheese, crumbled

1 ounce prosciutto, thinly sliced

1/8 pound mozzarella cheese, grated

1/8 pound fontina cheese, grated

2 teaspoons finely chopped chives

1/2 teaspoon dried oregano

2 teaspoons finely chopped parsley

1 egg

1/2 teaspoon pepper

1/2 cup olive oil

Mix goat cheese with prosciutto, mozzarella and fontina cheeses, chives, oregano, parsley, egg and pepper. Prepare pizza dough. Knead dough briefly and divide into 8 equal parts. On lightly floured surface, shape dough ovals approximately 6 1/2 x 7 1/2 inches. Brush olive oil on dough, leaving 1/2 inch free at edges. Brush 1/2-inch edge with water. Place 3 heaping tablespoons of filling on bottom half and fold over like a turnover. Press edges with tines of a fork to seal. Place on an oiled baking sheet. Repeat with remaining dough and filling. Brush each calzone again with olive oil. Let rise 30 minutes. Bake at 450 degrees for 25 to 30 minutes or until dough is puffed, golden brown and firm. Serve hot.

Makes 8 individual calzone.

CALZONE WITH WESTPHALIAN HAM

1 pizza dough recipe, page 190

3/4 pound Westphalian ham, thinly sliced

2 tomatoes, chopped and seeded

1/2 pound mozzarella cheese, grated

1 garlic clove, minced

1/2 cup minced fresh basil

Prepare pizza dough. Knead dough briefly on a lightly floured surface. Cut in half. Shape each half into a ball. Flatten and reshape with a rolling pin into a 1/4-inch thick oval. Layer half of the ham, tomatoes, cheese, garlic and basil on half of the oval. Fold in half and press the edges together with tines of a fork to seal. Repeat with the remaining ingredients to make another calzone. Place on an oiled baking sheet. Bake at 450 degrees for 25 to 30 minutes or until crust is golden brown. Slice each into 4 diagonal pieces and serve hot.

Makes 2 large calzone.

COOKIES AND DESSERTS

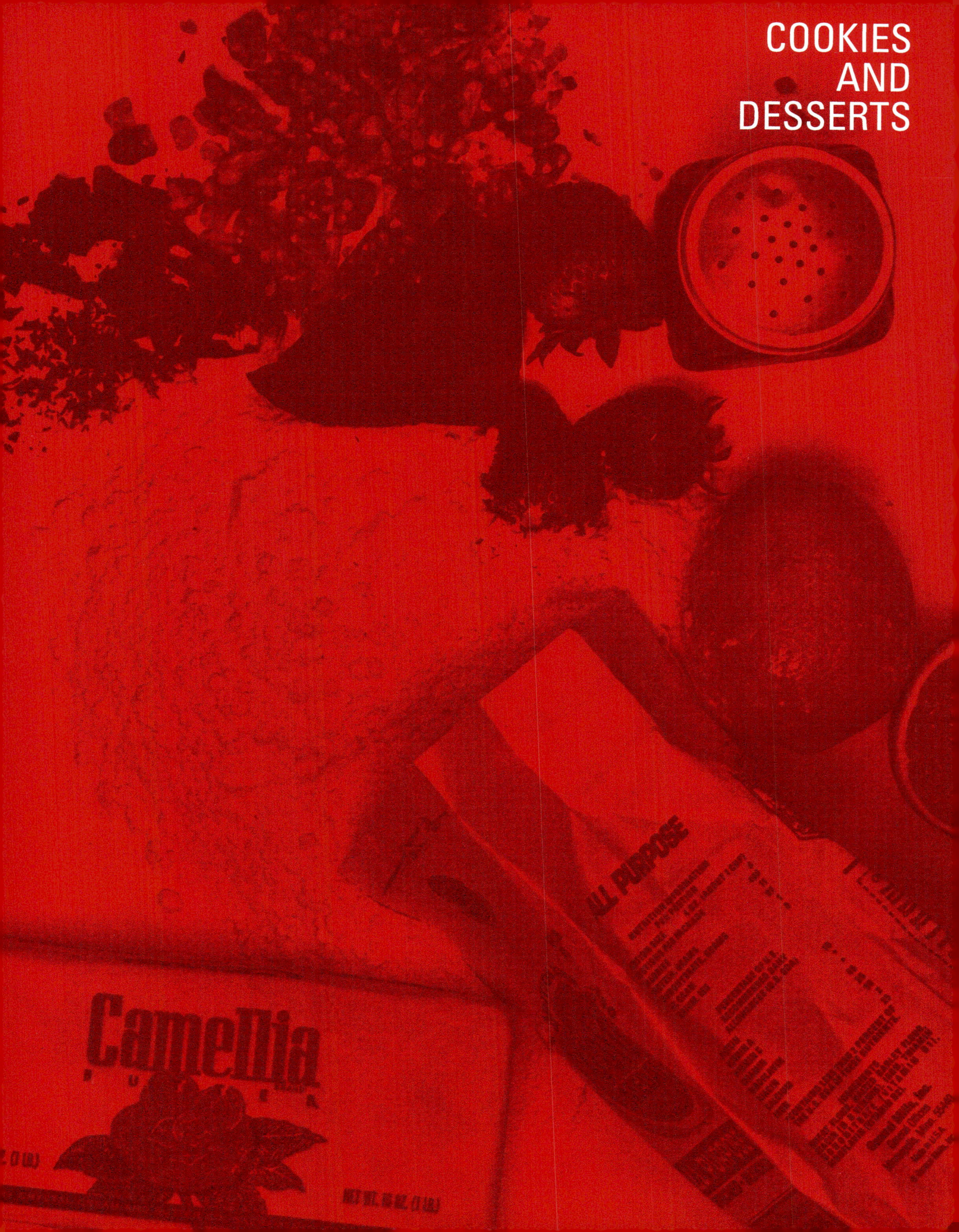

BROWN SUGAR SHORTBREAD PUFFS

1¼ cups butter, softened

1 cup firmly packed brown sugar

1 egg yolk

1 teaspoon vanilla

2¼ cups flour

Combine butter and brown sugar. Cream until light and fluffy. Add egg yolk and vanilla and mix until well blended. Gently spoon in flour. Stir until mixture forms a smooth dough. Drop by 1-inch rounded teaspoons onto ungreased cookie sheets. Bake at 350 degrees for 12 to 15 minutes or until lightly browned. Transfer to a rack to cool.

Makes 60.

GREEK BUTTER COOKIES

5½ cups flour

1¼ cups sugar

1 teaspoon baking soda

1 teaspoon baking powder

1¼ cups butter, softened

4 eggs

5 ounces evaporated milk

1½ teaspoons vanilla

½ cup sesame seeds

Sift together dry ingredients. Add butter and blend together by hand until mixture is smooth and the consistency of bread crumbs. In a separate bowl lightly beat 3 of the eggs and add to the flour mixture. Blend with hands. Add milk and vanilla. Knead until dough no longer clings to sides of bowl. Pinch off a piece of dough about the size of a large walnut and roll into a pencil-like strand about ½ inch thick and 7 inches long. Fold the strand in half. Leaving a tiny opening at the fold, turn each half of the strand around the other 2 or 3 times. Place twisted cookies 1 inch apart onto a cookie sheet which has been greased or lined with wax paper. Lightly beat remaining egg with 1 teaspoon water and brush egg mixture over the tops of the cookies. Sprinkle with sesame seeds. Bake at 350 degrees for 20 to 25 minutes or until lightly browned. Cool slightly before removing from cookie sheet. Cool thoroughly and store in an airtight container.

Makes 72.

COFFEE BARS

½ cup shortening

½ cup brown sugar

½ cup sugar

1 egg, beaten

½ cup hot coffee

1½ cups flour

½ teaspoon baking powder

½ teaspoon baking soda

½ teaspoon cinnamon

½ cup raisins

¼ cup chopped walnuts

ICING

1 cup powdered sugar

1 tablespoon melted butter

½ teaspoon vanilla

2 tablespoons hot coffee

Blend shortening, sugars and egg until creamy. Add hot coffee and stir well. Sift dry ingredients together and combine with sugar mixture. Add raisins and nuts. Turn batter into a 10 x 15-inch greased jelly roll pan. Spread evenly to ¼ inch thick. Bake at 350 degrees for 10 to 15 minutes. Combine icing ingredients and frost with icing while still warm.

Makes 48.

DELTA KIWI BARS

1¼ cups flour

½ cup powdered sugar

½ cup butter

1 cup granulated sugar

2 kiwis, peeled and puréed

2 eggs, beaten

1 teaspoon lime juice

½ teaspoon grated lime peel

½ teaspoon baking powder

Combine flour and ¼ cup of the powdered sugar. Cut butter into the flour mixture until it looks like cornmeal. Gently pat into a buttered 9-inch square pan. Bake at 350 degrees for 15 minutes. While crust bakes, combine granulated sugar, kiwi, eggs, lime juice, lime peel and baking powder. Pour over baked crust and return to oven. Bake for 25 minutes. Cool. Lightly sprinkle with remaining powdered sugar and cut into squares. As a variation, instead of puréeing all the kiwi, chop some for texture.

Makes 16.

CARMELITAS

1 cup plus 3 tablespoons flour

1 cup quick-cooking rolled oats

¾ cup brown sugar

¾ cup melted butter

½ teaspoon salt

½ teaspoon baking soda

6 ounces semisweet chocolate chips

½ cup chopped nuts

¾ cup butterscotch topping

Mix together 1 cup of the flour, oats, sugar, butter, salt and baking soda. Pat half of this mixture into a 9 x 12-inch pan. Bake at 350 degrees for 10 minutes. Remove from oven. Sprinkle with chocolate chips and nuts. Mix butterscotch topping with 3 tablespoons flour and warm slightly. Drizzle over nuts and chocolate chips. Cover with remaining oat/sugar mixture. Bake for 20 more minutes. Cool and cut into bars.

Makes 48.

MUD FLATS

12 ounces semisweet chocolate chips

½ cup butter

1 egg

½ cup superfine sugar

½ cup brown sugar

1 teaspoon vanilla

1 cup plus 1 tablespoon cake flour

½ teaspoon baking soda

½ teaspoon baking powder

½ teaspoon salt

¼ cup buttermilk

¼ cup chopped walnuts

The bigger the better!

In heavy pan melt 6 ounces of the chocolate chips and add butter, stirring constantly. In a bowl beat together egg, sugars and vanilla until creamy. Stir in chocolate mixture until well blended. Combine flour, baking soda, baking powder and salt. Alternately add dry ingredients and buttermilk to chocolate mixture. Stir in the remaining chocolate chips and nuts and chill. Drop by spoonfuls, any desired size, onto cookie sheets lined with parchment paper. Bake at 350 degrees for 8 to 10 minutes.

Makes 24 to 36.

SOUR CREAM BROWNIES

1 cup butter	$\frac{1}{2}$ teaspoon salt
4 tablespoons cocoa	$\frac{1}{2}$ cup sour cream
1 cup water	2 eggs
2 cups sugar	1 teaspoon baking soda
2 cups flour	

ICING

$\frac{1}{4}$ cup butter	$\frac{1}{2}$ teaspoon vanilla
2 tablespoons cocoa	$1\frac{3}{4}$ cups powdered sugar
3 tablespoons sour cream	

In a sauce pan melt butter, cocoa and water together. Remove from heat and set aside. In a mixing bowl combine sugar, flour and salt. Stir in cocoa mixture until well blended. Beat in sour cream, eggs and baking soda. Spread mixture into a 12 x 18-inch baking pan and bake at 400 degrees for 20 minutes. Remove from oven and cool slightly. Spread with icing while still warm. Cut into 2-inch squares.

Makes 54.

In a saucepan melt butter, cocoa and sour cream. Remove from heat and stir in vanilla. Slowly add powdered sugar, stirring until mixture is smooth.

CRÈME DE MENTHE SQUARES

$\frac{1}{2}$ cup cocoa	2 cups graham cracker crumbs
$1\frac{1}{4}$ cups butter	$\frac{1}{3}$ cup crème de menthe
$3\frac{1}{2}$ cups powdered sugar	$1\frac{1}{2}$ cups semisweet chocolate chips
1 egg	
1 teaspoon vanilla	

In a pan combine cocoa and $\frac{1}{2}$ cup of the butter. Heat and stir until blended. Remove from heat and add $\frac{1}{2}$ cup of the powdered sugar, egg and vanilla. Stir in cracker crumbs. Mix well and press into an ungreased 9 x 13-inch pan. Melt $\frac{1}{2}$ cup of the butter and add crème de menthe. Remove from heat. At low speed, beat in 3 cups powdered sugar. Carefully spread mixture over cracker crumb layer. Chill for 1 hour. Combine remaining $\frac{1}{4}$ cup butter with chocolate chips. Stir over low heat until melted. Spread over chilled mixture and chill again for 1 to 2 hours. Remove from refrigerator 15 minutes before cutting into squares.

Makes 48.

KAHLUA PECAN CAKES

$\frac{1}{2}$ cup unsalted butter	$\frac{3}{4}$ cup sugar
$\frac{1}{2}$ cup semisweet chocolate chips	1 teaspoon instant espresso powder
2 large eggs	$\frac{1}{2}$ cup chopped pecans
1 tablespoon Kahlua	24 large pecan halves
$\frac{1}{2}$ cup flour	

In a double boiler melt butter and chocolate chips. Stir until smooth. When cool, whisk in eggs, Kahlua, flour, sugar, espresso powder and chopped pecans. Line 24 mini muffin cups with paper muffin cups. Fill two-thirds full with batter. Place 1 pecan half in the center. Bake at 350 degrees for 20 minutes.

Makes 24.

GRAND MARNIER BARS

2 cups
unbleached flour

1/2 cup
powdered sugar

Grated rind of 1 orange

1 cup unsalted butter,
chilled and cut
into small pieces

2 tablespoons
shaved chocolate

4 large eggs

2 cups sugar

4 tablespoons
orange juice

2 tablespoons
Grand Marnier or
other orange liqueur

1 teaspoon
orange extract

1/4 cup flour

1/2 teaspoon
baking powder

Powdered sugar

In bowl of food processor fitted with steel blade combine flour, powdered sugar and orange rind. Process to combine well. Add butter and pulse until mixture resembles a coarse meal. Transfer mixture to an ungreased 10 x 14 x 2-inch baking pan. Spread to make a firm, even crust. This can be accomplished neatly by pressing the crumbs with a rectangular pan smaller than the one holding the crust. Bake for 20 to 25 minutes at 350 degrees until it just starts to brown. Remove to a rack and sprinkle shaved chocolate evenly over crust. Allow chocolate to melt. Beat eggs and sugar until light and fluffy. Lower speed, pour in orange juice, liqueur and extract. Beat until blended. Add flour and baking powder at low speed and mix until evenly blended. Pour mixture carefully over prepared crust. Return to oven for 20 to 25 minutes or until lightly browned and set. Check frequently during the first 15 minutes of baking so that you can puncture any large bubbles that may rise to the surface. While still hot, sprinkle generously with powdered sugar. Cool on a wire rack. Carefully cover cooled cookies with foil, pressing it to the outside edges of pan. Freeze for several hours. Cut around edges and into the desired number and shape of your choice. A Chinese cleaver is a good tool for cutting both the edges and bars. Keep in freezer or refrigerator until ready to serve.

Makes 32 bars.

FRANGELICO COOKIES

1 cup dark brown sugar

1 cup sugar

2 cups butter, softened

1 1/2 tablespoons
baking soda

1 tablespoon salt

4 eggs

1/4 cup
Frangelico liqueur

1/4 cup
Tia Maria liqueur

5 cups flour

32 ounces semisweet
chocolate chips

8 ounces
pecans, chopped

Cream together sugars, butter, baking soda and salt until light and creamy. Add eggs and liqueurs, a little at a time, until well blended. Add flour, chocolate chips and nuts. Mix until well blended. Drop by spoonfuls onto a greased cookie sheet and bake at 350 degrees for 10 to 15 minutes until golden brown.

Makes 48 large cookies.

GOBBLERS

1 cup butter, softened

2 cups brown sugar

2 cups sugar

6 eggs

1/2 tablespoon vanilla

1/2 tablespoon
corn syrup

1 1/2 pounds
peanut butter

4 teaspoons baking soda

9 cups quick-cooking
rolled oats

8 ounces semisweet
chocolate chips

8 ounces colored
M & M-type candies

To keep cookies soft, use real butter and don't forget the corn syrup.

Cream together butter and sugars. Beat in eggs, 1 at a time, until well blended. Mix in vanilla and corn syrup. Gradually add peanut butter, baking soda and oats. Stir in chocolate chips and M & M-type candies. Drop by large serving spoon or ice cream scoop, 6 cookies to a standard-sized cookie sheet. Bake at 350 degrees for 12 minutes. Do not overbake.

Makes 60.

CHOCOLATE PEARLS

1/2 cup butter, softened

1 pound
powdered sugar

2 teaspoons vanilla

2 cups chopped walnuts

1 cup coconut

6 ounces condensed milk

12 ounces semisweet
chocolate chips

1/4 pound paraffin

White chocolate, melted

Photograph, page 32.

Mix together butter, sugar, vanilla, walnuts, coconut and condensed milk. Chill for 1 hour. Remove from refrigerator and form into 1-inch sized balls. Chill again for 1 hour. Melt chocolate chips and paraffin together in a double boiler. One at a time, place a toothpick in each ball and dip into chocolate/paraffin mixture to coat. Using another toothpick as a pusher, place on chilled cookie sheet to set. Fill toothpick hole by swirling a small spoonful of chocolate over it. Drizzle white chocolate decoratively over the top.

Makes 36.

BLACK AND WHITE TRUFFLES

8 ounces dark
Belgian chocolate

1/4 cup hot
strong coffee

1 tablespoon
Grand Marnier,
whiskey or rum

White chocolate

Photograph, page 32.

In a double boiler melt dark chocolate over simmering hot water. While stirring, add coffee slowly. Mixture may turn grainy and thick. Don't worry! Add liquor and stir until blended. Remove from heat and set aside for 10 minutes. Form into balls or ovals. Place on a tray and chill for at least 1 hour. In a double boiler melt white chocolate very slowly over hot, but not boiling water. If chocolate gets too hot it will clump. If this happens, cool it slightly. When chocolate has melted, stick a toothpick into the center of the truffle and dip into the white chocolate. Place on a chilled cookie sheet to set. Decorate toothpick hole with extra white chocolate.

Makes 16.

HAPPY NEW YEAR COOKIES

8 ounces pitted dates

1/2 cup walnuts

2 teaspoons freshly grated orange rind

2 tablespoons Grand Marnier

36 wonton wrappers

4 cups oil

Powdered sugar

In a food processor chop dates and walnuts. Place in a bowl and stir together with orange rind and Grand Marnier. Knead mixture with fingers until it can be gathered into a ball. If mixture is too dry, moisten with more Grand Marnier. Fill each wonton wrapper with a small pinch of date/nut mixture, folding over each corner to make a square. Heat oil to 400 degrees in a wok. Fry 4 to 5 at a time, turning occasionally, for 2 to 3 minutes or until wontons are golden brown. Drain well and cool. Just before serving sprinkle with powdered sugar.

Note: The correct oil temperature is essential. If oil is too hot, foods will burn before they are cooked on the inside. If oil is too cold, foods will absorb the oil and become greasy. Check oil temperature by placing a wonton wrapper into the hot oil. If it sinks and rises immediately to the top, the oil is the right temperature.

Makes 36.

BUTTERSCOTCH CRUNCH ICE CREAM PIE

1 cup flour

1/4 cup quick-cooking rolled oats

1/4 cup brown sugar

1/2 cup butter

1/2 cup chopped nuts

12 ounces butterscotch or caramel sauce

1/2 gallon ice cream, mocha fudge, butterscotch ribbon, toffee or similar flavor, softened

Combine flour, oats and sugar. Cut in butter until mixture resembles coarse meal. Stir in nuts. Pat into a 9 x 13-inch pan and bake at 400 degrees for 15 minutes. Stir while warm to crumble. Cool. Spread half of the crumbs into a buttered 9-inch springform pan. Drizzle half of the caramel sauce over crumbs. Add the softened ice cream. Drizzle with remaining sauce and crumbs. Freeze until firm.

Serves 16.

FRESH LEMON ICE CREAM

1 cup heavy cream

1 egg

1 1/2 cups sugar

1/3 cup lemon juice

2 teaspoons grated lemon rind

Pinch of salt

1 1/3 cups milk

Raspberry purée, page 249

Combine cream and egg. Whip until thickened. Gradually add sugar and beat until mixture is almost stiff. Beat in lemon juice, rind, and salt. Stir in milk. Pour into an 8-inch square dish and freeze for 5 hours. Stir occasionally during the first hour. Serve in chilled dishes with raspberry purée, if desired.

Serves 6.

CARAMEL APPLE CAKE

1½ cups butter, softened

2 cups sugar

1 cup oil

3 eggs

2 teaspoons vanilla

3 cups flour

1 teaspoon baking soda

1 teaspoon salt

1 cup chopped pecans

4 cups peeled, cored and chopped apples, preferably Granny Smith

1 cup brown sugar

⅓ cup heavy cream

Cream ½ cup of the butter with sugar, oil and eggs. Add vanilla. Sift together flour, soda and salt. Fold into egg mixture. Add the pecans and apples. Spread mixture into a 9 x 13-inch pan. Bake at 350 degrees for 45 minutes. Combine the brown sugar, remaining 1 cup butter and cream in a small saucepan. Bring to a boil and cook 2 to 3 minutes, stirring constantly. Pierce the top of the hot cake with a fork and pour caramel sauce over all. Cool in pan.

Serves 12.

BRANDY APPLE SOUSED CAKE

4 apples, peeled, cored and finely chopped

½ cup brandy

2 eggs

2 cups sugar

½ cup oil

2 cups flour

2 teaspoons baking soda

2 teaspoons cinnamon

1 teaspoon nutmeg

¼ teaspoon cloves

1 teaspoon salt

1 cup chopped pecans or walnuts

Combine apples and brandy. Beat eggs, sugar and oil together until light and fluffy. Sift together flour, soda, spices and salt. Slowly add egg mixture to apple/brandy mixture. Stir in chopped nuts. Fold flour mixture lightly into batter. Divide between 3 buttered and floured 8-inch round pans. Bake at 350 degrees for 25 to 30 minutes. Remove from oven and cool.

Serves 8 to 12.

FROSTING

8 ounces cream cheese, softened

½ cup butter, softened

2 cups powdered sugar

2 teaspoons vanilla

1 cup chopped walnuts or pecans

Combine cream cheese and butter in a mixer until very creamy. While mixer is running slowly add the powdered sugar. When mixture looks like whipped cream, remove bowl from mixer and gently fold in, by hand, vanilla and nuts. Assemble cake by placing frosting between each layer and frosting the outside.

FRESH BERRIES WITH GRAND MARNIER SAUCE

2 cups sliced strawberries or whole raspberries, or a combination

1/2 cup plus 3 tablespoons sugar

5 egg yolks

1/4 cup plus 1 tablespoon Grand Marnier

1 cup whipping cream

1 teaspoon grated orange rind

In a small bowl toss berries with 1 tablespoon of the sugar. Set aside. In the top of a double boiler beat egg yolks and 1/2 cup of the sugar. Place over simmering water, stirring constantly, until sauce thickens. Add 1/4 cup of the Grand Marnier. Remove from heat and chill until cool. Whip cream until stiff. Add remaining 2 tablespoons of sugar. Fold yolk mixture and cream mixture together. Add remaining 1 tablespoon of Grand Marnier and orange rind. Spoon berries into serving bowls. Top with sauce and serve.

Serves 4.

CRANBERRY DELIGHT

2 cups fresh cranberries

1 1/2 cups sugar

1/2 cup chopped pecans

2 eggs

1 cup flour

Salt

1/4 cup shortening

1/2 cup melted butter

Blueberries may be substituted when cranberries are not available.

Mix together cranberries, 1/2 cup of the sugar and pecans. Pour into a greased 9-inch pie plate or square cake pan. Beat eggs until thick. Gradually add 1 cup sugar and beat well. Blend in flour and salt. Stir in shortening and butter. Pour over cranberry mixture. Bake at 350 degrees for 50 minutes until golden brown. Serve warm with whipped cream or softened ice cream.

Serves 8.

CANTALOUPE AND STRAWBERRIES WITH BROWN SUGAR CREAM

1 basket of strawberries

1 cantaloupe, seeded, peeled and cubed

2 cups sour cream

1/2 cup brown sugar

3 teaspoons triple sec

3 teaspoons vanilla

Fresh mint leaves for garnish

Combine sour cream, brown sugar, triple sec and vanilla in a bowl. Whisk until smooth and chill. Arrange strawberries and cantaloupe on a platter around the dipping sauce. Garnish with fresh mint leaves.

Serves 8.

MERINGUES WITH PASTRY CREAM AND FRESH FRUIT

4 large egg whites	Pastry cream, page 239
1/4 teaspoon cream of tartar	1 cup raspberries
Pinch of salt	1 cup blueberries
2/3 cup sugar	1 cup sliced strawberries
1 1/2 teaspoons vanilla	Raspberry purée, page 249
1/3 cup sugar	Apricot nappage, page 249

Photograph, page 32.

Using a 3-inch round cookie cutter, trace 10 to 12 circles on parchment paper. Place paper on a cookie sheet. Beat the egg whites slowly for 1 minute, until foaming. Beat in cream of tartar and salt. Gradually increase speed and beat until egg whites form soft peaks. Continue to beat while gradually adding the sugar. Keep beating until egg whites are stiff and shiny. Beat in the vanilla. Using a pastry bag with a toothed opening of 1/8 inch, pipe in circle outlines on baking sheet. Form 3 rings around the border of each, 1 on top of the other. Bake 1 1/2 to 2 hours at 200 degrees. Meringues should be a light ivory color. Adjust temperature to keep from browning. Baked and cooled meringues can be frozen in airtight containers. Fill meringues with pastry cream, frozen yogurt or ice cream. Combine fruit and spoon over the top. Ladle the raspberry purée on serving plates and place merringues on top. Fruit may be glazed with an apricot nappage.

Serves 10 to 12.

RASPBERRY WALNUT CHEESECAKE

CRUST

1 cup flour	1/2 cup sugar
1 cup walnuts	1/2 cup butter, chilled and cut into 1/2-inch slices

In food processor, mix flour, walnuts and sugar until walnuts are finely ground. Add butter and process until mixture forms a ball. Press into a 9-inch springform pan, making sides approximately 2 inches high.

FILLING

3 eggs	Juice of 1 lemon
1 pound cream cheese, softened	1 tablespoon vanilla
1/2 cup sugar	1/4 cup raspberry preserves

Mix eggs, cream cheese, sugar, lemon juice, vanilla and preserves together in a food processor. Pulse until mixture is smooth and creamy. Pour into crust. Bake at 350 degrees for 45 minutes. Set aside to cool.

TOPPING

3/4 cup sour cream	2 teaspoons vanilla
1/4 cup sugar	

While cheesecake is cooling, mix sour cream with sugar and vanilla. Spoon onto center of cooled cheesecake and return to oven for 10 minutes. Cool. Chill at least 3 hours, preferably overnight.

Serves 10 to 12.

PIÑA COLADA CHEESECAKE

CRUST

2 cups graham cracker crumbs	3 tablespoons sugar
	$^1/_3$ cup melted butter
$^1/_2$ cup finely chopped shredded coconut	

Combine graham cracker crumbs, coconut and sugar. Stir in the butter until moistened. Press crumbs on bottom and half-way up the sides of a 10-inch springform pan. Set aside.

FILLING

6 ounces crushed pineapple with heavy syrup	5 eggs
	2 egg yolks
2$^1/_2$ pounds cream cheese, softened	Rind of 1 lemon, grated
1$^1/_2$ cups sugar	$^1/_2$ cup cream of coconut
$^1/_3$ cup cornstarch	
	$^1/_3$ cup dark rum

Drain pineapple, reserving liquid. Beat cream cheese and sugar in mixing bowl until light and fluffy, about 10 minutes. Add cornstarch and beat in eggs and egg yolks, 1 at a time, until well blended. Mix in lemon rind, cream of coconut and rum. Stir in $^1/_2$ of the drained pineapple, reserving remaining for topping. Pour into prepared crust. Place in a pan of hot water and bake at 350 degrees for 1 hour and 15 minutes. Cool.

TOPPING

1 tablespoon cornstarch	$^1/_2$ cup coarsely chopped pecans
$^1/_4$ cup sugar	
	$^1/_2$ cup shredded coconut, toasted
$^1/_4$ cup dark rum	

Blend reserved pineapple juice and cornstarch in a medium saucepan until smooth. Stir in reserved crushed pineapple, sugar and rum. Bring to a boil, stirring constantly, until clear and thickened. Remove from heat and cool until warm to the touch. Spread over cake, sprinkle with nuts and coconut. Chill thoroughly.

Serves 12.

CHEESECAKE SQUARES

CRUST

$^3/_4$ cup butter, softened	$^1/_2$ cup light brown sugar
1$^1/_4$ cups flour	1$^1/_2$ cups ground pecan halves

Beat butter until creamy. Combine flour, brown sugar and pecans and add to butter. Mix to blend well. Dough should hold its shape. Press dough into the bottom only of a 10 x 15-inch jelly roll pan. Bake for 10 minutes at 350 degrees. Cool.

FILLING

1$^1/_2$ pounds cream cheese, softened	3 large eggs
	2 cups sour cream
1$^1/_2$ cups sugar	
3 teaspoons vanilla	Blueberries, raspberries or strawberry slices for garnish
Zest of 1 medium orange	

Beat cream cheese, 1$^1/_4$ cups of the sugar, 2 teaspoons of the vanilla and orange zest until well blended. Beat in eggs, 1 at a time, until mixture is smooth. Spread filling over crust. Bake for 20 minutes at 350 degrees. Top will be set but center will still be creamy. Cool on wire rack for 5 minutes. Stir together sour cream with remaining $^1/_4$ cup sugar and 1 teaspoon vanilla. Spread mixture carefully and evenly over cheesecake with rubber spatula. Bake 3 minutes longer. Cool on wire rack. Chill before serving. Cut into bite-sized pieces. Decorate each piece with a berry and serve in tiny paper muffin cups.

Makes 150 1-inch squares.

LEMON CHEESECAKE WITH STRAWBERRIES

CRUST

2 cups flour	1 cup unsalted butter
$^1/_2$ cup sugar	2 large egg yolks, beaten
2 tablespoons grated lemon rind	$^1/_2$ teaspoon vanilla

Combine flour, sugar and lemon rind in a bowl. Blend in butter until the mixture resembles coarse meal. Add the egg yolks and vanilla. Combine the mixture to form a dough. Remove the ring from a 10-inch springform pan. Press $^1/_3$ of the dough onto the bottom and bake at 400 degrees for 8 minutes. Cool on a rack. Return the ring to the pan and pat the remaining dough onto the sides of the pan, at least 2 inches high.

FILLING

24 ounces cream cheese, softened	1 teaspoon salt
	4 large eggs
$1^3/_4$ cups sugar	2 large egg yolks
1 teaspoon grated lemon rind	$^1/_4$ cup heavy cream
$^1/_2$ teaspoon vanilla	1 basket strawberries, halved, for garnish
3 tablespoons flour	

Beat the cream cheese with an electric mixer until smooth. Beat in sugar, lemon rind and vanilla. Beat in flour, salt and 4 eggs. Add the egg yolks, 1 at a time. Add cream and mix until smooth. Pour the filling into the prepared pan and place on a baking sheet. Bake at 425 degrees for 12 minutes. Reduce the heat to 300 degrees and continue baking for 60 minutes. Cheesecake will not be set. Cool on a wire rack. Before serving, garnish with fresh strawberry halves.

Serves 12.

WHITE CHOCOLATE CHEESECAKE

CRUST

$^1/_2$ cup unsalted butter, chilled and cut into 4 pieces	1 cup flour
	1 egg, beaten
1 cup sugar	

Photograph, page 2.

Place butter, sugar and flour in a food processor. Using the pulse switch, mix until the consistency of coarse meal. Add the egg and pulse again until a ball has formed. Chill for 1 hour. When cold, roll out a circle large enough to line the bottom of a small 6 to 7-inch springform pan with 4 inch sides. Prick the dough with a fork and bake at 350 degrees for 5 minutes. Remove and cool. Roll out the remaining dough and line the sides of the pan.

FILLING

24 ounces cream cheese	8 ounces white chocolate
1 cup sour cream	2 tablespoons heavy cream
1 cup sugar	Whole strawberries for garnish
$^1/_4$ cup flour	
1 teaspoon vanilla	Apricot nappage, page 249
2 eggs	

In a food processor place the cream cheese, sour cream, sugar, flour and vanilla. Purée until smooth, add eggs and purée once more. Slowly melt the white chocolate in a double boiler. When melted, stir in cream. With the food processor on, pour in the white chocolate mixture and purée until smooth. Pour the cheese mixture into the springform pan and bake at 350 degrees for 35 minutes. When the top becomes level the cheesecake is done. Turn off the oven and leave the cheesecake in the oven to cool, approximately 1 hour. Do not move or work with the cake until completely cooled. Remove the top layer of skin that has formed during baking. Arrange hulled strawberries over the top and glaze with an apricot nappage.

Serves 8.

SILK CHOCOLATE MOUSSE TORTE

CRUST

1½ cups crushed chocolate wafers	1 cup finely chopped walnuts
½ cup melted unsalted butter	

Try a minty variation by adding 3 tablespoons crème de menthe.

Mix wafers, butter and walnuts together and press into the bottom and up sides of a 9-inch pie pan or springform pan. Chill 1 hour or quick freeze for 20 minutes to set.

FILLING

1 cup butter, softened	2 teaspoons vanilla
1½ cups sugar	4 eggs
3 ounces unsweetened chocolate, melted and cooled	Sweetened whipped cream

Beat butter until smooth. Gradually beat in sugar until mixture is light and fluffy. Mix in chocolate and vanilla until mixture has a uniform color. Beat in eggs, 1 at a time, beating 3 to 5 minutes after each and scraping sides of bowl often. Beating every time is important. Pour mixture into the prepared pan and chill at least 6 hours, preferably longer. Run a sharp knife between pan and crust for easy removal. Garnish with sweetened whipped cream.

Serves 8 to 10.

KEY LIME PIE

1½ cups crushed chocolate wafers	¾ cup plus 2 tablespoons key lime juice
⅓ cup melted butter	4 teaspoons grated lime rind
3 eggs yolks	
2¼ cups condensed milk	

Mix chocolate wafers and butter and pat into a 9 or 10-inch pie plate. Freeze while preparing filling. In a medium bowl, beat the egg yolks until thick. Using a whisk, blend in condensed milk. Add the lime juice and rind. Mix well. Pour into prepared pie shell.

MERINGUE

3 egg whites	6 tablespoons sugar
1 teaspoon key lime juice	

Beat the egg whites until frothy. Add lime juice and beat until whites hold their shape. Add the sugar gradually, and beat until stiff. Spread mounds of meringue on top of pie, making sure meringue extends to all edges. Bake at 300 degrees for 12 to 15 minutes until golden. Cool and chill 4 to 5 hours.

Serves 8.

CHOCOLATE PEANUT BUTTER TORTE

CRUST

1 cup crushed chocolate wafers	1/4 cup melted butter
1/4 cup sugar	

Combine wafers, sugar and butter. Press into the bottom and halfway up sides of a 9-inch springform pan.

FILLING

2 cups creamy peanut butter	1 1/2 cups heavy cream
2 cups sugar	8 ounces semisweet chocolate
16 ounces cream cheese, softened	6 tablespoons hot coffee
2 tablespoons melted butter	Pecan or walnut halves for garnish
2 teaspoons vanilla	

Beat peanut butter, sugar, cream cheese, butter and vanilla with mixer until creamy. Whip heavy cream until soft peaks form and fold into peanut butter mixture. Spoon into crust and chill at least 6 hours. Melt chocolate and coffee in a double boiler over simmering water until chocolate is melted. Quickly spread on top of peanut butter filling. Place pecan or walnut halves in semi-circle around outer edge of pan. Chill again until firm. Run a thin hot knife between pan and torte to loosen. Release sides of pan and cut into thin slices. May be prepared 3 days in advance.

Serves 12.

CHOCOLATE ALMOND RUM TORTE

1 3/4 cups whole blanched almonds, toasted	3/4 cup butter, softened
1/2 cup plus 2 tablespoons sugar	5 eggs, separated
2 tablespoons flour	1 cup semisweet chocolate chips, melted
	1/4 cup rum

Reserve 1/4 cup whole almonds for garnish. Finely grind remaining 1 1/2 cups almonds in small batches in a blender or food processor. Combine ground almonds, 2 tablespoons of the sugar and flour. Set aside. In a large bowl cream butter. Add remaining 1/2 cup sugar and beat well. Beat in egg yolks, 1 at a time. Stir in chocolate and rum. Add ground almond mixture and blend. Beat egg whites until stiff but not dry and fold into almond mixture. Spread evenly into a greased and floured 9-inch springform pan. Bake at 350 degrees for 35 to 40 minutes or until toothpick inserted in center comes out clean. Run sharp knife around edge. Cool on wire rack for 10 minutes. Remove side of pan and cool completely.

CHOCOLATE RUM GLAZE

1/4 cup powdered sugar	1 tablespoon milk
1/2 cup semisweet chocolate chips, melted	1 tablespoon rum
3 tablespoons melted butter	

Beat together powdered sugar, chocolate, butter, milk and rum until smooth, adding more milk if necessary. Glaze when cake has cooled completely and garnish with reserved, whole almonds.

Serves 12.

WALNUT TORTE

6 eggs, separated

1 cup plus 1 tablespoon sugar

2 cups ground walnuts

1½ teaspoons vanilla

½ teaspoon salt

1 cup heavy cream

½ cup raspberry jam

Chopped walnuts for garnish

Beat egg yolks with 1 of the cup sugar. Blend in ground walnuts. Add 1 teaspoon of the vanilla and salt. Beat egg whites until stiff and fold into walnut mixture. Butter and flour 2 8-inch cake pans. Place an 8-inch parchment circle on the bottom of each. Pour batter into pans and bake at 350 degrees for 30 to 35 minutes. Invert pans on wire racks to cool. Whip cream with remaining ½ teaspoon vanilla and 1 tablespoon sugar. Spread 1 torte layer with jam and half of whipped cream. Place second layer on top and spread with remaining whipped cream. Sprinkle with chopped nuts.

Serves 10 to 12.

CHOCOLATE FUDGE TERRINE WITH CRÈME ANGLAISE AND RASPBERRY PURÉE

1⅓ pounds semisweet chocolate

6 eggs yolks

1 cup butter, softened

9 egg whites, room temperature

½ cup sugar

1 cup chopped pecans

Crème anglaise, page 249

Raspberry purée, page 249

Butter a 9 x 5-inch loaf pan. Over gently simmering water melt chocolate in the top of a double boiler until smooth. Transfer to a bowl and cool completely. Whisk egg yolks in the top of double boiler over gently boiling water until thick and pale, about 2 minutes. Remove from heat and whisk until completely cool. Using an electric mixer, beat butter in a large bowl until fluffy. Fold in melted chocolate, then egg yolks. Remove bowl from mixer, set aside and wash beaters. Using a clean bowl and beaters beat egg whites until soft peaks form. Add sugar, 1 tablespoon at a time. Beat until whites are stiff and shiny. Fold meringue into chocolate mixture. Pour into prepared pan. Sprinkle with pecans and press in lightly. Cover and chill until set, about 3 hours. Before serving, let soften slightly at room temperature. Cut terrine into thin slices. Serve with crème anglaise and raspberry purée.

Serves 8.

BOYSENBERRY GLAZED PIE

9-inch baked pie shell

1 quart or more fresh boysenberries

½ to 1 cup sugar

3 tablespoons cornstarch

Dash of salt

1 tablespoon butter

1 tablespoon lemon juice

Clean berries. Set some aside. Mash enough berries in food processor to make 2 cups of fruit. Strain through fine strainer or cheesecloth, reserving juice. Blend ½ to 1 cup of sugar, cornstarch and salt together. Add berry juice. Cook 15 minutes until mixture thickens, stirring constantly. Add butter and lemon juice. Cool. Spread thin layer of cooled filling in bottom of pie crust. Line with whole berries. Cover berries with filling. Repeat layers once more. Chill. Remove from refrigerator 15 minutes before serving.

Serves 6.

KAHLUA PECAN PIE

Pastry crust for
a 9-inch pie

1/4 cup butter, softened

3/4 cup sugar

1 teaspoon vanilla

2 tablespoons flour

3 eggs

1/2 cup Kahlua

1/2 cup dark corn syrup

3/4 cup evaporated milk

1 cup whole or
chopped pecans

1/2 cup heavy cream,
whipped, or ice cream

Pecan halves for garnish

Cream together butter, sugar, vanilla, and flour. Mix well. Beat in eggs, 1 at a time. Stir in Kahlua, corn syrup, evaporated milk and pecans. Mix well. Pour into prepared crust. Bake at 400 degrees for 10 minutes. Reduce heat to 325 and bake an additional 40 minutes, until firm. Remove and chill. To serve, top with whipped cream or ice cream and garnish with pecan halves.

Serves 6 to 8.

ALMOND TOFFEE TART

CRUST

2 cups flour

3 tablespoons sugar

3/4 cup butter

2 egg yolks

FILLING

1 1/2 cups
heavy cream

1 1/2 cups sugar

1/2 teaspoon
grated orange rind

1/4 teaspoon salt

2 cups sliced almonds

1/4 teaspoon
almond extract

Mix flour and sugar together. Cut in butter. Blend until mixture resembles coarse meal. Add egg yolks and mix until a dough forms a ball. Press evenly over the bottom and sides of an 11 or 12-inch fluted tart pan with removable bottom. Bake at 325 degrees for 10 minutes.

In a 2 or 3-quart saucepan, combine cream, sugar, orange rind and salt. Bring to a boil over high heat, stirring occasionally. Reduce heat to medium and cook sauce for 5 minutes, stirring often. Remove from heat and stir in almonds and almond extract. Pour the mixture over pastry. Bake a 12-inch tart at 375 degrees for 35 minutes or an 11-inch tart for 40 minutes, until lightly browned. Cool on a wire rack until warm to the touch. Slide a slender knife between pan and tart and remove pan.

Serves 12 to 18.

MEDITTERANEAN STRUDEL

1 pound phyllo dough

1/2 to 3/4 cup melted
unsalted butter

12 1/2 ounces
poppy seed filling,
found at specialty
grocery stores

In a buttered 9 x 13-inch baking dish, layer 6 phyllo sheets, brushing between each layer with melted butter. Spoon on poppy seed filling and spread it evenly. Layer 4 phyllo sheets, brushing between each layer with more melted butter. Spread Ricotta Cheese Filling over phyllo. Layer 4 more phyllo sheets, brushing between each with melted butter. Spread Apple Filling over phyllo. Cover with remaining phyllo sheets, brushing between each layer with melted butter, including the top sheet. Bake at 375 degrees for 1 hour or until golden brown. Cool for 10 minutes before cutting. Serve warm or cold.

Serves 12.

RICOTTA CHEESE FILLING

1 pint ricotta cheese

1 egg

1/4 cup sugar

Dash of nutmeg

1/2 teaspoon vanilla

1/2 cup golden raisins

1/2 cup coarsely
chopped walnuts

Stir cheese until smooth. Stir in egg, sugar, nutmeg and vanilla until well blended. Fold in raisins and nuts.

APPLE FILLING

6 apples, cored,
peeled and chopped

1/2 cup dry bread
crumbs or graham
cracker crumbs

1/2 cup sugar

2 teaspoons cinnamon

1/4 teaspoon nutmeg

1/4 teaspoon
ground cloves

Combine all ingredients in a large bowl.

ANGELA PIA

3 eggs, separated

1/2 cup sugar

2 tablespoons brandy

2 tablespoons rum

1 cup heavy cream

1 teaspoon vanilla

1 envelope
unflavored gelatin

Beat egg yolks until light lemon-colored. Add sugar gradually and beat until creamy. Add brandy and rum. Beat egg whites until stiff but not dry. Whip cream until stiff enough to stand in firm peaks. Add vanilla. Soften gelatin in 1/4 cup cold water for 5 minutes. Stir over hot water until gelatin dissolves completely. Stir thoroughly into egg yolk mixture. Fold in gently beaten egg whites and whipped cream. Spoon into cocktail glasses or small dessert bowls and chill until firm.

Serves 6.

CROQUEMBOUCHE

6 ounces shortcrust
pastry, page 238

16 large cream puffs,
page 238

4 cups chocolate pastry
cream, page 239

1¹/₂ cups raspberry
purée, page 249

2 cups sugar

¹/₂ cup water

1 basket raspberries

Chocolate shavings

Photograph, page 24. Technique, page 239.

Roll out the shortcrust pastry into a 10-inch circle, prick with a fork and bake in a preheated oven at 400 degrees for 5 minutes or until lightly browned. Cool. Meanwhile, fill the cream puffs with the chocolate pastry cream by making a hole in the bottom with a knife and, using an 18-inch pastry bag with small tip, fill each. To caramelize the sugar, place the sugar and water in a heavy skillet, and cook over low heat until a syrup is formed. Boil the syrup carefully. Remove from heat as soon as the syrup turns light brown. It will continue to cook as the croquembouche is being assembled. With a spoon lightly pour a little caramelized sugar on the shortcrust pastry and quickly place the cream puffs over the whole pastry in a circular pattern. Using the sugar as glue, quickly assemble the cream puffs into a pyramid. Once stacked, the caramelized sugar will be cooled enough to spin with an old fork. Hold the pan close to the croquembouche and, with the prongs of the fork, pull the sugar from the pan up and over the croquembouche and let it fall over the pyramid to form strands of sugar. Continue this procedure until a net of spun sugar covers all. If the sugar hardens before completion or if there is not enough caramelized sugar, repeat the procedure. Carefully place the croquembouche on a serving platter and garnish with fresh raspberries and chocolate shavings. To serve, break apart and divide among plates which contain raspberry purée.

Serves 8.

CAPPUCCINO TORTE

¹/₄ cup instant
coffee powder

1 tablespoon sugar

¹/₄ cup hot water

1¹/₂ pounds sweet
dark chocolate, chopped

1 pound unsalted
butter, softened

1 tablespoon cornstarch

8 eggs, separated

Pinch of salt

2 cups heavy cream

1 teaspoon vanilla

¹/₃ cup powdered sugar

12 candy coffee beans

Instant coffee powder
for garnish

Line a 9-inch springform pan with 2 crossing strips of foil. Press them firmly and neatly against the side and bottom of the pan. Dissolve coffee powder and sugar in water. Place chocolate in the upper pan of a double boiler and pour the prepared coffee over it. Melt chocolate, without stirring, over barely simmering water. In a mixing bowl cream butter with cornstarch. Add egg yolks and mix thoroughly. Add chocolate mixture and blend well. In another bowl whip egg whites and salt until soft peaks form and fold them into the chocolate mixture. Pour batter into the prepared pan and bake in a preheated 350-degree oven for 15 minutes. Turn off the oven, open door and cool cake in the oven. Chill. Whip the cream with vanilla and sugar. Unmold torte and invert on a serving dish. Frost with whipped cream, reserving 1 cup to make 12 rosettes around the cake. Top each rosette with a coffee bean. Sprinkle coffee powder over top.

Serves 12.

BAVARIAN APPLE TORTE

CRUST

¹/₂ cup butter	¹/₃ cup sugar
1 cup flour	¹/₄ teaspoon vanilla

FILLING

16 ounces cream cheese, softened	2 or 3 medium apples, peeled, cored and thinly sliced
³/₄ cup sugar	¹/₂ teaspoon cinnamon
2 large eggs	
1¹/₄ teaspoons vanilla	

This is best made a day ahead.

Combine butter, flour, sugar and vanilla in a food processor until it forms a ball. A few drops of water may be added. Remove and pat into the bottom and up the sides of a 9 or 10-inch springform pan. Bake at 350 degrees for 5 minutes. Remove and set aside to cool.

Mix cream cheese, ¹/₂ cup of the sugar, eggs and 1 teaspoon of the vanilla in food processor until smooth. Pour batter into cooled crust. Coat apples with remaining ¹/₄ cup of the sugar, cinnamon and ¹/₄ teaspoon of the vanilla. Layer in a circular pattern on top of cheesecake mixture. Apples may sink into filling. Bake at 450 degrees for 15 minutes. Reduce heat to 350 degrees and bake an additional 45 minutes. Remove from oven and cool. Chill for 4 to 6 hours before serving.

Serves 8 to 10.

RASPBERRY KIWI TART

CRUST

1¹/₂ cups flour	1 egg yolk
1 cup finely chopped almonds	¹/₂ teaspoon vanilla
3 tablespoons sugar	3 to 4 tablespoons ice water
¹/₂ cup butter, chilled and cut into small pieces	

Prepare crust by mixing flour, almonds and sugar in food processor. Blend well. Add butter, egg yolk and vanilla. Add water 1 tablespoon at a time, until dough sticks together. Chill. Press into an ungreased 13-inch tart pan. Bake at 350 degrees until crust begins to brown, about 20 minutes. Cool on wire rack. Remove from pan.

FILLING

¹/₄ cup sugar	2 tablespoons almond liqueur
3 tablespoons flour	¹/₂ cup heavy cream
2 envelopes unflavored gelatin	3 kiwis, peeled and sliced
¹/₄ teaspoon salt	1 cup fresh raspberries
2 eggs	10 ounces red currant jelly
1 egg yolk	2 tablespoons raspberry brandy
1¹/₂ cups milk	

Combine and mix sugar, flour, 1 envelope of the gelatin and salt in a 2-quart saucepan. Stir well. Beat eggs, egg yolk and milk together and stir into sugar mixture. Cook on low heat, stirring for 15 minutes, until gelatin dissolves and custard thickens to coat a spoon. Do not boil. Remove from heat and stir in almond liqueur. Chill until mixture mounds when dropped from a spoon. Beat cream until soft peaks form and fold into custard. Spread on top of crust. Chill for 1 hour. Arrange fruit on top of custard mixture, kiwis around the outside and raspberries in the middle. To make glaze, heat jelly, brandy and 1 envelope of the gelatin. Cook for 2 to 3 minutes or until thickened. Brush over top of dessert. Chill until serving.

Serves 8 to 10.

CRANBERRY TARTS

CRUST

5 tablespoons butter, softened	1 teaspoon vanilla
$^1/_2$ cup sugar	$1^1/_4$ cups flour
1 egg	3 ounces semisweet chocolate, melted in double boiler

With a wooden spoon, stir butter until creamy. Gradually beat in sugar. Stir in egg and vanilla. Add flour and blend until pastry forms a smooth ball. Cover and let stand for 20 to 30 minutes. On a lightly floured surface, knead for 1 minute. Roll out dough until $^1/_8$ inch thick. Cut to fit 6 4-inch tart pans. Press dough firmly against sides but do not stretch. Trim extra pastry from edges of tart pans. Bake at 350 degrees for 12 to 15 minutes or until lightly browned. Cool completely. Paint the bottom and sides of each tart shell with melted chocolate. Cool for 10 minutes or until hardened.

CRANBERRIES

2 cups cranberries, stems removed	$^1/_4$ cup orange juice
1 cup sugar	2 tablespoons grated orange rind

Combine all ingredients in a saucepan and cook until cranberries begin to pop. Chill until set.

FILLING

8 ounces cream cheese, softened	1 tablespoon Grand Marnier
3 tablespoons sugar	$^1/_2$ teaspoon vanilla

Combine all ingredients until blended. To assemble tarts place cream cheese filling on top of chocolate, and place cranberries on top of cream cheese filling. Chill before serving.

Makes 6 4-inch or 24 2-inch tarts.

LUSCIOUS LEMON TARTS

CRUST

5 tablespoons butter, softened	$1^1/_4$ cups flour
$^1/_2$ cup sugar	3 ounces semisweet chocolate, melted in double boiler
1 egg	
1 teaspoon vanilla	

Follow directions as given for Cranberry Tarts.

FILLING

1 cup sugar	2 eggs, beaten
$^1/_4$ cup butter	Whipped cream for garnish
$^1/_2$ cup lemon juice	Sugared fruit slices for garnish
1 tablespoon grated lemon rind	

Combine sugar, butter, lemon juice, lemon rind and eggs. Cook in double boiler over simmering water until mixture thickens. Prepare pastry shells as directed above. Using a baster, take filling from pan and squeeze into tart shells. Chill. Garnish with whipped cream and sugared fruit slice.

Makes 6 4-inch or 24 2-inch tarts.

CHOCOLATE MOUSSE BLANC ET NOIR

6 ounces sweet
chocolate, chopped

2 tablespoons
unsalted butter

4 egg yolks

1 cup sugar

2 ounces white
chocolate, chopped

1 quart heavy cream

Raspberry purée,
page 249

Place chopped sweet chocolate and butter in double boiler over simmering water until chocolate is completely melted and nicely blended. Beat egg yolks and sugar in bowl until thickened. Add the melted chocolate and stir in the chopped white chocolate. Whip the cream to form soft peaks. Fold the whipped cream into the chocolate mixture. Pour mixture into a 3-quart mold, cake or tart pan. Chill until set. Unmold and serve alone or with raspberry purée. As a variation, mousse may be piped into small, precooked tart shells.

Serves 10 to 12.

BLUEBERRY PUDDING

8 ounces puff pastry,
page 234

2 pints fresh blueberries,
rinsed and drained

$^3/_4$ cup sourdough bread,
cut into cubes no larger
than blueberries

4 eggs

1 teaspoon vanilla

1 teaspoon cinnamon

1 cup sugar

1 cup milk

Apricot nappage,
page 249

Roll out puff pastry on a lightly floured surface into a 14-inch circle, about $^1/_{16}$ inch thick. Place the pastry over a 10 x 2$^1/_2$-inch tart pan. Press to the edge of the tart pan. Line pan with parchment paper or aluminum foil and fill with pie weights. Bake in a preheated oven at 350 degrees for 10 minutes and remove the weights and paper. Bake again until slightly dry but not browned, about 5 minutes. Cool. It is important that there are not any holes in the crust because you will be pouring a custard into the pan. If there are some minor holes, patch them with raw dough left over from the scraps. Leave the crust in the tart base as you will be baking it 1 more time. Place the blueberries in a bowl and add the cubed bread. Toss them together so they are evenly mixed. Place the berries in the precooked tart shell. In a bowl, beat the eggs with the vanilla, cinnamon, and sugar. Bring the milk to a boil and add to the egg mixture. Stir until completely mixed. Pour the custard over the berries. Bake at 350 degrees for 45 minutes. When the custard begins to rise and there is no longer any raw custard visible, the blueberry pudding is done. Leave in the tart base until cool enough to handle. Remove from base by running a knife around the edge of the pan. From the bottom, gently push the base up through the top with even pressure. Glaze with an apricot nappage or serve with ice cream.

Serves 10.

RASPBERRY GRAND MARNIER SOUFFLÉ

1 teaspoon butter	1 cup egg whites
3 tablespoons sugar	1 cup fresh raspberries
6 ounces pastry cream, page 239	2 cups crème anglaise, page 249
4 tablespoons Grand Marnier	1 tablespoon powdered sugar
1 tablespoon chopped orange zest	Fresh orange zest for garnish

Photograph, page 22. Technique, page 241.

Preheat oven to 350 degrees. Rub the insides and outer rims of 2 soufflé cups, 3$\frac{1}{2}$ inches across by 2 inches deep, with butter and pour sugar in 1. While turning 1 cup, gradually pour the sugar into the other cup making sure that the edges and rim are coated with sugar. Set aside while preparing the soufflé mixture. In a bowl, mix thoroughly the pastry cream, 2 tablespoons of the Grand Marnier and orange zest. This mixture is the soufflé base. In another bowl beat the egg whites with a whisk until soft peaks form. Add half the beaten egg whites to the base and mix until smooth. With a spatula gently fold in the remaining egg whites until smooth once again. Fill the soufflé cups half way and place 10 raspberries in each. Set aside the remaining raspberries. Fill the cups to the top with the remaining soufflé batter and bake for 25 minutes or until golden brown with a level top. Meanwhile in a small skillet heat the crème anglaise carefully and add the remaining raspberries, saving 2 for garnish. Add 2 tablespoons of the Grand Marnier and pour into a sauce boat or creamer. When the soufflés are done carefully remove from oven and sprinkle with the powdered sugar. Top with a raspberry and fresh orange zest and serve immediately. Once presented remove the tops of the soufflés and pour in the crème anglaise sauce.

Serves 2.

ORANGE MOUSSE

1 envelope unflavored gelatin	Juice of 2 lemons, strained
$\frac{3}{4}$ cup water	Juice of 3 oranges, strained
$\frac{2}{3}$ cup sugar	4 large egg whites
Zest of 1 lemon	2 tablespoons triple sec or Cointreau
Zest of 2 oranges	

Soften gelatin in $\frac{1}{4}$ cup of the water. Bring $\frac{1}{2}$ cup water and sugar in a small saucepan to boil. Remove from heat, add gelatin mixture and stir until dissolved. Add zest and juice or approximately 1$\frac{1}{2}$ cups of liquid from lemons and oranges to gelatin mixture. Chill in refrigerator or freezer until thick. Whip egg whites until soft peaks form. Whisk triple sec or Cointreau into gelatin. Whip a heaping tablespoon of the egg whites into the gelatin mixture. Then fold in remaining egg whites. Spoon mousse into dessert dishes and chill before serving.

Serves 8.

RUM CHOCOLATE MOUSSE

6 ounces semisweet
chocolate chips

$^{1}/_{2}$ teaspoon
instant coffee

2 tablespoons water

$^{1}/_{4}$ teaspoon salt

4 eggs, separated

2 teaspoons dark rum

Melt chocolate in a double boiler over simmering water. Dissolve instant coffee in 2 tablespoons water. Add coffee and salt to chocolate. Beat egg yolks until thick and add rum. Combine yolks and chocolate mixture in a bowl. Whip egg whites until stiff and fold into chocolate mixture. Spoon into 6 individual cups and chill for at least 3 hours.

Serves 6.

GRAPEFRUIT ICE

4 cups water

2 cups sugar

$1^{1}/_{2}$ cups
grapefruit juice

8 tablespoons
lemon juice

Dash of salt

Grated lemon rind

2 egg whites,
stiffly beaten

Grapefruit shells

Mix all ingredients, except egg whites and grapefruit shells, together. Let stand in refrigerator, stirring occasionally, for 1 hour. Freeze. Remove to a large bowl and beat until frothy but not melted. Fold in egg whites and return to freezer, stirring occasionally. Food coloring may be added to the ice to add color. Serve in grapefruit shells. To prepare grapefruit shells, slice grapefruit in half and remove insides. Soak grapefruit shells in ice water for 15 minutes. Dry and store in refrigerator on waxed paper until ready to serve.

Serves 12.

FRESH FRUIT ICE

3 bananas, mashed

Juice of 3 lemons

3 cups water or 3 cups
pineapple juice
or $^{1}/_{2}$ of each

3 cups sugar

Juice of 3 oranges

1 teaspoon lemon rind

1 teaspoon orange rind

2 eggs, separated

Fresh mint for garnish

Heavy cream, whipped

Crystalized violets

Add lemon juice to bananas. Let stand while mixing water or pineapple juice, sugar, and orange juice. Add lemon and orange rinds. Beat the egg yolks and add to banana mixture and combine with juices. Beat egg whites until stiff and fold into mixture. Pour into a large bowl and freeze. Check mixture every 2 hours and mix until egg whites have combined with other ingredients. Freeze at least 12 hours. Garnish with mint, whipped cream and crystalized violets.

Serves 10 to 12.

STRAWBERRY SORBET

$^2/_3$ cup sugar

$^2/_3$ cup water

2$^1/_2$ pints ripe
strawberries,
puréed and chilled

2 tablespoons
Grand Marnier

2 tablespoons
lemon juice

1 tablespoon
lemon zest

Orange shells

Fruit slices and mint
leaves for garnish

Mix sugar and water in a small saucepan over medium-high heat. Stir until sugar is completely dissolved and syrupy. Remove from heat and chill. Purée fruit and all other ingredients, except orange shells, fruit slices and mint leaves. To freeze, use standard ice cream maker as directed or the following method: Place all ingredients in a bowl and place in freezer for 2 hours. Remove, break into chunks, and purée once again. Refreeze mixture for 40 minutes. Before serving, place in refrigerator to soften slightly. Serve scoops in hollowed orange shells and garnish with a slice of kiwi or other fruit and mint leaves.

Serves 8.

HONEYDEW SORBET

$^2/_3$ cup sugar

$^2/_3$ cup water

4 cups chunked
honeydew melon

5 tablespoons
lime juice

Zest of 2 to 3 limes

Cantaloupe

Mint leaves for garnish

Prepare and freeze sorbet as directed with Strawberry Sorbet. To serve, cut cantaloupe in half and scoop out seeds. Peel and slice in circles. Place sorbet in middle and garnish with a sprig of mint. Serve immediately.

Serves 8.

PINEAPPLE, LIME AND THYME SORBET

1 pineapple, peeled
and cored

4 limes, peeled

6 oranges, peeled

1 tablespoon sugar

$^1/_4$ cup chopped
fresh thyme

Cut fruit pulp into small pieces and puree in a food processor. Strain through a sieve into a 5-quart ice cream machine freezer or freezer-proof bowl. Add the sugar and thyme and stir. Add $^1/_4$ of the remaining pulp. Freeze as directed with Strawberry and Honeydew sorbets. To make a Lemon Mint Sorbet, substitute 4 lemons for limes and $^1/_4$ cup chopped fresh mint for the thyme.

Serves 8.

SPARKLING PINK PUNCH

24 ounces frozen pink
lemonade concentrate

12 ounces frozen orange
juice concentrate

20 ounces frozen
strawberries, thawed

6 cups water

2 quarts ginger ale

Strawberries and orange
slices for garnish

Combine all ingredients, except the ginger ale, and chill until ready to serve. Add ginger ale and serve in a punch bowl with strawberries and orange slices floating on top. As a variation substitute 2 bottles of champagne for 6 cups of water.

Serves 30.

CHRISTMAS CRANBERRY PUNCH

2 bottles champagne

1 quart cranberry juice

6 ounces frozen lime
concentrate, thawed

1 fifth brandy or gin

2 quarts lemon-lime
soda or ginger ale

1 cup sliced
strawberries for garnish

This is nice for Christmas, bridal showers, bachelor/bachelorette parties or any other celebration. Watch out for the kick!

Combine all ingredients, except strawberries, in a large punch bowl. Float strawberry slices on top.

Serves 25.

SANGRIA BLANCA

1 bottle dry
white wine, chilled

1/2 cup Cointreau

1/4 cup sugar

10 ounces club
soda, chilled

Ice cubes

1 lemon, thinly sliced

2 limes, thinly sliced

1 orange, halved
and thinly sliced

Combine wine, Cointreau and sugar until well blended in a glass pitcher. When ready to serve, stir in ice cubes and soda. Garnish with sliced fruit. Serve in clear, stemmed glasses.

Serves 6 to 8.

KIR CHAMPAGNE PUNCH

2 cups fresh or
frozen raspberries

32 ounces club
soda, chilled

1 cup crème de
cassis, chilled

3 bottles
champagne, chilled

Place half of raspberries in blender. Process until smooth and strain. Place remaining raspberries in punch bowl. Pour club soda, crème de cassis, raspberry purée and champagne into punch bowl very carefully. Stir gently. Serve at once.

Serves 12 to 16.

BOURBON SLUSH

7 cups water

2 tea bags

1 cup sugar

12 ounces frozen orange
juice concentrate

12 ounces frozen
lemonade concentrate

2 cups bourbon

Steep tea bags in 1 cup boiling water for 5 minutes. Discard tea bags. Add sugar to tea while it is still hot, stirring until it dissolves. Add orange and lemonade concentrates, bourbon and 6 cups cold water. Place in freezer-proof container and freeze until slushy. This will remain slushy because the liquor does not freeze. Serve in your favorite glass with a spoon.

Serves 10.

MAI TAIS BY THE GALLON

1 fifth light rum

1 fifth dark rum

³/₄ cup
orange Curacao

38 ounces unsweetened
pineapple juice

38 ounces orange juice

Skewers of fruit

These are perfect for the beach, tailgates and picnics since the mixture fits perfectly in a one gallon milk carton for easy storage.

Mix all ingredients in gallon container and chill. Serve over ice with skewered pineapple, cherry, orange wedges and lime.

Serves 16.

APRICOT PUNCH

4 teaspoons instant tea

¹/₄ cup sugar

12 ounces
apricot nectar

¹/₂ teaspoon
orange bitters

2 cups cold water

6 ounces frozen
lemonade concentrate

3¹/₂ cups ginger ale

Mix tea, sugar, nectar and bitters with cold water. Stir until sugar dissolves. Just before serving add lemonade concentrate and ginger ale. Stir until well blended.

Serves 6 to 8.

FRESH CRANBERRY PUNCH

1 gallon cranapple juice

4 quarts ginger ale

4 quarts club soda

1 cup cranberries,
finely chopped

Combine ingredients. Chill before serving.

Serves 16 to 18.

MINTY MELON PUNCH

PUNCH

6 ounces melon liqueur

2 ounces peppermint
schnapps

4 ounces wildberry
schnapps

3 quarts
lemon-lime soda

Mix the liqueurs together in a punch bowl. Add lemon-lime soda and stir until well mixed.

Serves 8.

PEPPERMINT ICE RING

2 ounces
peppermint schnapps

10 ounces
wildberry schnapps

3 ounces
blueberry schnapps

4 cups lemon-lime soda

2 lemons,
thinly sliced

8 strawberries,
thinly sliced

2 limes, thinly sliced

$1/2$ honeydew melon,
scooped into balls

$1/2$ cantaloupe,
scooped into balls

Fresh edible flowers

Mix the peppermint, wildberry and blueberry schnapps and lemon-lime soda together. Place one-fourth of the schnapps mixture, sliced fruits and flowers into a 6-cup ring mold and freeze. Remove mold from freezer. Pour remaining schnapps mixture into ring and return to freezer until completely frozen. To unmold ring, gently place in pan of warm water. Give the mold a slight twist and turn until ice moves freely. Float in punch bowl with punch for a festive summer picnic.

ORANGE PINEAPPLE PUNCH

46 ounces
pineapple juice

12 ounces frozen orange
juice concentrate

12 ounces frozen
lemonade concentrate

1 cup sugar

15 cups cold water

1 quart ginger ale

Strawberries, orange
slices and cherries
for garnish

Mix all ingredients together except ginger ale. Chill. Add ginger ale just before serving. Float strawberries, orange slices and cherries in punch.

Serves 30.

FROZEN TROPICAL BANANAS

4 cups ice	2 large very ripe bananas
1/2 cup Tia Maria	

Blend 2 cups of the ice, Tia Maria and 1 banana on high speed in a blender. Add the second banana and the remaining 2 cups of ice. Blend until smooth and serve.

Serves 4.

BERRY BANANA SMOOTHIE

4 large strawberries	2 tablespoon wheat germ
1/4 cup milk	1/2 banana
1/4 cup orange juice	Ice cubes
2 tablespoons berry yogurt	Strawberries for garnish

Purée strawberries in a blender. Add milk, orange juice, yogurt, wheat germ and banana. Add ice to measure 3 cups. Blend until smooth. Garnish with a whole strawberry.

Serves 4.

KAHLUA SMOOTHIE

3 tablespoons half and half	Ice cubes
6 tablespoons Kahlua	Nutmeg for garnish
3 tablespoons orange juice	Orange slices for ganish
2 scoops vanilla ice cream	

Place all ingredients, except ice, in a blender and process until blended. Add ice and continue to process until smooth. Garnish with nutmeg and a slice of orange.

Serves 4.

BRANDY MILK PUNCH

6 tablespoons brandy	3/4 cup milk
2 tablespoons crème de cacao	Nutmeg for garnish
Dash of vanilla	

Place all ingredients in a blender and process until smooth. Serve over ice and sprinkle top with nutmeg.

Serves 2.

GRANDPA'S EGGNOG

12 eggs, separated	1 pint brandy
2 cups sugar	2 quarts half and half
1 pint whiskey	1 quart vanilla ice cream
1 pint rum	

Although the directions suggest seasoning the blend for five days, it is delicious to drink right away. In fact, you may have none left in five days!

Due to the large quantity, mix the eggnog in 2 separate batches, using half the ingredients each time. In the large bowl of an electric mixer, beat 6 egg whites until foamy, gradually adding $1/2$ cup of the sugar. Beat until stiff and set aside. In a second bowl, beat 6 egg yolks with $1/2$ cup of the sugar until light and fluffy. Slowly add 1 cup each of liquors to the egg yolk mixture. Combine the yolk and egg white mixtures and 1 quart of the half and half. Repeat the entire procedure. Combine batches and pour over ice cream in a large bowl. When the ice cream has melted, bottle and chill for at least 5 days for best results before serving.

Makes 5 quarts.

ICE CREAM FIZZ

2 teaspoons powdered sugar	2 eggs
2 teaspoons granulated sugar	$3/4$ cup vodka or gin
3 tablespoons lemon juice	3 large scoops vanilla ice cream
	Ice cubes

Place ingredients, except ice, in a blender and process until smooth. Add ice cubes to fill the blender and blend until semi-frozen.

Serves 6.

BANANA FIZZ

1 cup milk	2 eggs
Juice of 1 large orange	$3/4$ cup gin or vodka
Juice of 1 lemon	20 ice cubes
3 tablespoons powdered sugar	Orange or lemon peel for garnish
1 ripe banana	

Blend milk, juices, powdered sugar and banana for 30 seconds. Add the eggs and blend for 30 seconds. Add liquor and ice and blend until semi-frozen. Garnish glasses with thinly sliced lemon or orange peel.

Serves 6.

LOTTA-COLADA

7 cups crushed ice	$1/4$ cup half and half
3 cups cubed fresh pineapple	2 cups rum
$2^3/4$ cups pineapple juice	Shredded coconut
15 ounces cream of coconut syrup	

In batches combine first 5 ingredients in blender and mix thoroughly. Add $1^1/2$ cups of the rum and blend 1 minute longer. Serve colada in chilled glasses rimmed with coconut. Top each drink with $1/2$ ounce of rum.

Serves 8 to 10.

MELON BALL SLAMMERS

2 tablespoons tequila	Splash of triple sec
3 tablespoons sweet and sour mix	Ice cubes
2 tablespoons melon liqueur	Lime, lemon and melon slices for garnish

Place all ingredients, except ice, in a blender and process until blended. Add ice and continue to process until slushy. Garnish with lime, lemon and melon slices.

Serves 4.

VODKA WASSAIL

Whole cloves	$1/2$ cup lemon juice
3 large oranges	10 cinnamon sticks
1 gallon apple juice	2 cups vodka
1 cup sugar	$1/4$ cup brandy

Insert cloves in oranges. Place in shallow baking dish and bake at 350 degrees for 30 minutes. Meanwhile, heat apple juice and sugar in a large kettle until bubbles form at the edge. Add lemon juice, cinnamon sticks and baked oranges. Simmer, covered, over low heat for 30 minutes. Add vodka and brandy and serve.

Serves 18.

BLEACHER BREW

4 cups apple juice	8 cloves
2 cinnamon sticks	1 to $1^1/2$ cups brandy

Place apple juice, cinnamon sticks and cloves in a large pot and bring to a boil. Add brandy and simmer for a few minutes. Remove from heat and serve hot or warm.

Serves 6 to 8.

HOT BUTTERED RUM

1 pound unsalted
butter, softened

1 pound light
brown sugar

1 pound
powdered sugar

2 teaspoons cinnamon

2 teaspoons nutmeg

1 quart vanilla
ice cream, softened

Light rum

Whipped cream

Cinnamon sticks

Combine butter, sugars and spices. Beat until fluffy. Add ice cream, stirring until well blended. Spoon mixture into a 2-quart freezer container. Freeze. When ready to serve, place 3 tablespoons of slightly thawed butter mixture and 3 tablespoons rum in a large mug. Fill with boiling water. Stir well. Top with whipped cream and serve with a cinnamon stick. Any unused butter mixture may be refrozen and used later.

Serves 24.

TOM AND JERRYS

6 eggs, separated

2 pounds powdered
sugar

2 drops oil of cinnamon

1 drop oil of clove

$\frac{1}{8}$ teaspoon baking soda

Rum

Brandy

Nutmeg for garnish

Beat egg yolks and gradually add powdered sugar. If the mixture is too stiff, add a little egg white. Add oils and soda. Beat the egg whites until stiff and fold into the egg yolk mixture. This batter may be kept in the freezer or refrigerator. When ready to serve, place 1 heaping tablespoon of the batter in a large mug or cup. Add 1 tablespoon rum and 1 tablespoon brandy and mix. Pour in boiling water and stir. Sprinkle with nutmeg.

Serves 24.

PANINI

5 medium ripe bananas

4 ounces frozen orange
juice concentrate

2 tablespoons
banana liqueur

1 cup sugar

Ice cubes

1 cup dark rum

Blend bananas, orange concentrate, banana liqueur, sugar and rum. Fill the blender with ice cubes and blend until semi-frozen.

Serves 6 to 8.

ENGLISH WASSAIL TEA

¹/₂ cup lemon juice	¹/₄ teaspoon nutmeg
1¹/₂ cups sugar	¹/₄ teaspoon cinnamon
5 tea bags	¹/₄ teaspoon allspice
1¹/₂ quarts water	2 quarts apple cider
2 cinnamon sticks	1 quart pineapple juice
¹/₄ teaspoon ground cloves	

Boil lemon juice and sugar for 5 minutes. Place tea bags in boiling water, add lemon/sugar mixture and steep for 5 minutes. Remove tea bags and discard. Place cinnamon sticks, cloves, nutmeg, cinnamon and allspice in a cheesecloth bag. Add bag to hot tea and simmer 10 minutes. Remove from heat and let stand for 2 hours. Remove cheesecloth bag and discard. Mix cider and pineapple juice into cooled mixture and simmer 1 hour. Remove from heat and steep for an additional 8 hours. Reheat and serve warm.

Serves 16.

CRANBERRY TEA

6 tea bags	2 cups cranberry juice
4 cups water	¹/₂ cup orange juice
³/₄ cup sugar	¹/₃ cup lemon juice
¹/₄ teaspoon allspice	Peppermint sticks
¹/₄ teaspoon cinnamon	
¹/₄ teaspoon nutmeg	

Steep tea and spices in 2¹/₂ cups boiling water for 5 minutes and strain. Add sugar and stir to dissolve. Add remaining ingredients and 1¹/₂ cups water. Heat just to boiling. Serve hot with peppermint sticks as stirrers. May be stored in refrigerator and reheated.

Serves 6 to 8.

PERUVIAN HOT CHOCOLATE

4 ounces semisweet chocolate	Grated rind of 1 orange
¹/₂ cup water	1 stick cinnamon
¹/₂ gallon milk	¹/₂ cup sugar
1 teaspoon vanilla	

In a double boiler, melt chocolate with water. Remove from heat and combine with the milk, vanilla, orange peel, cinnamon and sugar. Bring to a boil over low heat. Boil for 1 minute. Cool. Chill for at least 24 hours. Remove the cinnamon stick and the chocolate "skin" that forms on the surface. Reheat mixture and serve.

Serves 8 to 10.

TECHNIQUE

A major challenge for anyone who loves to cook is mastery of professional techniques which give confidence and polish to the home chef. In this section basic techniques of food preparation such as meat cutting and boning, stock and sauce preparation, pastry handling and garnishing will be demonstrated. Practice and sensible equipment are keys to success in these areas. Once these culinary techniques have been mastered the home cook will be amazed at the grand feasts that can be quickly and efficiently prepared and served to the delight of family and guests.

The mastery of culinary techniques can be very frustrating without proper equipment. Although it does not take a tremendous amount of equipment to stock the home kitchen, all cooking implements should be carefully selected for strength, durability and versatility. Pots and pans should be heavy and made of stainless steel, cast iron or aluminum with handles that are riveted, not spot welded. Good knives are a necessity. Many professional chefs prefer knives of forged steel with handles which are riveted to the blade. Anyone who has visited a culinary equipment shop knows that there are literally thousands of gadgets and utensils available. All cooks have their favorites, but as with pots and pans, strength, durability and versatility are essential in selecting utensils.

Have fun experimenting with these techniques. Enjoy the failures as well as the success. If the first attempt to bone a leg of lamb fails, make lamb stew. If the choux paste does not puff up enough for cream puffs, deep fry the rest and dust with powdered sugar. Cooking should be creative and satisfying, so be inventive and enjoy learning these professional skills.

Opposite: Pheasant Galantine

CUTTING AND BONING TECHNIQUE

POULTRY BONING

Boning and cutting one's own meats has its advantages in both economy and quality control. Special cuts of meat cost more. And why leave the bones and trimmings at the butcher's shop when they have such wonderful uses in the home kitchen. Beef or lamb bones, when removed, can be roasted with mirepoix until browned and then placed in the pot for a delicious stock. Meat trimmings are the basis for many forcemeats and mousselines.

1. Disjoint wing and thigh by cutting down through both sides of back.

2. Cut carcass away from breast carefully on both sides.

3. Cut wings off and remove thigh bone. Lay flat and continue recipe as directed.

BUTTERFLIED LEG OF LAMB

1. Place the leg of lamb on a board with the large end down. Hold the narrow end.

2. Make a cut to the elbow as close to the bone as possible. From the elbow cut down to the hip and expose the joint. Carefully work the joint free by cutting through the tendons. Carefully cut through the carti-lage to separate the joint, remove the hip side of the joint, and set aside for trimmings.

3. Work the knife around the elbow and leg bone by making small cuts to free the bone.

4. Once the bone is removed, lay the leg flat, skin side down. Remove any undesirable sinew or fat. Cut across the large thick portion of the leg being careful not to go all the way through. Lay open and prepare with stuffing or spices and sear or barbecue as the recipe may require.

CROWN OF LAMB

1. Lay the half-rib of lamb fat side down, and remove the chime bones, which are sections of the back bone that remain attached when cut in half.

2. Stand rib on end with bones facing up. Cut down along and against the bone to the loin. Be careful not to cut into the loin.

3. Save the flap, as the extra meat can be used in stock or sausage.

4. Cut away meat between ribs by slicing along each side of rib bones. Save any extra meat for stock or sausage.

5. Sear in a hot skillet with oil and butter.

6. When cool enough to handle, bring the ends of the loin together to form crown.

7. Tie securely with kitchen string.

8. Cover the tips of the ribs with foil to prevent burning. Roast at 350 degrees for 20 minutes or according to specific recipe instruction.

FORCEMEAT TECHNIQUE

MOUSSELINES

GALANTINES

Grinding and processing of meats developed in the sixteenth and seventeenth centuries. In those days people worked very hard for even small amounts of food, and they had to use every edible part of every piece of meat they could get. They puréed and chopped bits of meat, mixed them with vegetables and grains. These mixtures were then cooked in their own stock or baked crusts. Puréed meat and vegetables baked in a tureen became what we now call a pâté en terrine. Chopped meat with vegetables baked in a crust is now known to us a pâté en croûte. Ballottines or galantines came about when pieces of meat were wrapped and tied in a cloth and cooked in their own stock. Many dishes that are widely enjoyed today were developed during this period.

Forcemeat is one element all pâtés, galantines and ballottines have in common. Forcemeat is a seasoned mixture of raw or cooked meats, seafood, or vegetables which has been chopped or ground, then used as a stuffing. Sausage is a forcemeat, and so is pâté. The possibilities for forcemeat combinations are endless and bound only by the cook's imagination.

MOUSSELINE

4 ounces uncooked meat, skinned and boned	1/4 cup butter, softened
1/2 cup egg whites	2 teaspoons salt
	1 cup heavy cream

A mousseline is a simple purée of meat or seafood mixed with egg, salt and cream. The mousseline can be folded together with a forcemeat and baked to create delicious pâté. It can also be used in soufflés and formed into quenelles. The following is a basic recipe for mousseline. It is possible to use any uncooked meat and most seafoods successfully.

Depending upon the application, the amount of cream may be adjusted. For a firm mousseline, to be used as a binding agent for a forcemeat, use less cream or none at all. For a lighter mousseline to be used in a soufflé or a quenelle, use more cream. Note that the cream content should not exceed the volume of puréed meat. In that case the mousseline would not be able to hold shape.

When using a coarse meat such as veal, add some chicken to the purée. This will help to give the mousse a smoother texture. If using previously frozen fish, add some fresh scallops to the purée to help the texture. Due to the chemical reaction of iodine naturally found in shellfish, fresh lobster and fresh prawns do not work well as the base for mousseline. Instead, make the mousseline using white fish or scallops. Steam or poach the shellfish and then dice. The cooked and diced shellfish can then be folded into the mousseline with delicious results.

Purée meat in food processor. Add egg whites and purée again until smooth. Add butter, a little at a time, until fully incorporated. With machine running add salt and cream gradually. Refrigerate.

Makes 2 1/2 cups.

GALANTINE APPLICATION

A galantine is created when mousseline is mixed with a forcemeat and then rolled up in a larger flat piece of meat, wrapped in cheesecloth and baked in a water bath called a bain-marie. A bain-marie is a very slow and gentle way to cook pâtés, mousselines, and egg preparations. The bain-marie method can be used in the oven or stove top.

Photograph, page 228. Recipe, page 60.

1. Bone the pheasant and trim away excess fat. Trim half the breast away. Chop half and purée the other. Set aside for forcemeat.

2. Place the pheasant breast flat on a 12-inch square of cheesecloth.

3. Prepare forcemeat using chopped and puréed pheasant and remaining ingredients.

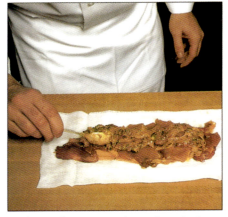

4. Spoon forcemeat mixture lengthwise down the center of the whole breast.

5. Gently lift the edge of the cheesecloth and tightly roll up the pheasant and forcemeat.

6. Complete the roll and tie the ends securely with kitchen string. Bake in a bain-marie according to recipe directions.

PUFF PASTRY

Puff pastry is truly the most versatile and impressive of all pastry crusts. Its preparation is by comparison more involved and difficult than other pastries, but it is well worth the effort. The origin of puff pastry is disputed. The French perfected the preparation, but the actual method dates back to ancient Greece. The theory of puff pastry is quite simple. Thin layers of dough consisting of flour and water are separated by layers of fat: butter, shortening, goose fat or margarine. During the cooking process the fat keeps the layers separate, and the heat creates steam which in turn "puffs" the dough. Puff pastry may be used in many ways from hors d'oeuvres to entrées to desserts. Properly prepared it is light, crisp, and cooks to a golden brown. It can be used as a crust for meats and fillings. It can also be used as a fleuron, a small pastry cut into a special shape and served as a garnish in dishes which are served with a sauce. Once prepared, puff pastry may be stored in the refrigerator for several days or in the freezer for up to a month. For best results it should be placed in the refrigerator to thaw to prevent butter from melting.

Puff pastry should be cool when rolling and shaping. Roll the pastry evenly and avoid working the dough too much, because if the layers of dough and fat become one, the pastry will lose the ability to "puff." If the pastry is to be filled after it has been baked or used as a garnish such as a fleuron, it should be cooked ahead of time and allowed to dry. If used for encasing a pâté or a mousseline en croûte, prepare the recipe for the fillings first, and then remove the pastry from the refrigerator for use. If the recipe calls for a cooked filling, it should be cooled before being encased in the pastry. Use an egg wash of 2 parts slightly beaten egg to 1 part milk or water for glazing the pastry. As the pastry cooks the egg wash will give shine to the golden brown crust. A small amount of egg wash also can act as an adhesive when used between layers of rolled puff pastry.

PUFF PASTRY

4¹/₂ cups flour	1¹/₂ cups water
1 teaspoon salt	¹/₂ pound butter
1 teaspoon sugar	

Place flour on a pastry board and make a well in the center. Pour the water, salt and sugar into the well, blend, and quickly work into a ball. Knead until a smooth dough is formed, adding water if dough is too dry or flour if dough is too moist. It should be soft and pliable but not wet. Shape into a ball and follow photo instructions on the next page.

Makes 1 pound.

PUFF PASTRY TECHNIQUE

1. Shape prepared dough into a ball and cut a cross into the top.

2. Sinking fingers into the center of the cross, pull down the edges forming four arms.

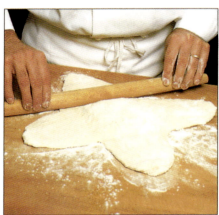

3. Roll out the arms to a thickness of ¹/₂ inch, leaving the center 2 inches thick.

4. In the center place ¹/₂ pound block of butter.

5. Fold arms of dough over butter .

6. Dust with flour and roll into a rectangle.

7. Fold by thirds toward the center. Refrigerate 15 minutes.

8. Repeat steps 6 and 7 four times.

SALMON MOUSSELINE EN CROÛTE

1. Roll pastry to size and cut in half.

2. Mound mousseline in oval shape over spinach and salmon strips. Cover with additional salmon, spinach and pastry.

3. Form seal around salmon with hands.

4. Cut pastry into fish shape and brush with egg wash.

5. Create fish scale motif using a pastry tip.

6. After baking, slice at a slant to show all layers.

BEGGARS' POUCHES

1. Roll out puff pastry and cut into 1¹/₂-inch squares. Place filling in the center of each square. Lift one corner of each square and roll over filling toward opposite corner, forming cylinders with pointed open ends.

2. Bring up the open ends and twist, forming a "pouch."

3. Tie with a strip of wilted chive, and deep fry according to recipe directions.

PASTRY CRUST

SHORTCRUST PASTRY

1 cup flour	1/2 cup unsalted butter, very cold
1 cup sugar, granulated or powdered	1 egg

Sweet or savory, a wonderful flaky pastry crust has endless versatility. Anything baked within a crust becomes a delicious surprise when served. And who can resist the wonderful aroma of a pie or tart baking. Making the perfect pastry crust takes practice and patience, but if one carefully follows the directions, the results will be very satisfying.

On a floured pastry board: Mix the flour and the sugar into a pile. With the back of a spoon make a well in the center. Break the egg into the well. Cut the cold butter into small pieces and place on the flour around the egg. With the edge of a spatula cut all the ingredients until they resemble coarse sand. With cold hands knead into a ball. Wrap in plastic and chill for 30 minutes. When chilled, roll and cut into any shape. Bake in a preheated oven at 375 degrees 15 to 20 minutes until browned.

In a food processor: Place flour, sugar and the cold butter in the processor bowl. Add the egg and pulse until the dough kneads itself into a ball. Remove and wrap with plastic wrap. Chill as above.

Makes 1 10-inch tart shell.

CHOUX PASTE

1 1/2 cups milk (water may be substituted)	Pinch of salt
2 tablespoons sugar	1 1/2 cups flour
1/2 cup unsalted butter	5 to 6 eggs

In a 2-quart saucepan bring milk, sugar, butter and salt to a boil. When it has boiled, add the flour and stir with a wooden spoon until the dough no longer sticks to the sides of the pan. Add eggs, 1 at a time, stirring completely after each addition. Once completed the dough should be semi-firm, smooth and glossy. Transfer to a pastry bag and pipe onto a buttered and floured baking sheet in desired shapes. The choux paste will double in size as it bakes. Bake in a preheated oven at 350 degrees for 30 minutes or until golden brown. Once cooked, turn off the oven and let cool with the oven door ajar. This recipe is suitable for profiteroles, eclairs and cream puffs. Once cooled, they can be filled with whipped cream, custards and mousses. Choux paste is also wonderful fried and simply served with powdered sugar.

Makes 16 large cream puffs or 36 profiteroles.

CROQUEMBOUCHE

1. Puncture bottoms of cream puffs and fill with chocolate pastry cream using large pastry tube. Place filled cream puffs on baked shortcurst pastry base.

2. Using caramelized sugar as a "glue" place cream puffs in a circle around the perimeter of the base.

3. Continue building pyramid using caramelized sugar generously.

4. When pyramid is completed, hold the pan of caramelized sugar close to the pyramid and draw fine strands of sugar up and over the structure. Garnish according to recipe directions.

SPUN SUGAR

2 cups granulated sugar	
1/2 cup water	

Place the sugar and water in a heavy 12-inch skillet and cook over low heat until syrup is formed. Boil carefully and remove from heat when caramelized sugar is light brown. When it has cooled and thickened a bit, dip the tines of a fork into the syrup and pull straight up a few times. If the strands of caramelized sugar solidify before falling back into the pan, it is ready to spin. Place the tines of the fork into the sugar and allow some excess sugar to cling to the fork. Pull straight up and over a clean surface. At arm's length let the sugar fall to the surface while spinning the fork. The sugar will form a pile of thin strands as it falls. Repeat this several times so that it accumulates into a pile of very fine strands of spun sugar. Use it as the recipe directs.

PASTRY CREAM

10 egg yolks	1 cup flour
1 cup sugar	1 quart milk
1 tablespoon cornstarch	1 vanilla bean or 1 tablespoon vanilla

In a bowl beat the egg yolks with the sugar until pale. Add the flour and cornstarch and mix into a smooth paste. Bring the milk and vanilla bean to a boil and pour half the hot milk into the egg mixture and stir. Add the rest of the milk and continue to cook over a double boiler while beating with a whisk. When thick, transfer to a plastic container and sprinkle with granulated sugar to prevent a skin from forming. Cool before refrigerating. Once the pastry cream has cooled, it can be flavored with anything. To make a chocolate cream, simply add melted chocolate and stir vigorously. Then fold in whipped cream. If stored properly, pastry cream will keep in the refrigerator for up to 5 days.

Makes 5 cups.

SOUFFLÉ

There is perhaps no greater triumph for the home chef than the mastery of the soufflé. The presentation of a perfect soufflé is a delicious accomplishment and a testament to culinary skill and finesse. Many cooks avoid the soufflé, because the technique must be exact and carefully applied. Some feel that the potential for failure is too great. How-ever, if one understands a few basic principles, there will be few frustrations in the preparation of this exciting dish.

A soufflé is simply a base mixture, sweet or savory, into which whipped egg whites have been very carefully folded. As this mixture cooks, the air trapped in the egg white ex-pands, causing the soufflé to rise. It is important to remember that the ratio of egg whites to base should be 2 to 1 by volume, not by weight. The trick to achieving a smooth, moist soufflé is to add the whipped egg whites in two parts. Half are added to thin out the base a bit so that the remaining egg whites will blend in easily without breaking down. It is also critical to whip the egg whites into soft peaks and then to pro-ceed quickly with the rest of the preparation. If the egg whites are too stiff, they will not be able to expand as they cook and the soufflé will be dry. Any soufflé must be baked in a round or oval dish, because as the soufflé rises it slides along the smooth sides of the dish. A soufflé baked in a square or rectangular dish would catch in the corners causing irregular cooking and an odd shape. A frozen soufflé is not cooked, but it follows the same principle in that air has been trapped in the whipped cream that is added to the base to give volume.

The base for a soufflé can be made from puréed meats, shellfish, vegetables, or cheeses mixed with a thick béchamel sauce or bound with egg yolks. The bases can be prepared in advance and kept cool until the whipped egg whites are added. At that point they must be cooked immediately and served as soon as possible. A sauce complementing the base of the soufflé is ususally served as an accompaniment. When serving the soufflé, the top crust is removed and set aside while the sauce is poured into the center. Another method is to make a hole in the crust with the back of a spoon and pour the sauce into the center of the soufflé.

Sweet soufflés are made from a base consisting of pastry cream to which any of the fol-lowing may be added: melted chocolate, liqueur or fruit purée. Whole or chopped fruit or nuts may be added when filling the soufflé dish. Crème anglaise is the most popular sauce for sweet soufflés.

SOUFFLÉ TECHNIQUE

1. Add zest of orange to pastry cream.

2. Beat egg whites to soft peaks.

3. Add half the egg whites and mix together. Then fold in remaining egg whites.

4. Fold gently to keep the soufflé batter smooth.

5. Fill cups half full with batter.

6. Add whole raspberries.

7. Fill cups to top rim and bake.

8. Garnish with powdered sugar, orange zest and raspberry.

STOCKS AND SAUCES

A sauce is a seasoned liquid which is served as an accompaniment to food enhancing its flavor. Sauce can be hot or cold, sweet or savory. The word "sauce" comes from the Latin word "salus" which means salted or seasoned. In fine restaurants where reputations are built upon the excellence of the sauces served, chefs are constantly preparing the stocks which are the basis for all sauces. A stock is a broth that has been made from cooking meat, fish or poultry bones with a combination of vegetables and herbs called bouquet garni or mirepoix. These stocks are reduced to make demi-glace, a rich concentration of the original stock which is used as a sauce base. Home chefs need spend only a few days a year to prepare enough stock for almost all sauce needs. The stocks can be frozen in small quantities for months and used whenever a special sauce is called for in a recipe. A sauce adds sophistication to simple cooked meats or vegetables. A sweet sauce makes a plain dessert very special by adding color and flavor. Two sauces of different colors and the same consistency can literally be painted onto the dish to create a dramatic effect.

Opposite: Chicken with Foie Gras and Port Wine

MIREPOIX &
BOUQUET GARNI

Mirepoix is a combination of vegetables which adds depth to soups and stock preparations. Named after the eighteenth century Duc de Levis-Mirepoix, this combination usually consists of carrot, onion and celery. Try mirepoix to enhance the flavor of meats and seafoods.

Bouquet garni is a wonderful addition to stocks and soups. Typically, bouquet garni is made up of parsley, thyme and bay leaf. These herbs are wrapped together in muslin or tied securely and dropped into the stock pot. The bouquet garni is then removed just before serving.

A creative cook can invent variations of the mirepoix and bouquet garni to suit the palate. Bundles of vegetables can be braised with meat or seafood, then used to garnish the serving platter. In this way the mirepoix not only enhances the flavor of the meat during cooking, but also becomes an attractive garnish and a delicious vegetable addition to the meal.

STOCKS

BROWN STOCK

5 pounds veal bones, split in half and cut into 3-inch pieces	8 garlic cloves, halved
1 pound carrots, chopped	6 fresh tomatoes, halved
1 celery stalk, chopped	3 bay leaves
4 large yellow onions, quartered, with skins on	1/4 cup fresh thyme
	1 teaspoon whole peppercorns

Brown stock, also called "espagnole," is a wonderfully rich veal stock that is very aromatic. From this stock Demi-glace and Glace de viande can be made.

In a roasting pan place the bones and a mirepoix of carrots, onions, celery, garlic and tomatoes. Roast at 450 degrees until the bones and onions are well browned. Pour off grease and place bones and vegetables in a 10-quart stock pot. Place the empty roasting pan on a stove top with 2 inches of water and bring to a boil, scraping the bottom to remove the concentrated drippings. Pour this liquid into the stock pot and add the bay leaves, thyme and peppercorns. Add cold water up to 3 inches from the top. Bring stock to a simmer, skimming the fat every hour. Simmer the stock for 6 hours. When it has reduced by half, strain and set aside. With the bones still in the pot, refill with water once again and repeat the cooking process. Strain the second stock and discard bones. Add the first stock to the second and reduce by half.

DEMI-GLACE

5 quarts brown stock	2 tablespoons cornstarch mixed with 1 tablespoon water
4 cups red wine	
2 tablespoons chopped shallots	1/2 cup butter
	Salt and pepper

A Demi-glace is a half-glaze. It is used as the foundation for many meat and poultry sauces as well as a glaze. When cooking poultry and meats, all one needs to do is to deglaze pan with reserved marinade or wine and bring to a boil. Add Demi-glace, fresh vegetables and herbs and serve immediately.

Place the red wine and shallots in a 10-quart pot and reduce by half. Add the brown stock and bring to a rolling boil and reduce by half. Make the cornstarch roux. It should be a smooth paste that feels dry to the touch but still runny. Pour the roux into the boiling stock and stir completely. Add the butter and season with salt and pepper.

GLACE DE VIANDE

1 quart brown stock

Glace de viande is a rich stock reduction used to enhance meat sauces in both flavor and depth. To make glace de viande reduce brown stock by three-fourths or until it coats the back of a spoon. Caution must be used as it can burn easily. It may be necessary to transfer into a smaller pot to complete the process. Once the glace is made, it should be stored in an airtight container and chilled. Glade de viande will keep indefinitely if stored properly. Glace de viande may also be used on its own as a meat glaze.

POULTRY STOCK

2 pounds chicken bones	1 garlic bulb, halved
2 carrots, chopped	1 bay leaf
6 celery stalks, chopped	1 teaspoon whole peppercorns
2 yellow onions, chopped	1 tablespoon fresh thyme

Chicken bones may be replaced with veal bones to achieve a white veal stock. Depending on how these stocks are used, their color can be adjusted during the second phase of cooking. As the poultry stock is reduced, it turns a golden color and has a spectacular flavor. A white veal stock should not be reduced to the point that it will change color.

Place all of the ingredients in a 5-quart stock pot and fill with cold water to 2 inches from the top. Slowly bring to a simmer. Skim any fat from the surface, and continue cooking for 4 hours or until reduced by one quarter. Strain and use as desired.

FISH STOCK

2 pounds white fish, cod, halibut or bass bones and heads	1 whole bulb garlic, cut in half
2 carrots, chopped	10 juniper berries
6 celery stalks, chopped	1 bay leaf
2 yellow onions, chopped	1 cup dry white wine

Place all ingredients in a 5-quart stock pot and fill with cold water to 2 inches below the rim. Bring to a simmer very slowly so that the stock will remain clear. When the pot reaches the gentle simmer, remove from heat and strain through a sieve. Reserve the stock and discard all other ingredients.

CONSOMMÉ

2 quarts any cold stock	2 stalks celery, finely chopped
2 carrots, finely chopped	5 egg whites, slightly beaten
1 onion, finely chopped	

A consommé is a clarified stock. It is used in the preparation of aspic and clear soups.

Combine vegetables with the egg whites and stir into cold stock. Very slowly bring mixture to a simmer, stirring occasionally. Do not boil. As the stock heats, the egg whites will cook, trapping and collecting the bits of vegetable and meat within the stock and leaving the liquid clear. The egg whites will float to the surface of the stock forming a "raft." Once the raft has formed, strain the liquid through cheesecloth.

ENTRÉE SAUCES

BUTTER SAUCES

It is important to remember a few points when making sauces. First of all, never add salt to a liquid that is to be reduced. As the volume of the liquid decreases, the proportion of salt to liquid increases, therefore making the liquid too salty. Salt cannot be removed from a stock or sauce. Seasonings, herbs and flavorings should be added just before the sauce is served. In the reduction of liquid, if the liquid evaporates beyond half the volume of fat, the sauce will separate. Simply add more liquid to bring back the balance in the demi-glace. The addition of butter will increase the volume of a sauce, but it will also change the color and flavor and may not be appropriate in certain preparations.

BEURRE BLANC SAUCE

1 cup dry white wine	1 tablespoon heavy cream
1 teaspoon chopped shallots	½ cup butter

These butter sauces are simple accompaniments to any grilled, poached or baked fish.

In a skillet over high heat reduce the wine and shallots by two-thirds. Reduce heat and add cream. Bring to a boil and add butter while stirring. Once the butter has melted, remove from heat and serve. To hold sauce at preferred temperature, transfer to a container and place in a bain-marie. This will prevent the sauce from separating.

VARIATIONS

Champagne/Dill Beurre Blanc: Substitute champagne for white wine and add 1 tablespoon fresh dill just before serving.

Pesto Beurre Blanc: Add 1 tablespoon pesto to sauce after the addition of butter.

Pistachio/Green Onion Beurre Blanc: Add 1 tablespoon shelled pistachios and 1 tablespoon thinly sliced green onions after the addition of butter.

Corn/Horseradish Beurre Blanc: Add 1 tablespoon cooked fresh corn and 1 teaspoon horseradish just before serving.

SAUCE MEUNIÈRE

½ cup butter	2 tablespoons chopped parsley
Juice of 1 lemon	

In a skillet melt butter over medium heat until it turns golden brown. Add lemon and parsley. Serve over fish, chicken or rabbit.

BELLE MEUNIÈRE

¼ cup diced tomatoes	¼ cup sliced mushrooms

To the above recipe add tomatoes and mushrooms.

SWEET AND SAVORY RELISHES

APPLE MINT MARMALADE

2 large Granny Smith apples, peeled, cored and cut into pieces	2 tablespoons white vinegar
1/2 cup sugar	1 teaspoon cracked peppercorns
1/2 cup water	1 tablespoon chopped fresh mint leaves

In a medium saucepan, cook the apples with the sugar and water for 10 minutes, or until syrupy. Stir in the vinegar, peppercorns and mint leaves. Continue to cook, stirring often, for an additional 5 to 10 minutes. Serve with lamb or poultry.

Makes 2 cups.

GINGER PEAR CONSERVE

8 pounds pears, peeled and sliced	1 tablespoon grated orange rind
4 pounds sugar	4 lemons, thinly sliced and julienned
1/2 pound fresh ginger, peeled and thinly sliced	

Add sugar and ginger to the pears. Set aside in a mixing bowl for approximately 8 hours or overnight. Add orange rind and lemons. In a large kettle bring mixture to a boil, stirring constantly. Reduce heat and simmer until mixture thickens, approximately 2 1/2 to 3 hours. Stir occasionally. Pour conserve into sterilized jars and seal.

Makes 11 cups.

CRANBERRY CHUTNEY

1 pound fresh cranberries	1 teaspoon ginger
1 cup raisins	1/2 teaspoon ground cloves
2/3 cup sugar	1 medium onion, chopped
1 cup water	1 medium apple, peeled and chopped
1 tablespoon cinnamon	1/2 cup thinly sliced celery

Combine cranberries, raisins, sugar, water and spices in a large sauce pot and cook over medium heat for about 15 minutes or until cranberries pop. Stir in onions, apple and celery. Simmer 15 minutes longer until mixture thickens. Cool and chill until ready to serve. Chutney keeps nicely for 2 weeks in the refrigerator and can be frozen for longer periods.

Makes 4 cups.

DESSERT SAUCES

CRÈME FRAÎCHE

3 parts heavy cream	1 part buttermilk

Place in glass container. Cover and let sit at room temperature for at least 24 hours. Refrigerate for up to 3 days. Crème fraîche can be served over fresh fruit and berries and can be flavored with honey and fruit purées. It can also be used for sauce design.

CRÈME ANGLAISE

2 cups milk	½ cup sugar
5 egg yolks	1 teaspoon vanilla

In a small saucepan, bring milk to a boil. In a double boiler, beat the egg yolks, sugar and vanilla until pale yellow. Stir the hot milk into the egg yolk mixture, half at a time, and cook over simmering water, while stirring with a spatula, until mixture thickens. Remove and chill. Crème anglaise can be served warm with soufflés or cold with fresh fruit or chocolate pâte.

FRUIT PURÉES

1 pint berries	½ cup water
½ cup sugar	½ teaspoon lemon juice

Blueberries, currants and raspberries make the prettiest purées. These berries have a low water content, are rich in flavor, high in pectin and thicken quickly. Any of the three colors, or a combination of all three, provides a striking contrast when used to make designs with crème anglaise or crème fraîche. Purées can be used also to flavor whipped creams, pastry creams, crème anglaise and ice creams.

Bring all ingredients to a boil. Purée and strain. Reserve for sauce design or to serve with desserts.

CARAMEL SAUCE

½ cup sugar	1 tablespoon butter
½ cup plus 2 tablespoons water	

Bring sugar and ½ cup of the water to a boil. Reduce until golden brown. Very carefully, drizzle in, while stirring, 2 tablespoons water. Stir in butter and blend well. Serve warm .

BRANDY SAUCE

1 cup sugar	2 tablespoons butter
¼ cup brandy	

Place sugar on high heat in a skillet. Stir until sugar melts. As soon as it turns golden brown in color, add brandy. While the mixture flames, stir carefully. When the flame dies down, whisk in butter.

CHOCOLATE SAUCE

4 ounces chocolate	¼ cup butter
1 cup cream, warmed	1 tablespoon any liqueur

Melt chocolate in double boiler. Add warmed cream and stir until blended. Whisk in butter and liqueur.

APRICOT NAPPAGE

5 pounds fresh apricots	Water
5 cups sugar	

Place apricots and sugar in a 10-quart pot and fill with water to cover. Bring to a boil and simmer 3 to 4 hours. Pour through a sieve and drain, reserving liquid. Discard apricots. Return liquid to the pot and reduce until it is thick enough to coat the back of a wooden spoon. Place in an airtight container, covering with paraffin if desired. To glaze, warm a small amount of the apricot nappage and brush with a pastry brush. Use apricot nappage to glaze fruit, seal pastries and crusts. It will help berries keep longer at room temperature.

FINAL TOUCHES

Anyone who loves to cook knows the many pleasures associated with the preparation of food. Whether one is accomplished and inventive or a strict recipe follower, cooking should be fun and satisfying. Just what turns a good meal into something special is a subject for debate, because cooking and eating are individual delights. And it is the individual touch that marks an excellent cook. Each person brings something remarkable to the kitchen. . . a talent for gardening, a mastery of culinary technique, artistry in presentation or simply the ability to bring the right people together for the pure enjoyment of food and company. Whether it is to be a casual picnic in a sunny park or an elegant dinner in a dramatic dining room, special individual touches, simple or elaborate, make the occasion memorable.

CARROT HEARTS

1. Peel and trim carrot, rounding sides and coming to a point for the bottom of the heart.

2. Make a "V" cut down the length of the carrot and round off any sharp edges.

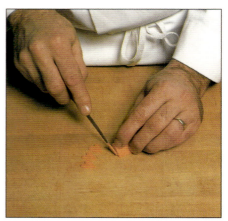

3. Thinly slice the carrot hearts.

PEPPER POINTS

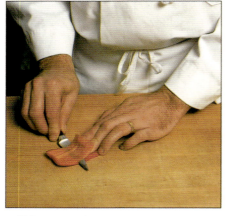

1. Trim inside flesh from pepper to make a smooth surface.

3. Thinly slice lengthwise, keeping the bottom of the slices attached. Fan pepper points.

2. Make "V" cuts across the inside of the pepper.

ZUCCHINI FLOWERS

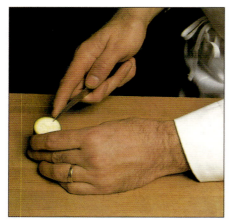

1. With the point of a knife, make a slit and "V" cut down the zucchini.

2. Continue around the entire zucchini, making 7 or 8 "V" cuts.

3. Slice zucchini to desired thickness.

SAUCE DESIGN

1. Make dots of light sauce in a circular pattern.

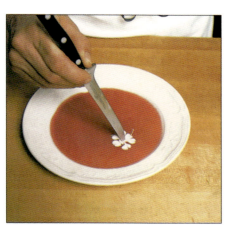

2. Run the point of the knife outside to inside to form the flower petals.

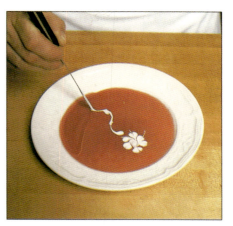

3. Make a stem using additional light sauce.

4. In a zig-zag pattern form leaves.

5. Run knife point from the end of the leaf through the stem.

6. To make a string of hearts, place drops of light sauce in a line. Then run a knife through the string of dots.

7. To make a spider web pattern, place semi-circles of light sauce on a darker sauce.

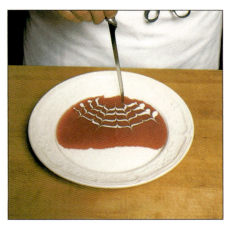

8. Run knife through semi-circles alternately outside to inside, then inside to outside.

FINAL THOUGHTS

From the very beginning, the production of *CELEBRATE!* was a collaborative effort. For four years members of the Sacramento community and members of The Junior League united with one common goal—to create the very best cookbook possible. Professional food writers and food enthusiasts helped to refine our concepts for the book. Their knowledge of food trends was invaluable. Local retailers generously lent silver, china and other serving and preparation vessels to enhance the visual impact of *CELEBRATE!* Professionals in graphic design, photography, publishing and food styling dedicated their talents to the success of this book. Our membership triple-tested each of the thousands of recipes submitted, so that only those of the highest quality would be included in the book.

Expert chefs shared the secrets of their art and the wisdom of their experience to give *CELEBRATE!* a professional polish. We were particularly fortunate to work with Mitchell Miller, a premier Northern California chef. His well-known style based on practical experience and European influence was invaluable to the production of this cookbook. Once only a vision shared, *CELEBRATE!* became a beautiful reality— a testament to community collaboration and cooperation at its best.

Whatever the level of skill or experience, the most important aspect of cooking is that it be ultimately pleasurable. In producing *CELEBRATE!* we hoped to excite those culinary talents that you, our readers, possess. We wanted to encourage creativity and yet ensure success. We hoped each of you would find something new to carry with you into your own kitchen to share with your family and friends. Good company and good food are the main ingredients of any special occasion. So celebrate often, and may *CELEBRATE!* be part of all your special occasions.

THE JUNIOR LEAGUE OF SACRAMENTO

A HISTORY OF SERVICE TO THE SACRAMENTO COMMUNITY

The Junior League of Sacramento has been active in the growth and development of the Sacramento community for more than sixty-five years. First known as the Charity League, in 1938 this group of volunteers planted the first seeds of women's activism in Sacramento with its support of the Fairhaven Home for Unwed Mothers and a children's ward at the Sacramento County Hospital. In 1942, the group was chartered as The Junior League of Sacramento. Among the League's first projects were The Children's Receiving Home of Sacramento and Children's Theatre. These two projects remain vital today, perfect examples of the League's vision and sustainability.

As the community grew through the 1950s and 1960s, so did The Junior League of Sacramento. Our League was instrumental in providing enrichment for children by originating the Junior Museum and Fairytale Town, a family activity center still popular today. Education and training of community volunteees has been a major focus of the League. Over the years The JLS broadened its areas of voluntarism to the arts by developing the Crocker Art Museum Docent Program and establishing the Sacramento Regional Arts Council. The Junior League of Sacramento was instrumental in the historical preservation of Old Sacramento. Restored on its original site along the Sacramento River, it is a Northern California landmark and popular destination for visitors to the area.

In the 1970s and 1980s, The JLS continued its preservation and arts efforts but redirected a good deal of energy to the health and welfare of families. The Child Abuse Council, the Cystic Fibrosis Clinic and Sacramento Valley Eye Bank were all touched by the hands of dedicated volunteer women of The Junior League. Recognizing the potential of combining strengths with other organizations, our League was instrumental in establishing The Sacramento Regional Foundation (now known as the Sacramento Regional Community Foundation). This foundation attracts funds from various entities to be redistributed within our community. Building on this success, other collaboratives were created such as The Sacramento Crisis Nurseries, the Child Abuse Prevention Council and The Sacramento Children's Home.

Keeping in mind our vision statement, *"Enhancing the well-being of children through the dedicated action of volunteers,"* The Junior League of Sacramento has awarded grants to a number of community organizations that provide support to the youth of our community. Among them are Child Abuse Council's Family Cooperative and the Greater Sacramento Mentoring Coalition. In 2000, The Junior League of Sacramento was honored by automaker BMW and The Association of Junior Leagues International with a Community Impact Merit Award for its work in development of The Crisis Nursery.

In 2006, The Junior League of Sacramento helped to develop the concept for the Sacramento Children's Museum. SCM was envisioned as an innovative, hands-on, play-based museum, designed especially for young childen. Its intent is to provide them with a place to enjoy learning, while providing parents and caregivers with resources and support. The Junior League of Sacramento is proud to be a founding member of The Children's Museum, the first of its kind in the Sacramento area.

The JLS has always understood the importance of public advocacy for issues of concern in our focus areas. Our location, in the state's capital city, has been a tremendous advantage. Our League was instrumental in the establishment of the State Public Affairs Committee, a committee that has become a model for those in other states.

As the community needs grow, so does our dedication to fund-raising. We are proud of our development history. From a doll auction in the 1940s, through years of very successful rummage sales, on to fashion shows, grand opening events, and designer showhouse tours, our members have worked tirelessly to earn those much-needed dollars that go back into our community.

First published in 1991, *CELEBRATE!* is an excellent example of the dedication of Junior League volunteers to raise funds to support JLS projects. *CELEBRATE!* was reprinted in 2007 to commemorate our sixty-fifth anniversary. The Junior League of Sacramento is proud to *CELEBRATE!* the Sacramento community and its volunteers.

REPRINT COOKBOOK COMMITTEE

CHAIRS
Christy Ahdan
Gloria Knopke

COMMITTEE MEMBERS
Jane Adams
Cheryll Cochrane
Christa Dyck
Nancy Greenwood
Cathy Levering
Kristen Oliver
Carrie Temple

SPECIAL THANK YOUS

The Junior League of Sacramento wishes to thank the following individuals and businesses for their unending advice, contributions and good spirit throughout the CELEBRATE! project.

BUSINESSES AND INDIVIDUALS

APPLE COMPUTER INC.

CAL CENTRAL PRESS
Scott Keilholtz
Steve Stuart

FISCHER TILE & MARBLE INC.

GREBITUS & SONS JEWELERS
Beth Grebitus

GWEN AMOS DESIGN
Gwen Amos
Michele Cable
Mark Olsztyn

HARBOR VILLAGE RESTAURANT, SAN FRANCISCO

JENSEN PHOTOGRAPHY
Keith Jensen

KOLB COMMUNICA-TIONS
Steve Kolb

PRECISION MARINE

S. J. FOSTER LINENS

TRAINOR & ASSOCI-ATES, INC.
Paulette Trainor

WILLIAM GLEN
Glen Forbes
Bill Snyder

WILLIAMS-SONOMA INC.

ZELLERBACH PAPER COMPANY

SACRAMENTO AREA RESTAURANTS AND CULINARY SPECIALISTS

BIBA
Biba Caggiano

CALIFORNIA FAT'S
Lina Fat

CHINOIS EAST WEST
David Soo Hoo

ETTORE'S EUROPEAN BAKERY
Ettore Ravazzolo

KAY LEE'S MANDARIN RESTAURANT
Kay Lee Helmrich

JOSEPH & PAULETTE KREISS

MAD DOG BAKERY
Terrie Green

MAX'S OPERA CAFE
Lewis & Susie Orlady

MITCHELL'S TERRACE
Mitchell B. Miller

PARAGARY'S
Kurt Spataro

QUINTESSENT QUISINE
Nancy Harvey
Cathy Levering

THE SACRAMENTO BEE
Elaine Corn

THE SACRAMENTO UNION
Gloria Glyer

WULFF'S FRENCH RESTAURANT
Ann Shelton
Horace & Helen Wulff

RECIPES SUBMITTED BY:

Anne Adams
Lois Anderson
Camilla Andrews
Gail Ankele
Marilyn Arnholt
Ann Ashbrook
Lisa Auble
Gail Bailey
Mindy Bazlen
Leigh Beermann
Susan Bell
Shelia Bennett
Anne Biegler
Stephanie Biegler
Donna Blessley
Shirley Bonuccelli
Rebecca Boris
Linda Wenker Boutin
Bonnie Bowman
Jim Bowman
Judy Boyko
Mary Brady
Marolyn Brandon
Cathleen Brew
Kiefie Breuer
Heather Browne
Ellen Bruno
Lisa Wargo Bruzzone
Pauline Buck
Dornie Burr
Elisabeth Bush
Biba Caggiano
Happy Callis
Yolanda Campbell
Ken Carle
Martha Carle
Jenny Catchot
Jean Luc Chassereau
Karen Clark
Marilyn Clark
Cheryll Cochrane
Patti Codiga
Cecile Cook
Sandra Cook
Karine Corrigan
Nancy Corum
Carolyn Coughlin
Linda Coward
Betty Cripe
Stephanie Cripe
Diane Cronan
Meg Crow
Jeannie Crowther
Judy Culbertson
Bobbie Cuttle

Jack Cuttle
Jan Daneke
Maryly Darsie
Lisa Daum
Carol Davis
Diana Diana
Chris Day
Bev Deary
Alison DeFazio
Denise Dewey
Carol Dierkoph
Ilene Dillon
Julie DiLoreto
Marge Dolcini
Sheryl Downing
Lisa Dubois
Carol Duke
Elizabeth Breuner
Bonnie Elliot
Kari Ellison
Kristine Elmer
J. P. Eltorai
Molly Evangelisti
Marty Fair
Toni Farrell
Lina Fat
Karen Feathers
Mardy Fellenz
Dianne Ferrell
Tracy Fike
Jayne Finkbohner
Nancy Fisher
Suzie Fisher
Cindi Fores
Merrin Forsgren
Nina Fox
Dorie Fraser
Kathie Frasier
Jeannie Frisch
Alma Fulster
Bev Geremia
Patty Gibson
M. Gonzales
Tina Goodridge
Beth Grebitus
Sue Groefsema-Jones
Kathy Gunz
Caroline Gwerder
Marit Haarberg-Doucet
Bernice Hagen
Laura Hale
Louise Hammill
Ann Hargrove
Karin Klove Harris
Tina Harris

Linda Hayward
Suzanne Hegland
Ruth Ann Henderson
Kristin Higgins
Helen Home
Ann Hoover
Juanita Irwin
Barbara Jack
Lindy Jack
Sue Jack
Marijane Jacobs
Susan James
Patsy Johnson
C. Breck Jones
Hely Jones
Mrs. W. Raymond Jones
Jane Jonsson
Kate Judson
Patti Kaufman
Linda Kelly
Marilyn Kennedy
Ann Kerr
Lynda Khasigian
Janet Kiener
Marie Kimble
Cecily Kingston
Marget Kingston
Elsa Klein
Gloria Knopke
Lise Knox
Joseph Kreiss
Paulette Perfumo Kreiss
Sharon Kueneke
Mary Kurowski
Theresa Kwong
Sevim Larsen
William Latham
Cynthia Leathers
Mr. & Mrs. James
    Leathers
S. Leir
Pam Lester
Catherine Miller Levering
Cathy Bowman Levering
Evie Lieb
Dorothy Lien
Kim Lien
Allison Lintner
Carolyn Long
Inger Lonnerdal
Eileen Lotz
Laura Lyon-Diepenbrock
Carol Luery
Jeanie MacAulay
Barbara Mackey

Pam MacLeod
Mad Dog Bakery
Rula Manikas
Anita Seipp Marmaduke
Severina Marsh
Carol Martin
Barbara McConnell
Jenifer McDonald
Tricia Meister
Gayle Merksamer
Kathy Metzger
Katie Mietus
Georgia Mikacich
Kathy Milan
Anita Miller
Mitchell Miller
Nancy Miller
Julie Monroe
Linda Montoya
Rebecca Moore
Mary Beth Morris
Carolyn Mowlds
Cynthia Mulit
Cindy Mullins
Tammy Murray
Cheryl Nativo
Joyce Nein
Julie Nelson
Ann Boyd Newman
Cindy Nolan
Kitty O'Neil
Susie Orlady
Carol Penney
Janet Perry
Debra Pevey
Jane Plant
Debra Ponzek
Sue Popp
Pamela Rainforth
Ettore Ravazzolo
Diana Reed
Becky Regan
Suzy Reynolds
Jaime Riker-Andrews
Chris Rodvold
Betty Rooney
Barbara Root
Susan Salow
Sandy Sanderman
Sue Geise-Sawicki
Jody Schauer
Janet Schei
Marilyn Scheid
Amy Scherschligt
May Scherschligt

Bonnie Schwabe
Linda Scott
Mark Scribner
Gerene Shafer
Ann Shelton
Cherie Shimek
Sara Shuper
Lillian Sioukas
Cindy Slagle
Betty Carragher Smith
Jennifer Smith
Kit Smith
Nancy Smith
Bill Snyder
David Soo Hoo
Kurt Spataro
Helen Star
Melinda Stawicki
Kimberly Stewart
Peggy Strickland
Sue Strong
Nancy Szydelko
Judy Tandy
Fred Teichert
Nancy Tennyson
Erna Thompson
Willadean Thompson
Linda Tochterman
Leslie Toms
Susan Tonkin
Kim Tozer
Paulette Trainor
Linda Turner
Carrie Twitchell
B. J. Ueltzen
Barbara Vanaman
Sue Vitiello
Carol Vodak
Millie VonWald
Lynn Waggoman
Karen Wiese
Jane Wheeler
Diane Whitfield
Pam Wilczek
Ann Ryan Wilson
Janet Wilson
Jeanine Wilson
Lenore Winston
Linda Wodarski
Debbie Wong-Okabe
Helen Wulff
Melinda Wulff

RECIPES TESTED BY:

David Abbott
Anne Adams
Joyce Adamson
Susan Aichele
Ruth Ann Anderson
Camilla Andrews
Cathy Arostegui
Barbara Bailey
Gail Bailey
Mary Barber
Diane Barker
Jennifer Barnes
Barrett Junior High
  School, Mrs. Pickman's
  8th Grade
Lynn Bartlett
Mindy Bazlen
Susan Bell
Carol Bennett
Susan Benson
Connie Berg
Leslie Berger
Stephanie Biegler
Barbara Bilbrey
Donna Blessley
Carol Bone
Deborah Bonuccelli
Jackie Bossert
Anne Bowlus
Carol Bowman
Theresa Boyes-Peot
Cathleen Brew
Dornie Burr
Elisabeth Bush
Paule Butler
Happy Callis
Ken Carle
Martha Carle
Kim Cherry
Karen Clark
Marilyn Clark
Kassy Clifford
Cheryll Cochrane
Patti Codiga
Lillian Colombero
Marilyn Combrink
Tina Costella
Linda Coward
Stephanie Cripe
Diane Cronan
Sue Crosby
Judy Culbertson
Suzy Cummings
Bobbie Cuttle
Kim Cuttle
Shawn D'Alesandro

Lisa Daum
Diana Davis
Jodi Davis
Laurie Davis
Sue Davis
Chris Day
F. Michael Dell
Denise Dewey
Ilene Dillon
Bob Distler
Meg Distler
Tanya Dolphin
K. Donegan
Lisa Dubois
Cindy Dunning Jakle
Brenda Duppong
Michele Egan
Mary Ellingson
Bonnie Elliot
Gail Ellison
Kari Ellison
Kris Elmer
J. P. Eltorai
Molly Evangelisti
Toni Farrell
Lina Fat
Mardy Fellenz
Dianne Ferrell
Jayne Finkbohner
Ann Fish
Birgit Fladager
Penny Ford
Cindi Fores
Sue Fores
Kathie Frasier
Jean Frioux
Jeannie Frisch
Alma Fulster
Karen Galster
Sue Galster
Leslie Gandy
Liz Garland
Bev Geremia
Maureen Gianelli
Sally Gibson
Marlene Gidaro
Lori Grammatico
Betty Gray
Sue Groefsema-Jones
Sue Gross
Kathy Gunz
Joanne Gustafson
Theresa Guenther
Caroline Gwerder
Lynn Hall
Gail Halverson

Louise Hammill
Cathy Harned
Karin Klove Harris
Ann Hart
Laura Heidt
Nina Henderson
Ruth Ann Henderson
Catherine Hogan
Helen Home
Ann Hoover
Carol Houston
Janet Howard
Lilie Hudson
Barbara Jack
Toni James
Emilia Jankowski
Brenda Johnson
Hely Jones
Louise Jones
Jane Jonsson
Joyce Jonsson
Veronica Jordan
Mary Beth Judisch
Eve Justice
Jennifer Justice
Sue Karacozoff
Bryan Kelley
Linda Kelley
Barbara Kennedy
Ben Kimbrough
Cecily Kingston
Marget Kingston
Laura Klotz
Gloria Knopke
Lise Knox
Joseph Kreiss
Paulette Perfumo-Kreiss
Theresa Kwong
Terri Lyn Larsen
Sevim Larsen
Janet Leader
Cynthia Leathers
Beth Leonard
Cathy Bowman Levering
Lisa Levering
Robin Lewis
Kim Lien
Vrada Lindsley
Allison Lintner
Elizabeth Livingston
Carolyn Long
Nancy Long
Eileen Lotz
Laura Lyon-Diepenbrock
Jeanie MacAulay
Pam MacLeod

Wendy Mains
Barbara Manfield
Rula Manikas
Jeri Mann
Anita Seipp Marmaduke
Barbara McConnell
Lynn McDaniel
Jenifer McDonald
Donna McFadyen
Suzanne Meek
Tricia Meister
Wendy Meyer
Nancy Miller
Linda Montoya
Lisa Moore
Mary Beth Morris
Carolyn Mowlds
Cynthia Mulit
Cindy Mullins
Tammy Murray
Cheryl Nativo
Nancy Nelle
Julie Nelson
Susan Nelson
Tanya Newell
Cindy Nolan
Margaret Noisworthy
Sue Olson
JoEllen Opfer
Lewis Orlady
Susie Orlady
Faye Osborn
Ethel Parrington
Barbara Peitzmann
Carol Penney
Mary Peot
Janet Perry
Debra Pevey
Lauren Poage
Carolyn Poli
Erin Porter
Marie Provencial
Pamela Rainforth
Avery Rambo
Sue Rambo
Becky Regan
Nancy Reid
Gary Richardson
Jaime Riker-Andrews
Betty Robinson
Chris Rodvold
Darleen Roland
Kent Rounds
Linda Rowe
Norene St. Louis
Sue Geise Sawicki

Carole Schauer
Jody Schauer
Melanie Schauer
Marilyn Scheid
Amy Scherschligt
Marilyn Schiveley
Teri Scholle
Kathy Shadburn-Butler
Patty Shanley
Beryl Shepard
Cherie Shimek
Sara Shuper
Jan Silsby
Vicki Silverbach
Suzie Simas
Jennifer Smith
Kit Smith
Nancy Smith
Suzie Smits
Terri Smythe
Kim Spare
Helen & Carl Spilman
Julie Steacy
Melinda Stawicki
Lauren Stenvick
Melissa Stepanick
Katie Stille
Rene Stwora-Hail
David Swartz
Leslie Swartz
Nancy Szydelko
Judy Tandy
Timothy Taylor
Barbara Thomas
Regina Thomas
Erna Thompson
Susan Tonkin
Carrie Twitchell
B. J. Ueltzen
Krista Vernon
Sue Vlautin
Lynn Waggoman
Marlene Ward
Karen Werth
Pamela Whipp
Diane Whitfield
Joanne Wiedermann
Gary Wiese
Karen Wiese
Janet Wilson
Linda Wodarski
Mary Wolleson
Catherine Wynne
Cynthia Yerger
Joe Yerger
Lynn Zakskorn

INDEX

**JUNIOR LEAGUE OF
SACRAMENTO**
Women building better communities®

To purchase additional copies of

CELEBRATE!

visit our Web site at www.jlsac.org.